**Test Prep Series**

# GRE®
## Master Wordlist:
### 1535 Words for Verbal Mastery

| **1535** essential words for complete preparation

| **Learn** to use the words in the right context through sample sentences

| **List** of synonyms and antonyms you are going to need in the exam

| **Build** a deeper understanding by knowing the parts of speech the words belong to

VIBRANT PUBLISHERS

# GRE® Master Word List: 1535 Words for Verbal Mastery

© 2018, By Vibrant Publishers, USA. All rights reserved. No part of this publication may be reproduced or distributed in any form or by any means, or stored in a database or retrieval system, without the prior permission of the publisher.

ISBN-10: 1-946383-41-4
ISBN-13: 978-1-946383-41-9
Library of Congress Control Number: 2012916199

This publication is designed to provide accurate and authoritative information in regard to the subject matter covered. The Author has made every effort in the preparation of this book to ensure the accuracy of the information. However, information in this book is sold without warranty either expressed or implied. The Author or the Publisher will not be liable for any damages caused or alleged to be caused either directly or indirectly by this book.

Vibrant Publishers books are available at special quantity discount for sales promotions, or for use in corporate training programs. For more information please write to **bulkorders@vibrantpublishers.com**

Please email feedback / corrections (technical, grammatical or spelling) to **spellerrors@vibrantpublishers.com**

To access the complete catalogue of Vibrant Publishers, visit **www.vibrantpublishers.com**

GRE is the registered trademark of the Educational Testing Service (ETS) which neither sponsors nor endorses this product.

# Table of Contents

| | | | |
|---|---|---|---|
| Chapter 1 | Abase – Aplomb | | 7 |
| Chapter 2 | Apocalyptic – Bemused | | 17 |
| Chapter 3 | Benediction – Centaur | | 27 |
| Chapter 4 | Centrifuge – Concomitant | | 37 |
| Chapter 5 | Concord – Denigrate | | 47 |
| Chapter 6 | Denouement – Epistemologist | | 57 |
| Chapter 7 | Epitaph – Gawk | | 67 |
| Chapter 8 | Genealogy – Impolitic | | 77 |
| Chapter 9 | Importune – Legerdemain | | 87 |
| Chapter 10 | Lethargic – Nocturnal | | 97 |
| Chapter 11 | Noisome – Plauditory | | 107 |
| Chapter 12 | Plebeian – Repudiate | | 117 |
| Chapter 13 | Requiem – Slew | | 127 |
| Chapter 14 | Slough – Tensile | | 137 |
| Chapter 15 | Tepid – Viscous | | 147 |
| Chapter 16 | Vitiate – Zephyr | | 157 |

This page is intentionally left blank

Dear Student,

Thank you for purchasing **GRE® Master Word List: 1535 Words for Verbal Mastery**. We are committed to publishing books that are content-rich, concise and approachable enabling more students to read and make the fullest use of them. We hope this book provides the most enriching learning experience as you prepare for your **GRE** exam.

Should you have any questions or suggestions, feel free to email us at **reachus@vibrantpublishers.com**

Thanks again for your purchase. Good luck for your GRE!

- Vibrant Publishers Team

**facebook.com/vibrantpublishers**

---

**40% OFF**

on MockTestPrep's – 3 Tests Pack for the GRE® Exam

**Coupon: 3TESTS**

www.mocktestprep.com

**Valid through 01/31/2019**

# Other GRE Books in Test Prep Series

**Verbal Insights on the GRE General Test**
ISBN: 978-1-946383-36-5

**Analytical Writing Insights on the GRE General Test**
ISBN: 978-1-946383-39-6

**GRE Analytical Writing: Solutions to the Real Essay Topics - Book 1**
ISBN: 978-1-946383-26-6

**GRE Analytical Writing: Solutions to the Real Essay Topics - Book 2**
ISBN: 978-1-946383-29-7

**Math Insights on the GRE General Test**
ISBN: 978-1-946383-38-9

**GRE Text Completion and Sentence Equivalence Practice Questions**
ISBN: 978-1-946383-32-7

**GRE Reading Comprehension: Detailed Solutions to 325 Questions**
ISBN: 978-1-946383-30-3

**GRE Master Word List: 1535 Words for Verbal Mastery**
ISBN: 978-1-946383-41-9

**GRE Word List: 491 Essential Words**
ISBN: 978-1-946383-40-2

**6 Practice Tests for the GRE**
ISBN: 978-1-946383-34-1

**GRE Words in Context: List 1**
ISBN: 978-1-946383-42-6

**GRE Words in Context: List 2**
ISBN: 978-1-946383-43-3

**GRE Words in Context: Challenging List**
ISBN: 978-1-946383-44-0

**Conquer the GRE: Stress Management & A Perfect Study Plan**
ISBN: 978-1-946383-45-7

For the most updated list of books visit
# www.vibrantpublishers.com

facebook.com/vibrantpublishers

# Chapter 1

## (Abase – Aplomb)

*This chapter covers the following words along with their part of speech, pronunciation, synonyms and antonym, if applicable. Sample usage of the word is also illustrated.*

abase
abash
abdicate
aberrant
abeyance
abjure
abnegation
abominate
abrasive
abridge
abrogate
abscission
abscond
abstain
abstemious
abstinence
abstruse
abut
accede
accessible
accessory
acclivity
accolade
accord
accost
accouter
accretion
accrue
acerbity
acidulous
acoustics
acquiesce
acquittal
acrophobia
actuarial
actuate
acuity
acumen
adage
addendum
addle
adhere
adjunct
adjuration
adroit
adulation
adventitious
adversity
advocate
aerie
affable
affiliation
affluence
agglomeration
aggressor
agnostic
alacrity
alchemy
allay
allege
allegory
alleviate
altruistic
ambidextrous
ambiguous
ambivalence
ambrosia
ameliorate
amenable
amenities
amnesty
amok
amphitheater
amplify
anachronism
analgesic
anarchist
anathema
anathematize
ancillary
animadversion
animosity
anneal
annihilate
annotate
annuity
anodyne
anoint
anonymity
antagonistic
antecede
antediluvian
anthropologist
anthropomorphic
anticlimax
antidote
antipathy
antithesis
aphasia
aphorism
aplomb

**ABASE** (v) *[uh-BEYS]*

*Syn:* lower; humiliate

*Ant:* exalt; elevate; honor; raise; promote

*Usage:* To add insult to injury, he further *abased* her by throwing the report at her in the presence of the rest of the staff.

**ABASH** (v) *[uh-BASH]*

*Syn:* embarrass

*Ant:* encourage; cheer; animate; embolden; incite

*Usage:* The writer felt *abashed* seeing the amount of attention he was receiving.

**ABDICATE** (v) *[AB-di-keyt]*

*Syn:* renounce; give up; relinquish

*Ant:* occupy; retain; maintain

*Usage:* He *abdicated* his entire estate and retired into the forest, spending the rest of his life in a log cabin.

**ABERRANT** (adj) *[uh-BER-uh nt]*

*Syn:* abnormal; deviant

*Ant:* normal

*Usage:* Normally a calm and steady worker, recently Jim's behavior has been noted to be *aberrant*.

**ABEYANCE** (n) *[uh-BEY-uh ns]*

*Syn:* suspended action; inactivity; cessation; suspension

*Ant:* continuance

*Usage:* But these rights of adulthood are in *abeyance* during the period of pupilage or nonage.

**ABJURE** (v) *[ab-JOO r]*

*Syn:* renounce; repudiate; retract

*Ant:* claim; assert; profess; vindicate; retain; maintain, hold

*Usage:* To save his skin, he simply *abjured* every statement they had made, humbling under their pressure.

**ABNEGATION** (n) *[ab-ni-GEY-shuh n]*

*Syn:* repudiation; self-sacrifice; relinquishment

*Ant:* assertion; retention; maintenance; hold

*Usage:* But this *abnegation* of responsibility is bringing with it the anarchy, chaos, and violence in society.

**ABOMINATE** (v) *[uh-BOM-uh-neyt]*

*Syn:* loathe; hate

*Ant:* love; abide

*Usage:* He has such a loathsome personality that any sane person would *abominate* him.

**ABRASIVE** (adj) *[uh-BREY-siv]*

*Syn:* caustic; corrosive; rubbing away; tending to grind down or abrade; causing irritation, annoyance, or bad feelings

*Ant:* calm; mild; soothing; likable

*Usage:* The builder explained that the material was *abrasive* and hence would easily crumble to powder.

**ABRIDGE** (v) *[uh-brij]*

*Syn:* condense or shorten

*Ant:* lengthen, append

*Usage:* The key issues are listed below in an *abridged* version of the mail sent to him.

**ABROGATE** (adj) *[AB-ruh-geyt]*

*Syn:* abolish; nullify

*Ant:* approve; establish; sanction; support

*Usage:* It was Abraham Lincoln who took the initiative to *abrogate* slavery in America.

**ABSCISSION** (n) *[ab-SIZH-uhn]*

*Syn:* removal by cutting off, as in surgery; separation; section

*Ant:* joining; recombination

*Usage:* The doctor explained that the planned *abscission* of the patient's toe was a necessary amputation to save his life from the spreading infection.

# Chapter 1

**ABSCOND** (v) *[ab-SKOND]*

*Syn:* depart secretly and hide

*Ant:* appear; emerge; show; stay; remain

*Usage:* The culprit is said to be *absconding* with the bank robbery proceeds.

**ABSTAIN** (v) *[ab-STEYN]*

*Syn:* refrain; hold oneself back voluntarily from an action or practice

*Ant:* participate; act; consume

*Usage:* On every Tuesday of the month, Jim *abstains* from consuming meat and alcohol.

**ABSTEMIOUS** (adj) *[ab-STEE-mee-uh s]*

*Syn:* Sparing in eating and drinking; temperate

*Ant:* intemperate; gluttonous; greedy

*Usage:* Roderick chooses to remain *abstemious* when the rest of his colleagues meet up for drinks.

**ABSTINENCE** (n) *[AB-stuh-nuhns]*

*Syn:* self-restraint; restraint from eating, drinking, having sex, or indulging any other appetites

*Ant:* indulging; consumption; participation

*Usage:* Spiritual ascetics preach a complete *abstinence* from the pleasures of world.

**ABSTRUSE** (adj) *[ab-STROOS]*

*Syn:* obscure; profound

*Ant:* evident; visible; obvious

*Usage:* It's clever, fun and makes a fairly *abstruse* point very neatly for even the most inexperienced to understand.

**ABUT** (v) *[uh-BUHT]*

*Syn:* border upon; adjoin

*Ant:* separate

*Usage:* A gravel terrace *abuts* the rear of the main house with a further brick path to the side of the farmhouse kitchen.

**ACCEDE** (v) *[ak-SEED]*

*Syn:* agree; approve; assent

*Ant:* antagonize, dissent; demur; protest

*Usage:* Shelly *acceded* to the request of Jill and stayed back for group study.

**ACCESSIBLE** (adj) *[ak-SES-uh-buh l]*

*Syn:* easy to approach; obtainable

*Ant:* inaccessible; hard to reach

*Usage:* The cliff-top at Skorda is easily *accessible* through a ski lift.

**ACCESSORY** (n) *[ak-SES-uh-ree]*

*Syn:* additional object; useful but not essential thing

*Ant:* necessity; essential item

*Usage:* Today a trendy cell phone is not just a gadget, but also a fashion *accessory* to flaunt in public.

**ACCLIVITY** (n) *[uh-KLIV-i-tee]*

*Syn:* sharp upslope of a hill; ascent

*Ant:* declivity; descent

*Usage:* It is delightfully situated on a bold *acclivity*, one mile east of the church, looking down on the village.

**ACCOLADE** (n) *[AK-uh-leyd]*

*Syn:* award of merit; recognition of accomplishment

*Ant:* criticism; demerits

*Usage:* She has been winning many *accolades* for her achievements.

**ACCORD** (n) *[uh-KAWRD]*

*Syn:* agreement; treaty

*Ant:* difference; disagreement; withholding; refusal; denial

*Usage:* The talks between the two Presidents led to an *accord* with a number of new agreements being signed by the two countries.

**ACCOST** (v) [uh-KAWST]

Syn: approach and speak first to a person

Ant: shun; pass; elude; ignore; avoid

Usage: Just as she was emerging from the bank, two men *accosted* her, grabbed her handbag, and made off in a waiting car.

**ACCOUTER** (v) [uh-KOO-ter]

Syn: equip; outfit

Ant: disrobe;

Usage: Her primary job was to fashionably *accouter* the women in the royal household.

**ACCRETION** (n) [uh-KREE-shuh n]

Syn: growth; increase; addition

Ant: shrinkage; deduction; decrease

Usage: There was no point in attempting *accretion* of more wealth when he knew that everything his affluent parents owned would eventually be handed down to him.

**ACCRUE** (v) [uh-KROO]

Syn: accumulate; pile up; grow; collect

Ant: divest; shrink; decrease; lose

Usage: There was no point in attempting to *accrue* more wealth when he knew that everything his affluent parents owned would eventually be handed down to him.

**ACERBITY** (n) [uh-SUR-bi-tee]

Syn: bitterness of speech and temper; harshness; severity

Ant: sweetness; mellowness; mildness

Usage: The party members showed *acerbity* in their harsh criticism of the leader's Divide and Rule policy.

**ACIDULOUS** (adj) [uh-SIJ-uh-luhs]

Syn: slightly sour; sharp; caustic

Ant: sweet; sugary

Usage: People around Sheena are terrified of her *acidulous* tongue.

**ACOUSTICS** (n) [uh-KOO-stiks]

Syn: science of sound

Usage: The ceiling slanted down toward the screen to improve *acoustics*.

**ACQUIESCE** (v) [ak-wee-ES]

Syn: assent; agree without fuss; comply

Ant: dissent; demur; object; protest; resist; oppose

Usage: After a lot of pressure, the President decided to *acquiesce* to the people's demands and moved to withdraw the troops.

**ACQUITTAL** (n) [uh-KWIT-l]

Syn: deliverance from a charge

Ant: conviction

Usage: The mafia don called for a huge celebration on account of his *acquittal* of all felony charges.

**ACROPHOBIA** (n) [ak-ruh-FOH-bee-uh]

Syn: fear of heights

Usage: Jack did not join his friends for mountaineering as he suffered from *acrophobia*.

**ACTUARIAL** (adj) [AK-choo-er-ee]

Syn: calculating; pertaining to insurance statistics

Usage: The *actuarial* statistics show that people are living into a higher age these days than ten years back.

**ACTUATE** (v) [AK-choo-eyt]

Syn: motivate; impel; incite

Ant: dissuade; prevent; deter; hinder; discourage

Usage: Bob was *actuated* toward committing the crime because of his heavy debts.

**ACUITY** (n) [uh-KYOO-i-tee]

Syn: sharpness

*Ant:* stupidity

*Usage:* His sense of *acuity* and acumen was amazingly sharp even at this age.

**ACUMEN** (n) *[uh-kYOO-muh n]*

*Syn:* mental shrewdness; discernment; keen insight

*Ant:* stupidity; lack of awareness

*Usage:* His sharp sense of business *acumen* has always been admired by people.

**ADAGE** (n) *[AD-ij]*

*Syn:* wise saying; proverb

*Ant:* absurdity; ambiguity; foolishness; nonsense

*Usage:* That "experience is the parent of wisdom," is an *adage,* the truth of which is recognized by all mankind.

**ADDENDUM** (n) *[uh-DEN-duh m]*

*Syn:* an addition or a supplement

*Ant:* subtraction

*Usage:* This year, the company has put in a new *addendum* to the existing set of regulations to deal with new technology issues.

**ADDLE** (v) *[AD-l]*

*Syn:* muddle; confuse; drive crazy; become rotten

*Ant:* clarify; explain; clear up

*Usage:* Ken became *addled* by all this talk because he just couldn't understand what Lori was saying.

**ADHERE** (v) *[ad-HEER]*

*Syn:* stick fast

*Ant:* disjoin; not conform

*Usage:* However, dates will still need to be strictly *adhered* to if we hope to meet the due date.

**ADJUNCT** (n) *[AJ-uhngkt]*

*Syn:* something added on or attached

*Ant:* something removed

*Usage:* Lastly, the lawyer made another *adjunct* to the will on the advice of the client.

**ADJURATION** (n) *[aj-uh-REY-shuh n]*

*Syn:* solemn urging; appeal

*Ant:* denial; refusal; disavowal

*Usage:* Broken-hearted with the verdict, the captain decided to make an *adjuration* to a higher court.

**ADROIT** (adj) *[uh-DROIT]*

*Syn:* skillful

*Ant:* awkward; clumsy; unskillful; inexpert; lubberly

*Usage:* Being an army officer's daughter, she was quite *adroit* at all the physical exercises they asked her to do.

**ADULATION** (n) *[aj-uh-LEY shuh n]*

*Syn:* flattery; admiration; overenthusiastic praise; sycophancy

*Ant:* criticism; abuse

*Usage:* By now, the film star was sick of all the fawning *adulation* he was drawing.

**ADVENTITIOUS** (adj) *[ad-vuh n-tish-uh s]*

*Syn:* accidental; casual; extrinsic

*Ant:* deliberate; intrinsic; planned

*Usage:* That they would meet like this at a coffee shop after twenty years of being separated was too *adventitious* to believe.

**ADVERSITY** (n) *[ad-VUR-si-tee]*

*Syn:* poverty; misfortune; bad luck

*Ant:* fortune; good luck; prosperity

*Usage:* They say the true strength of man is measured in times of hardship and *adversity.*

**ADVOCATE** (v) *[AD-vuh-keyt]*

*Syn:* urge; plead for; support

*Ant:* counter; discourage; impede

*Usage:* What was really shocking to the pacifists was that he *advocated* the use of violence in their protests.

**AERIE** (n) [air-ee]

*Syn:* nest of a large bird of prey

*Usage:* The vulture was winging his way at a high altitude toward his *aerie* atop the mountain.

**AFFABLE** (adj) [AF-uh-buh l]

*Syn:* easily approachable; warm; genial; friendly

*Ant:* contemptuous; disdainful; discourteous;, impolite, callous

*Usage:* Jim had seemed like an *affable* gentleman to me but his neighbor told me he was often rude to her.

**AFFILIATION** (n) [uh-fil-ee-EY-shuh n]

*Syn:* joining; association; alliance

*Ant:* separation; estrangement

*Usage:* The local university has an *affiliation* to the University of Wisconsin.

**AFFLUENCE** (n) [AF-loo-uh ns]

*Syn:* abundance; wealth

*Ant:* dearth

*Usage:* Even before entering the mansion, the family's *affluence* was clearly obvious from the value of the various imported cars parked outside.

**AGGLOMERATION** (n) [uh-glom-uh-REY-shuh n]

*Syn:* collection; heap; jumble; cluster

*Ant:* individual item

*Usage:* Now, the site is an oasis of green space in an *agglomeration* of urban sprawl.

**AGGRESSOR** (n) [uh-GRES-er]

*Syn:* attacker

*Ant:* victim

*Usage:* The United Nations received much support for taking robust action against an *aggressor* nation.

**AGNOSTIC** (n) [ag-NOS-tik]

*Syn:* one who is skeptical of the existence of a god or any ultimate reality

*Ant:* believer

*Usage:* There was no celebration for Easter in their house because they were *agnostics*.

**ALACRITY** (n) [uh-LAK-ri-tee]

*Syn:* cheerful promptness; eagerness; celerity; willingness; cheerfulness

*Ant:* aversion; slowness; repugnance; reluctance; unwillingness

*Usage:* On hearing the good news, the three of them rose to their feet with such *alacrity* that he was stunned.

**ALCHEMY** (n) [AL-kuh-mee]

*Syn:* medieval chemistry; sorcery

*Ant:* science

*Usage:* I studied *alchemy* and new age ideas at first, and then yoga.

**ALLAY** (v) [uh-LEY]

*Syn:* assuage; relieve; alleviate; calm; pacify

*Ant:* dispute; provoke; agitate; arouse

*Usage:* "Don't worry; I am here with you," he said, *allaying* her fears.

**ALLEGE** (v) [uh-LEJ]

*Syn:* state without proof

*Ant:* contradict; deny; disprove; refute; gainsay

*Usage:* Later they even dared to *allege* that he had helped the prisoner to escape.

**ALLEGORY** (n) [AL-uh-gawr-ee]

*Syn:* story in which characters are used as symbols; fable

*Ant:* fact; history

*Usage:* Aesop's fable of the hard-working ant and lazy grasshopper presents an *allegory* showing the value of planning, working, and saving.

(Abase – Aplomb)

**ALLEVIATE** (v) [uh-LEE-vee-eyt]

Syn: relieve

Ant: exacerbate; aggravate; increase; augment; embitter

Usage: With great patience, he set out to *alleviate* their uneasiness.

**ALTRUISTIC** (adj) [al-troo-IS-tik]

Syn: unselfishly generous; concerned for others

Ant: frugal; miserly

Usage: Because of his *altruistic* nature he has no qualms about donating even millions to charity.

**AMBIDEXTROUS** (adj) [am-bi-DEK-struh s]

Syn: capable of using either hand with equal ease

Ant: right-handed; left-handed

Usage: *Ambidextrous* design makes working more comfortable, whether you mouse with your left or right hand.

**AMBIGUOUS** (adj) [am-BIG-yoo-uh s]

Syn: unclear or doubtful in meaning; obscure; uncertain

Ant: indisputable; obvious; unequivocal; unambiguous

Usage: It would be far more sensible to write clear, lucid statements than *ambiguous* statements, which would only serve to confuse the reader.

**AMBIVALENCE** (n) [am-BIV-uh-luh ns]

Syn: the state of having contradictory or conflicting emotional attitudes

Ant: certainty; decisiveness

Usage: Paul was faced with deep *ambivalence* toward the prevailing culture.

**AMBROSIA** (n) [am-BROH-zhuh]

Syn: food of the gods

Usage: After weeks of eating bland, tasteless food, the dinner cooked by Zoya felt as good as *ambrosia* to Neil.

**AMELIORATE** (v) [uh-MEEL-yuh-reyt]

Syn: improve

Ant: injure; spoil; mar; debase; deteriorate

Usage: The weather *ameliorated* toward the evening, with a beautiful sunset and pleasant temperatures.

**AMENABLE** (adj) [uh-MEE-nuh-buh l]

Syn: readily managed; willing to be led

Ant: independent; irresponsible; determinate; agreeable

Usage: "Provided I find the terms *amenable* I shall sign the document," said Paul.

**AMENITIES** (n) [uh-MEN-i-tees]

Syn: comforts; conveniences; luxuries; niceties

Ant: discomforts

Usage: Even the most basic *amenities* were not available in that village.

**AMNESTY** (n) [AM-nuh-stee]

Syn: pardon; forgiveness;

Ant: conviction; censure; blame

Usage: On seeing the powerful mayor arriving at the town square, the prisoners begged for *amnesty*.

**AMOK** (adj) [uh-MUHK]

Syn: in a state of rage

Ant: calm; relaxed; organized

Usage: The bull ran *amok* on the grounds after being speared by the matador.

**AMPHITHEATER** (n) [AM-fuh-thee-uh-ter]

Syn: open oval building with tiers of seats

Ant: enclosed theater

Usage: In Rome, our primary agenda had been to make a visit to the *amphitheater* for a performance under the stars.

**AMPLIFY** (v) [AM-pluh-fahy]

Syn: broaden or clarify by expanding; intensify; make

stronger

*Ant:* abridge; condense; summarize; curtail

*Usage:* The noise only served to *amplify* the pain that had already brought her to tears.

**ANACHRONISM** (n) [uh-NAK-ruh-niz-uh m]

*Syn:* something or someone misplaced in time

*Usage:* His manner of working was so steeped in Victorian times that it appeared to be an *anachronism*.

**ANALGESIC** (adj) [an-l-JEE-zik]

*Syn:* causing insensitivity to pain

*Usage:* The pain was so severe that Peter had to opt for an *analgesic* pill.

**ANARCHIST** (n) [AN-er-kist]

*Syn:* person who seeks to overturn the established government; advocate of abolishing authority

*Ant:* conservative; moderate

*Usage:* The *anarchist* predicted chaos and disorganization on the path toward their ultimate goal of a new regime.

**ANATHEMA** (n) [uh-NATH-uh-muh]

*Syn:* abomination; enemy

*Ant:* love

*Usage:* Taxes are *anathema* to most people.

**ANATHEMATIZE** (v) [uh-NATH-uh-muh-tahyz]

*Syn:* curse

*Ant:* bless

*Usage:* The new copier-printer *anathematizes* the employees; they refuse to go near it.

**ANCILLARY** (adj) [AN-suh-ler-ee]

*Syn:* serving as an aid or accessory; auxiliary

*Ant:* primary; fundamental

*Usage:* There was an *ancillary* clause in the will, which stated that unless and until she was married, she wouldn't be able to inherit the estate.

**ANIMADVERSION** (n) [an-uh-mad-VUR-zhuhn]

*Syn:* critical remark; accusation; censure; criticism

*Ant:* commendation; praise

*Usage:* The news of mass tree killing excited *animadversion* and severe criticism among the environmentalists.

**ANIMOSITY** (n) [an-uh-MOS-i-tee]

*Syn:* active enmity; strong dislike; hostility

*Ant:* concord; companionship; harmony; regard

*Usage:* "I bear no *animosity* towards you," Richard said to Fred as they shook hands to settle their differences.

**ANNEAL** (v) [uh-NEEL]

*Syn:* reduce brittleness and improve toughness by heating and cooling; harden; temper

*Ant:* soften; weaken

*Usage:* The crisis Wanda was going through only served to *anneal* and make her stronger.

**ANNIHILATE** (v) [uh-NAHY-uh-leyt]

*Syn:* destroy almost entirely; vanquish; abolish

*Ant:* perpetuate; preserve; foster; protect

*Usage:* Filled with a desire for revenge, Gordon swore to *annihilate* every family member of his son's killers.

**ANNOTATE** (v) [AN-uh-teyt]

*Syn:* comment; make explanatory notes

*Ant:* obscure; confuse

*Usage:* The professor asked the students to *annotate* their essays with suitable remarks and references.

**ANNUITY** (n) [uh-NOO-i-tee]

*Syn:* yearly allowance

*Usage:* The siblings then began quarreling among themselves for their *annuity* from their dead father's estate.

**ANODYNE** (adj) [AN-uh-dahyn]

Syn: soothing; calming

Ant: exciting; exhilarating

Usage: The book is rather too *anodyne* and uninteresting.

**ANOINT** (v) [uh-NOINT]

Syn: consecrate

Usage: The senior priest *anointed* John as the new pontiff.

**ANONYMITY** (n) [an-uh-NIM-i-tee]

Syn: state of being nameless; obscurity

Ant: fame; visibility

Usage: The biggest advantage of Internet social clubs is that they offer *anonymity* so that people can mix about without disclosing their identities.

**ANTAGONISTIC** (adj) [an-tag-uh-NIS-tik]

Syn: hostile; opposed

Ant: friendly; loving

Usage: The child's attitude would expectedly be *antagonistic* towards the new stepmother taking her own mother's place.

**ANTECEDE** (v) [an-tuh-SEED]

Syn: precede

Ant: follow

Usage: There were some *anteceding* conditions to be fulfilled before she would be inducted into the company as a partner.

**ANTEDILUVIAN** (adj) [an-tee-di-LOO-vee-uh n]

Syn: antiquated; extremely ancient; prehistoric

Ant: modern; state-of-the-art; new

Usage: Wayne was too old-fashioned and anachronistic; he belonged to *antediluvian* times.

**ANTHROPOLOGIST** (n) [an-thruh-POL-uh-jist]

Syn: a student of the history and science of mankind

Usage: Jimmy is studying to become an *anthropologist* and anxiously anticipates his first visit to an excavation field.

**ANTHROPOMORPHIC** (adj) [an-thruh-puh-MAWR-fik]

Syn: having human form or characteristics

Usage: A new breed of scientists claim there are *anthropomorphic* or human-like creatures on the planet Pluto.

**ANTICLIMAX** (n) [an-ti-KLAHY-maks]

Syn: letdown in thought or emotion

Ant: climax; excitement

Usage: After the exciting and lively beginning, the dull ending of the movie was a huge *anticlimax* to us.

**ANTIDOTE** (n) [an-ti-doht]

Syn: remedy to counteract a poison or disease; cure; solution

Ant: pain; disease; injury

Usage: News from friends could provide the refreshing *antidote* you need to your bout of depression.

**ANTIPATHY** (n) [an-TIP-uh-thee]

Syn: extreme aversion; dislike; distaste; enmity

Ant: affinity; amity; sympathy; attraction; harmony

Usage: The two warring brothers have a great amount of *antipathy* toward each other.

**ANTITHESIS** (n) [an-TITH-uh-sis]

Syn: contrast; direct opposite of or to

Ant: equivalence; likeness; counterpart; equal

Usage: The book was a complete *antithesis* to what he'd expected it to be.

**APHASIA** (n) [uh-FEY-zhuh]

Syn: loss of speech due to injury or illness

Ant: talkativeness

Usage: Nina was diagnosed as suffering from *aphasia*, a

form of brain damage that limited her use or understanding of words or their meanings.

## APHORISM (n) *[AF-uh-riz-uh m]*

*Syn:* adage; belief; proverb; pithy maxim

*Ant:* absurdity; ambiguity; nonsense

*Usage:* It was another of his famous *aphorisms,* that life is never fair and that we must know the rules to play it well.

## APLOMB (n) *[uh-PLOM]*

*Syn:* poise; assurance

*Ant:* discomposure; nervousness; apprehension

*Usage:* Jenny walked into the room full of *aplomb*, brimming with confidence.

# Chapter 2

## (Apocalyptic –Bemused)

*This chapter covers the following words along with their part of speech, pronunciation, synonyms and antonym, if applicable. Sample usage of the word is also illustrated.*

| | | |
|---|---|---|
| apocalyptic | ascribe | axiom |
| apocryphal | asinine | azure |
| apogee | askance | bacchanalian |
| apoplexy | askew | badinage |
| apostate | asperity | baleful |
| apothecary | assail | ballast |
| apothegm | assiduous | bandy |
| apotheosis | assuage | bane |
| appall | asteroid | baneful |
| appease | astigmatism | barb |
| append | astringent | bard |
| appraise | asunder | barefaced |
| apprehensive | asymmetric | baroque |
| apprise | atavism | barrage |
| approbation | atheistic | barterer |
| appurtenances | atrocity | bastion |
| aquiline | attenuate | bate |
| arabesque | attest | bauble |
| arable | attribute | bawdy |
| arbitrate | atypical | beatific |
| arboretum | audacious | beatify |
| arcane | augment | beatitude |
| archaic | augury | bedraggle |
| archetype | aureole | begrudge |
| archives | auspicious | beguile |
| argot | austere | behoove |
| arid | authenticate | belabor |
| armada | automaton | beleaguer |
| arrears | autopsy | belittle |
| arroyo | avalanche | bellicose |
| articulate | avenge | bemoan |
| artifice | avert | bemused |
| ascendancy | avocation | |
| asceticism | avuncular | |

**APOCALYPTIC** (adj) *[uh-pok-uh-LIP-tik]*

*Syn:* prophetic; pertaining to revelations; ominous

*Ant:* insignificant; unimportant

*Usage:* Everything was going too badly; it felt like an *apocalyptic* moment.

**APOCRYPHAL** (adj) *[uh-POK-ruh-fuh l]*

*Syn:* untrue; made up

*Ant:* authentic; genuine; verified; attested; undisputed

*Usage:* The means by which Gary had secured the job was most likely *apocryphal*.

**APOGEE** (n) *[AP-uh-jee]*

*Syn:* highest point; apex; acme; zenith

*Ant:* nadir

*Usage:* The vineyard's sales had reached its *apogee* in the 90s before suffering from conflict with other local growers.

**APOPLEXY** (n) *[AP-uh-plek-see]*

*Syn:* stroke; loss of consciousness followed by paralysis

*Ant:* consciousness

*Usage:* Bob's sudden *apoplexy* was the calm, but deadly symptom indicating he was having a stroke.

**APOSTATE** (n) *[uh-POS-teyt]*

*Syn:* one who abandons his religious faith or political beliefs

*Ant:* faithful; believer

*Usage:* After the priest's death, a large number of people turned *apostates*, forsaking their religion for good.

**APOTHECARY** (n) *[uh-POTH-uh-ker-ee]*

*Syn:* druggist

*Usage:* Armed with the doctor's prescription, I headed towards the nearest *apothecary*.

**APOTHEGM** (n) *[AP-uh-them]*

*Syn:* pithy, compact saying; aphorism

*Ant:* absurdity; nonsense

*Usage:* Every saying of Uncle George is revered by us as if it were an *apothegm* of golden wisdom.

**APOTHEOSIS** (n) *[uh-poth-ee-OH-sis]*

*Syn:* elevation to godhood; deification; an ideal example of something

*Ant:* exclusion; condemnation

*Usage:* Last year around this time, David Beckham was the object of *apotheosis*, but this year he's just another fallen idol.

**APPALL** (v) *[uh-PAWL]*

*Syn:* dismay; shock

*Ant:* calm; comfort; console; innervate

*Usage:* We were *appalled* to see the sad state Lynette's mother had been reduced to.

**APPEASE** (v) *[uh-PEEZ]*

*Syn:* pacify or soothe; relieve

*Ant:* embitter; annoy; irritate; perturb; roil

*Usage:* Some primitive tribes believe that animals must be sacrificed in order to *appease* the gods.

**APPEND** (v) *[uh-PEND]*

*Syn:* attach; supplement

*Ant:* subtract; take away

*Usage:* It was unanimously decided by the board of directors to *append* the new clause to the regulations document.

**APPRAISE** (v) *[uh-PREYZ]*

*Syn:* estimate value of

*Ant:* ignore

*Usage:* Even with her eyes closed, Lynn could tell that she was being *appraised* by Gary.

**APPREHENSIVE** (adj) *[ap-ri-HEN-siv]*

*Syn:* fearful; discerning

*Ant:* trusting; bold

*Usage:* My mother was more than a little *apprehensive* about the stranger who, according to her, seemed to be following us.

**APPRISE** (v) *[uh-PRAHYZ]*

*Syn:* inform; tell; advise

*Ant:* keep secret

*Usage:* No matter what the consequence would be, we knew we had to *apprise* the boss about the loss of data.

**APPROBATION** (n) *[ap-ruh-BEY-shuh n]*

*Syn:* approval; praise

*Ant:* criticism; disapprobation; denial; censure; refusal

*Usage:* She desperately sought *approbation* for her actions from her peers.

**APPURTENANCES** (n) *[uh-PUR-tn-uh ns s]*

*Syn:* subordinate possessions

*Ant:* principal items

*Usage:* We decided to buy at one go the whole set of *appurtenances* that would be needed for our new venture.

**AQUILINE** (adj) *[AK-wuh-lahyn]*

*Syn:* curved; hooked

*Ant:* straight

*Usage:* Wilma was characterized by her above-average height and sharp, *aquiline* features.

**ARABESQUE** (n) *[ar-uh-BESK]*

*Syn:* style of decoration involving intertwined plants and abstract curves

*Usage:* Each contains a variation on *arabesque* design with green ivy spiraling on a white background.

**ARABLE** (adj) *[AR-uh-buh l]*

*Syn:* fit for growing crops; farmable

*Ant:* infertile; fallow

*Usage:* The plains, with their alluvial soil, are more *arable* for these kinds of crops.

**ARBITRATE** (n) *[AHR-bi-treyt]*

*Syn:* judge; decide

*Ant:* contest; dispute

*Usage:* Sam is often asked to *arbitrate* the issue between the two teams.

**ARBORETUM** (n) *[ahr-buh-REE-tuh m]*

*Syn:* botanic garden; place where different tree varieties are exhibited

*Usage:* Nina has an awesome *arboretum* with some rare eucalyptus, cypress, and pine trees.

**ARCANE** (adj) *[ahr-KEYN]*

*Syn:* secret; mysterious; known only to the initiated

*Ant:* straightforward; obvious; clear

*Usage: Arcane* matters discussed only between the two of us had somehow been leaked out to the press.

**ARCHAIC** (adj) *[ahr-KEY-ik]*

*Syn:* antiquated

*Ant:* modern

*Usage:* Her sense of dressing seemed *archaic* and old-fashioned.

**ARCHETYPE** (n) *[AHR-ki-tahyp]*

*Syn:* prototype; primitive pattern; typical

*Ant:* atypical

*Usage:* Father William was the *archetypal* Catholic priest.

**ARCHIVES** (n) *[AHR-kahyvs]*

*Syn:* public records; place where public records are kept

*Usage:* Newspaper *archives* are the best place to look for old, outdated articles.

**ARGOT** (n) [AHR-goh]

Syn: jargon; slang

Ant: standard language

Usage: We had devised a new kind of *argot* among us and when we spoke in it, few others would understand what we spoke of.

**ARID** (adj) [AR-id]

Syn: dry; barren; dull; unimaginative

Ant: wet; moist; rainy; fertile

Usage: Surviving in the *arid* desert for the next ten days was a huge challenge John had to face.

**ARMADA** (n) [ahr-MAH-duh]

Syn: fleet of warships

Usage: A new fleet of ships had been added to the *armada* making it the best in the world.

**ARREARS** (n) [uh-REER s]

Syn: debt; obligation

Ant: paid in full; excess

Usage: The family was in deep *arrears* so they decided to mortgage the house.

**ARROYO** (n) [uh-ROI-oh]

Syn: gully; ravine

Ant: hillock

Usage: Martha and Jim had spent many happy days in their childhood playing in the mud of the *arroyo* adjacent to their house.

**ARTICULATE** (adj) [ahr-TIK-yuh-lit]

Syn: effective; distinct; coherently spoken

Ant: unclear; unintelligible

Usage: Because she can put across her thoughts so *articulately*, Kay was chosen to represent the sales team at the debate contest.

**ARTIFICE** (n) [AHR-tuh-fis]

Syn: deception; trickery

Ant: fairness; candor; honesty

Usage: Quite often, *artifice* wins over people faster than honesty.

**ASCENDANCY** (n) [uh-SEN-duh n-see]

Syn: controlling influence; domination

Ant: weakness; inferiority

Usage: King George failed to retain his *ascendancy* over the revolting masses.

**ASCETICISM** (n) [uh-SET-uh-siz-uh m]

Syn: doctrine of self-denial

Ant: indulgence

Usage: To practice *asceticism* one needs to have a very strong will and resolve.

**ASCRIBE** (v) [uh-SKRAHYB]

Syn: refer; attribute; assign

Ant: deny; disconnect; dissociate

Usage: Though she does at times seem very careless, it was not fair to *ascribe* the mistake to her alone.

**ASININE** (adj) [AS-uh-nahyn]

Syn: foolish; stupid

Ant: intelligent; smart

Usage: That she could be so stupid and *asinine* was a huge surprise for me.

**ASKANCE** (adj) [uh-SKANS]

Syn: with a sideways or indirect look

Ant: directly

Usage: They looked *askance* at Harry, wondering how in the world he would accomplish the feat.

**ASKEW** (adj) [uh-SKYOO]

Syn: crooked; slanted; awry

Ant: straight

*Usage:* At the end of the short but very bumpy ride, Paula's hat was *askew* and strands of her hair were falling all over face.

**ASPERITY** (n) *[uh-SPER-i-tee]*

*Syn:* sharpness (of temper)

*Ant:* mildness; gentleness; sweetness; softness; pleasantness

*Usage:* It was not appropriate for her to use such *asperity* while talking to young Peter; the poor little kid was hurt.

**ASSAIL** (v) *[uh-SEYL]*

*Syn:* assault

*Ant:* applaud

*Usage:* The new Grand Slam champion was *assailed* with all sorts of questions at the press conference.

**ASSIDUOUS** (adj) *[uh-SIJ-oo-uh s]*

*Syn:* diligent; persevering

*Ant:* lazy; negligent

*Usage:* Sara is a committed, hardworking and *assiduous* worker.

**ASSUAGE** (v) *[uh-SWEYZH]*

*Syn:* ease or lessen (pain); satisfy (hunger); soothe (anger)

*Ant:* estrange; excite; increase; provoke; inflame; incite; stimulate

*Usage:* The dentist talked to her gently and *assuaged* her fears before starting to work on her sore tooth.

**ASTEROID** (n) *[AS-tuh-roid]*

*Syn:* small planet

*Usage:* The report in the science digest spoke about how the earth would be affected if there were an *asteroid* strike.

**ASTIGMATISM** (n) *[uh-STIG-muh-tiz-uh m]*

*Syn:* eye defect that prevents proper focus

*Ant:* sightedness

*Usage:* After giving me a series of eye tests, the ophthalmologist told me that I have *astigmatism*.

**ASTRINGENT** (adj) *[uh-STRIN-juh nt]*

*Syn:* binding; causing contraction; harsh

*Ant:* bland; mild

*Usage:* Her sharp, caustic remarks acted like an *astringent* on his delicate feelings.

**ASUNDER** adv *[uh-SUHN-der]*

*Syn:* into parts; apart

*Ant:* completely

*Usage:* The bullet hit her body with such force that her arms were torn *asunder* from her torso.

**ASYMMETRIC** (adj) *[ey-suh-ME-trik]*

*Syn:* not identical on both sides of a dividing central line

*Ant:* symmetric; balanced

*Usage:* A recent survey discovered that people who have *asymmetric* facial features are not as attractive as those with balanced features.

**ATAVISM** (n) *[AT-uh-viz-uh m]*

*Syn:* reversal; resemblance to remote ancestors rather than to parents; deformity returning after passage of two or more generations

*Usage:* Suddenly there was an *atavism* of fortunes and overnight he rose from a pauper to a millionaire.

**ATHEISTIC** (adj) *[ey-thee-IS-tik]*

*Syn:* denying the existence of god

*Ant:* faithful; spiritual

*Usage:* Brian has begun to exhibit *atheistic* behavior and refuses to visit the church anymore.

**ATROCITY** (n) *[uh-TROS-i-tee]*

*Syn:* brutal deed

*Ant:* kindness

*Usage:* On the prison island of Alcataraz, numerous unspeakable *atrocities* were committed on prisoners.

**ATTENUATE** (v) *[uh-TEN-yoo-eyt]*

*Syn:* make thin; weaken; contract

*Ant:* expand; increase; intensify; strengthen

*Usage:* The tight corset only seemed to *attenuate* her figure making her look thinner than ever.

**ATTEST** (v) *[uh-TEST]*

*Syn:* testify; bear witness

*Ant:* refute; disprove; oppugn; deny

*Usage:* Anyone who knows Jim well would *attest* to the fact that he is a good father.

**ATTRIBUTE** (v) *[UH-trib-yoot]*

*Syn:* ascribe; explain; accuse

*Ant:* vindicate; exonerate; absolve

*Usage:* "We would like to *attribute* our success to you, Sir," said the students, brimming with gratitude.

**ATYPICAL** (adj) *[ey-TIP-i-kuhl]*

*Syn:* not normal

*Ant:* typical; normal

*Usage:* His *atypical*, violent behavior caused his mother great alarm.

**AUDACIOUS** (adj) *[aw-DEY-shuh s]*

*Syn:* daring; bold

*Ant:* cowardly; timid; feckless; diffident; introverted

*Usage:* Her *audacious* behavior shocked the entire crowd.

**AUGMENT** (v) *[awg-MENT]*

*Syn:* increase; add to

*Ant:* reduce: diminish: deduct

*Usage:* She has decided to take up another part-time job to *augment* her income.

**AUGURY** (n) *[AW-gyuh-ree]*

*Syn:* omen; prophecy

*Ant:* luck; providence

*Usage:* Her sense of *augury* allows her to predict events in an uncanny and bizarre way.

**AUREOLE** (n) *[AWR-ee-ohl]*

*Syn:* sun's corona; halo

*Usage:* Michael arrived into the room looking like a radiant angel with an *aureole* around his blond head.

**AUSPICIOUS** (adj) *[aw-SPISH-uh s]*

*Syn:* favoring success; faring well for the future; propitious

*Ant:* inauspicious; unpropitious; discouraging

*Usage:* It seemed a very *auspicious* moment to propose to her, so he immediately did that.

**AUSTERE** (adj) *[aw-STEER]*

*Syn:* forbiddingly stern; severely simple and unornamented

*Ant:* indulgent; genial; luxurious; mild; dissipated

*Usage:* A nun's simple and *austere* lifestyle was just not Gina's cup of tea; she was too used to material comforts.

**AUTHENTICATE** (v) *[aw-THEN-ti-keyt]*

*Syn:* prove genuine

*Ant:* disprove

*Usage:* The bank refused to let him inside the locker vault unless he *authenticated* his identity.

**AUTOMATON** (n) *[aw-TOM-uh-ton]*

*Syn:* mechanism that imitates actions of humans

*Ant:* human

*Usage:* Don't work so hard as to become an *automaton* following a mechanical routine.

**AUTOPSY** (n) *[AW-top-see]*

*Syn:* examination of a dead body; post-mortem

*Ant:* biopsy; examination of living tissue

*Usage:* The police wanted permission from Dana's mother to perform an *autopsy* which they said would determine the cause and exact time of death.

**AVALANCHE** (n) *[AV-uh-lanch]*

*Syn:* great mass of falling snow and ice

*Usage:* You felt something might come soon but nobody expected the *avalanche*.

**AVENGE** (v) *[uh-VENJ]*

*Syn:* take vengeance for something; retaliate

*Ant:* forgive

*Usage:* Bill has his chance to *avenge* the defeat in the Thursday singles final.

**AVERT** (v) *[uh-VURT]*

*Syn:* prevent; turn away

*Ant:* allow

*Usage:* For having taken the efforts to *avert* a major disaster with his quick presence of mind and courage, Sgt. Jim Bellows was awarded a gold medal.

**AVOCATION** (n) *[av-uh-KEY-shuh n]*

*Syn:* secondary or minor occupation; hobby

*Ant:* idleness; leisure; holiday

*Usage:* Cooking seems to be her favorite *avocation*.

**AVUNCULAR** (adj) *[uh-VUHNG-kyuh-ler]*

*Syn:* like an uncle; able

*Usage:* The reason women tend to confide easily in Bill is his *avuncular* features, which they say remind them of their uncles.

**AXIOM** (n) *[AK-see-uh m]*

*Syn:* self-evident truth, requiring no proof

*Ant:* fallacy

*Usage:* It is a sad fact today that many youngsters are not aware of the classic timeless *axioms*, which were articulated decades ago.

**AZURE** (adj) *[AZH-er]*

*Syn:* sky blue; cerulean

*Ant:* sky

*Usage:* His dreamy and *azure* eyes made many women swoon in their sky blue intensity.

**BACCHANALIAN** (adj) *[bak-uh-NEY-lee-uh]*

*Syn:* drunken

*Ant:* sober

*Usage:* Young Croft's *bacchanalian* tendencies had his aristocratic father seriously worried about his excessive drinking.

**BADINAGE** (n) *[bad-n-AHZH]*

*Syn:* teasing conversation

*Ant:* seriousness

*Usage:* The night was filled with the merry-making and *badinage* of the young men.

**BALEFUL** (adj) *[BEYL-fuh l]*

*Syn:* deadly; having a malign influence; ominous

*Ant:* pleasant

*Usage:* He kept casting *baleful* glances at her every now and then.

**BALLAST** (n) *[BAL-uh st]*

*Syn:* heavy substance used to add stability or weight

*Ant:* lightness

*Usage:* Extra *ballast* was attached to the boat to assure it would stay upright

**BANDY** (v) *[BAN-dee]*

*Syn:* discuss lightly or glibly; exchange (words) heatedly

*Ant:* discuss seriously

*Usage:* The brothers like to *bandy* insults back and forth every night before they fall asleep.

**BANE** (n) *[beyn]*

*Syn:* cause of ruin; curse

*Ant:* boon; benefit

*Usage:* Whether video blogging recently launched by Google will be a boon or *bane* is yet to be seen.

**BANEFUL** (adj) *[beyn-fuhl]*

*Syn:* destructive; causing ruin or death

*Ant:* advantageous; beneficial; fortunate

*Usage:* Mohammed was a believer in the *baneful* influence of the evil eye.

**BARB** (n) *[bahrb]*

*Syn:* sharp projection from a fishhook, etc; openly cutting remark

*Ant:* bluntness

*Usage:* When irate, she would use her words like sharp *barbs*, which could really hurt people.

**BARD** (n) *[bahrd]*

*Syn:* poet

*Usage:* Robert Burns, the poet, is Scotland's best-loved *bard*.

**BAREFACED** (adj) *[BAIR-feyst]*

*Syn:* shameless; bold; unconcealed

*Ant:* careful; quiet; shamed

*Usage:* I could not believe that she would escape with such a *barefaced* lie but she did.

**BAROQUE** (adj) *[buh-ROHK]*

*Syn:* highly ornate

*Ant:* simple, unadorned

*Usage:* The mansion was built in *baroque* fashion with columns and arcades.

**BARRAGE** (n) *[buh-RAHZH]*

*Syn:* barrier lay down by artillery fire

*Ant:* deluge

*Usage:* A *barrage* of bullets hit the bunker, throwing the soldiers to the ground.

**BARTERER** (n) *[BAHR-ter-er]*

*Syn:* trader

*Usage:* When John discovered that Matthew was a *barterer*, he wished to learn from him more about trade and negotiations.

**BASTION** (n) *[BAS-chuh n]*

*Syn:* fortress; defense; fortification

*Ant:* weakness

*Usage:* The troops decided to line up along the *bastion*, which offered them a vantage point of view.

**BATE** (v) *[beyt]*

*Syn:* let down; restrain; lessen

*Ant:* add

*Usage:* The students waited for the year-end results with *bated* breath.

**BAUBLE** (n) *[BAW-buh l]*

*Syn:* trinket; trifle

*Ant:* item of significance

*Usage:* Billy had gone through endless adventures and hardships in search of the diamonds but ended up with only a few *baubles* and gems that weren't worth much.

**BAWDY** (adj) *[BAW-dee]*

*Syn:* indecent; obscene

*Ant:* serious; upstanding

*Usage:* The sailors loved to unwind at the pub, drinking beer and sharing *bawdy* jokes.

**BEATIFIC** (adj) *[bee-uh-TIF-ik]*

*Syn:* giving bliss; blissful

*Ant:* miserable; sorrowful; unhappy

*Usage:* The pope bestowed a *beatific* smile upon them thrilling their hearts.

**BEATIFY** (v) *[bee-AT-uh-fahy]*

*Syn:* bless or sanctify

*Ant:* condemn; curse; damn

*Usage:* The contract blesses, canonizes and *beatifies* this slip of paper as the total sum due.

**BEATITUDE** (n) *[bee-AT-i-tood]*

*Syn:* blessedness; state of bliss

*Ant:* grief; misery; sorrow; unhappiness

*Usage:* When the Smiths finally reached the Virgin Mary shrine and beheld her carved angelic face, they felt no end of *beatitude* and bliss.

**BEDRAGGLED** (adj) *[bi-DRAG-uh ld]*

*Syn:* wet thoroughly; stained with mud; fatigued

*Ant:* energized; refreshed

*Usage:* Despite Jim's insistence that he had gotten into a mishap, the hotel doorman refused to let him in, seeing his *bedraggled* appearance.

**BEGRUDGE** (v) *[bi-GRUHJ]*

*Syn:* resent; envy

*Ant:* affirm; allow; concede

*Usage:* We weren't so petty-minded as to *begrudge* Kylie her hard-won success.

**BEGUILE** (v) *[bi-GAHYL]*

*Syn:* mislead or delude; pass time

*Ant:* be honest

*Usage:* Regardless of whether they are friends or strangers, Carmen can easily *beguile* anyone, winning them over with her duplicity.

**BEHOOVE** (v) *[bi-HOOV]*

*Syn:* be suited to; be incumbent upon

*Ant:* disagree

*Usage:* It doesn't *behoove* a girl from such an affluent family to be talking in this manner.

**BELABOR** (v) *[bi-LEY-ber]*

*Syn:* explain or go over excessively or to a ridiculous degree; attack verbally

*Ant:* relax; simplify

*Usage:* With cruel, harsh words they *belabored* the importance of the code of conduct they had raised her to follow…and she had broken.

**BELEAGUER** (v) *[bi-LEE-ger]*

*Syn:* besiege or attack; harass; annoy

*Ant:* leave alone

*Usage:* Faced with bankruptcy of his company, the director was *beleaguered* with pressures and tensions of all kinds.

**BELITTLE** (v) *[bi-LIT-l]*

*Syn:* disparage or depreciate; put down

*Ant:* build up; praise

*Usage:* It was not right of Jake to *belittle* his neighbor's achievements in this manner.

**BELLICOSE** (adj) *[BEL-i-kohs]*

*Syn:* warlike

*Ant:* peaceful

*Usage:* His *bellicose* and arrogant behavior was beginning to get on everybody's nerves.

**BEMOAN** (v) *[bih-MOHN]*

*Syn:* lament; express disapproval of

*Ant:* gloat; be happy

*Usage:* I could *bemoan* the lack of articles but I won't; my pleas fall on deaf ears.

**BEMUSED** (adj) *[bi-MYOOZD]*

*Syn:* confused; lost in thought; preoccupied; absentminded

*Ant:* attentive

*Usage:* He could see that she hadn't been paying attention at all when she gave a *bemused* look in response to his query.

# Chapter 3

## (Benediction – Centaur)

*This chapter covers the following words along with their part of speech, pronunciation, synonyms and antonym, if applicable. Sample usage of the word is also illustrated.*

| | | |
|---|---|---|
| benediction | bowdlerize | candor |
| benefactor | brackish | cantankerous |
| benevolent | braggadocio | cantata |
| benign | brandish | canto |
| benison | brawn | capacious |
| bequeath | breach | capitulate |
| berate | brevity | capricious |
| bereft | brindled | carafe |
| besmirch | bristling | carapace |
| bestow | brooch | carcinogenic |
| betroth | brunt | careen |
| bicameral | brusque | caricature |
| bicker | buccaneer | carnal |
| biennial | bucolic | carousal |
| bifurcated | buffoonery | carrion |
| bilious | bugaboo | cartographer |
| billowing | bulwark | caste |
| bivouac | bungle | castigation |
| blandish | burgeon | casual |
| blandishment | burlesque | cataclysm |
| blasé | burly | catapult |
| blasphemous | burnish | catechism |
| blatant | buttress | catharsis |
| blighted | cabal | caucus |
| bludgeon | cache | caulk |
| blurt | cacophonous | cavalcade |
| bluster | cadaver | cavil |
| bohemian | cadence | celibate |
| boisterous | cadge | censorious |
| bolster | cajole | centaur |
| bombastic | caliber | |
| boorish | callow | |
| bouillon | calorific | |
| bountiful | cameo | |
| bourgeois | canard | |

**BENEDICTION** (n) *[ben-i-DIK-shuh n]*

*Syn:* blessing

*Ant:* malediction; curse; disapproval; censure; execration

*Usage:* They waited for hours so that they could get the Cardinal's *benediction* for the newborn.

**BENEFACTOR** (n) *[BEN-uh-fak-ter]*

*Syn:* gift giver; patron

*Ant:* malefactor

*Usage:* An anonymous *benefactor* has left the bereaved and impoverished family a huge sum of money that will see them through this dark phase.

**BENEVOLENT** (adj) *[buh-NEV-uh-luh nt]*

*Syn:* generous; charitable

*Ant:* niggardly; miserly; cruel

*Usage:* James Mender was a kindly, *benevolent* man and often gave out large sums of his income to various charities.

**BENIGN** (adj) *[bi-NAHYN]*

*Syn:* kindly; favorable; not malignant

*Ant:* malignant

*Usage:* I had never come across such a *benign*, caring person before; I was overwhelmed by his kind gesture.

**BENISON** (n) *[BEN-uh-zuh n]*

*Syn:* blessing

*Ant:* execration; anathema

*Usage:* When the priest uttered the holy *benison*, tears streamed down the faces of people in the congregation.

**BEQUEATH** (v) *[bi-KWEETH]*

*Syn:* leave to someone by a will; hand down

*Ant:* take

*Usage:* Wallace *bequeathed* his whole property to his daughter and retired to the mountains to lead a secluded life.

**BERATE** (v) *[bi-REYT]*

*Syn:* scold strongly; reprimand

*Ant:* commend

*Usage:* Jane's mother *berated* her all day for disobeying her instructions and wandering off into the woods alone.

**BEREFT** (adj) *[bi-REFT]*

*Syn:* deprived of; lacking; desolate because of a loss

*Ant:* full; happy

*Usage:* Suddenly *bereft* of his great power, the former tycoon now sank deep into depression.

**BESMIRCH** (v) *[bi-SMURCH]*

*Syn:* soil; defile

*Ant:* honor; compliment

*Usage:* Mike did not dare enter the town after the townsfolk discovered that it was he who had *besmirched* young Jenny's reputation.

**BESTOW** (v) *[bi-STOH]*

*Syn:* give

*Ant:* take away

*Usage:* In recognition of his contributions to the country's economy, the college decided to *bestow* upon him an honorary doctorate.

**BETROTH** (v) *[bi-TROHTH]*

*Syn:* become engaged to marry; marry

*Ant:* divorce; leave; separate

*Usage:* They are to be *betrothed* this weekend and married next month.

**BICAMERAL** (adj) *[bahy-KAM-er-uh l]*

*Syn:* two-chambered, as a legislative body

*Ant:* unicameral

*Usage:* It was decided that a *bicameral* legislature of a Senate and House of Representatives would be formed.

# Chapter 3

**BICKER** (v) [BIK-er]

*Syn:* quarrel

*Ant:* agree; converse; chat

*Usage:* They spent the whole night *bickering* and arguing about the money.

**BIENNIAL** (adj) [bahy-EN-ee-uh l]

*Syn:* every two years

*Ant:* annual

*Usage:* This function is a *biennial* event, the last event being held two years ago.

**BIFURCATED** (adj) [BAHY-fer-keyt-ed]

*Syn:* divided into two branches; forked

*Ant:* undivided; whole

*Usage:* The road is *bifurcated* into two streets, thus adding more confusion to first-time visitors.

**BILIOUS** (adj) [BIL-yuh s]

*Syn:* suffering from indigestion; irritable

*Ant:* healthy

*Usage:* People tend to keep away from him because of his *bilious* nature and short temper.

**BILLOWING** (adj) [BIL-oh-ing]

*Syn:* swelling out in waves; surging

*Ant:* compact; shrinking

*Usage:* The *billowing* smoke from burning houses was a dreadful sight.

**BIVOUAC** (n) [BIV-oo-ak]

*Syn:* temporary encampment

*Ant:* permanent quarters

*Usage:* To rest for the night, we built a *bivouac* at the base of the mountain with tarpaulin and poles.

**BLANDISH** (v) [blan-dish]

*Syn:* cajole; coax with flattery

*Ant:* allow

*Usage:* The students *blandished* the guard into letting them through the college gate at night.

**BLANDISHMENT** (n) [BLAN-dish-muh nt]

*Syn:* flattery

*Ant:* disgust

*Usage:* Fed up with the saleswoman's *blandishments*, we bought two of the items even though we didn't actually need them.

**BLASÉ** (adj) [blah-ZEY]

*Syn:* bored with pleasure or dissipation

*Ant:* enthusiastic; excited

*Usage:* Having such a *blasé*, relaxed attitude even in the presence of the boss will do Jack no good.

**BLASPHEMOUS** (adj) [BLAS-fuh-muh s]

*Syn:* profane; impious

*Ant:* pious

*Usage:* His speech was so offensive and *blasphemous* that even before he was halfway through it, the crowd was aiming rotten tomatoes at him.

**BLATANT** (adj) [BLEYT-nt]

*Syn:* flagrant; conspicuously obvious; loudly offensive

*Ant:* soft; noiseless; quiet; reserved; refined

*Usage:* She flirted with him *blatantly*, without any qualms.

**BLIGHTED** (adj) [blahyt-ed]

*Syn:* suffering from a disease; destroyed

*Ant:* healthy

*Usage:* Everything he owned had been *blighted* in a few seconds during the bombing, but he was glad to escape with his life.

**BLUDGEON** (n) [BLUHJ-uh n]

*Syn:* club; heavy-headed weapon

*Usage:* The solid, wooden club could be used as a *bludgeon* against the bear if one were to attack him.

**BLURT** (v) *[blurt]*
*Syn:* utter impulsively
*Ant:* stay silent
*Usage:* Trembling with fear, the man *blurted* out the truth about the robbery.

**BLUSTER** (v) *[BLUHS-ter]*
*Syn:* blow in heavy gusts; bully
*Ant:* be modest
*Usage:* Do not *bluster* about dead theology or throw Calvin's name around in derision; just read the words themselves in the Bible.

**BOHEMIAN** (adj) *[boh-HEE-mee-uhn]*
*Syn:* unconventional
*Ant:* conventional
*Usage:* It used to attract true *bohemians*; now it attracts tired London media types.

**BOISTEROUS** (adj) *[BOI-ster-uh s]*
*Syn:* violent; rough; noisy
*Ant:* peaceful; calm; serene; self-possessed
*Usage:* The party was *boisterous* and loud, as usual.

**BOLSTER** (v) *[BOHL-ster]*
*Syn:* support; reinforce
*Ant:* hinder; obstruct; prevent
*Usage:* They *bolstered* their favorite participant's spirits by cheering for him at the top of their lungs.

**BOMBASTIC** (adj) *[bom-BAS-tik]*
*Syn:* pompous; using inflated language
*Ant:* humble
*Usage:* Making *bombastic* statements is easy enough; to prove that you really possess knowledge is quite tough.

**BOORISH** (adj) *[BOO R-ish]*
*Syn:* rude; clownish
*Ant:* pleasant; polite
*Usage:* Keith is rather too aggressive and *boorish*.

**BOUILLON** (n) *[BOO L-yon]*
*Syn:* clear beef soup
*Usage:* She offered him the bowl of piping hot *bouillon*, which he grabbed eagerly, for he had been famished for days.

**BOUNTIFUL** (adj) *[BOUN-tuh-fuh l]*
*Syn:* abundant; graciously generous
*Ant:* scarce
*Usage:* Anne is a kind, generous soul and loves to donate *bountiful* gifts.

**BOURGEOIS** (adj) *[boo r-ZHWAH]*
*Syn:* middle-class; selfishly materialistic; dully conventional
*Ant:* aristocratic
*Usage:* It was quite *bourgeois* for Anne Marie to chatter with the townsfolk so casually; after all, she was a blue-blooded aristocrat.

**BOWDLERIZE** (v) *[BOHD-luh-rahyz]*
*Syn:* expurgate; cleanse; purge
*Ant:* allow; permit
*Usage:* To Peter's horror, his masterpiece of a novel had been badly *bowdlerized* by the novice editor.

**BRACKISH** (adj) *[BRAK-ish]*
*Syn:* somewhat saline; stagnant
*Ant:* moving
*Usage:* The lost hikers found a *brackish* stream and risked drinking from it despite the salty taste of the water.

**BRAGGADOCIO** (n) *[brag-uh-DOH-shee-oh]*

*Syn:* boasting

*Ant:* humility

*Usage:* By now, we were all tired and bored by Ken's *braggadocio* and boasting.

**BRANDISH** (v) *[BRAN-dish]*

*Syn:* wave around; flourish

*Ant:* not show

*Usage: Brandishing* a large knife, he demanded cash, then escaped on the pedal bike.

**BRAWN** (n) *[brawn]*

*Syn:* muscular strength; sturdiness

*Ant:* weakness

*Usage:* Brains are better than *brawn* any day.

**BREACH** (n) *[breech]*

*Syn:* breaking of contract or duty; fissure or gap

*Ant:* wholeness

*Usage:* The primary code of conduct in the group must never suffer from a *breach*.

**BREVITY** (n) *[BREV-i-tee]*

*Syn:* conciseness

*Ant:* lengthiness; longevity; permanence

*Usage: Brevity* is the soul of wit.

**BRINDLED** (adj) *[BRIN-dld]*

*Syn:* tawny or grayish with streaks or spots

*Ant:* solid-colored

*Usage:* A fine, *brindled* animal was following Mary.

**BRISTLING** (adj) *[bris-uhl-ing]*

*Syn:* rising like bristles; showing irritation

*Ant:* calm

*Usage:* By the time Jenny reached home after her date, it was way past midnight and her father was *bristling* with anger.

**BROOCH** (n) *[brohch]*

*Syn:* ornamental clasp

*Usage:* Among the various ornaments in her jewelry box, the most precious one was the gold *brooch* given to her by her grandmother.

**BRUNT** (n) *[bruhnt]*

*Syn:* main impact or shock

*Usage:* He took the full *brunt* of the wolves' attack.

**BRUSQUE** (adj) *[bruhsk]*

*Syn:* blunt; abrupt

*Ant:* courteous; polite

*Usage:* His manner of speaking was *brusque* and curt.

**BUCCANEER** (n) *[buhk-uh-neer]*

*Syn:* pirate

*Usage:* Later, the governors of Caribbean islands such as Jamaica paid the *buccaneers* to attack Spanish treasure ships and ports.

**BUCOLIC** (adj) *[byoo-KOL-ik]*

*Syn:* rustic; pastoral

*Ant:* urban

*Usage:* Walt Whitman loved to ramble for hours through the *bucolic* man countryside.

**BUFFOONERY** (n) *[buh-FOO-nuh-ree]*

*Syn:* clowning

*Ant:* seriousness

*Usage:* The man was a disciplinarian and would not tolerate any *buffoonery*.

**BUGABOO** (n) *[BUHG-uh-boo]*

*Syn:* bugbear; object of baseless terror; fear

*Ant:* bravery

*Usage:* Mike dismissed my fears as a *bugaboo* and promptly went off to sleep again.

**BULWARK** (n) *[BOOL-werk]*

*Syn:* earthwork or other strong defense; person who defends

*Ant:* weak point

*Usage:* The soldiers took up positions along the *bulwark*.

**BUNGLE** (v) *[BUHNG-guhl]*

*Syn:* mismanage; blunder

*Ant:* manage well; succeed

*Usage:* Peter was bound to *bungle* the operation; he is such a clumsy, careless man.

**BURGEON** (v) *[BUR-juh n]*

*Syn:* grow forth; send out buds

*Ant:* atrophy

*Usage:* The venture seems to be *burgeoning* day by day.

**BURLESQUE** (v) *[ber-LESK]*

*Syn:* give an imitation that ridicules

*Ant:* perform seriously

*Usage:* He decided to *burlesque* the unbearable conditions, using humor to point out the need for improvements.

**BURLY** (adj) *[BUR-lee]*

*Syn:* husky; muscular

*Ant:* diminutive

*Usage:* The henchman was hefty and *burly*; his mere appearance sent shivers down our spine.

**BURNISH** (v) *[BUR-nish]*

*Syn:* make shiny by rubbing; polish

*Ant:* dull

*Usage:* The table had been *burnished* with wax in preparation for his visit.

**BUTTRESS** (v) *[BUH-tris]*

*Syn:* support; prop up

*Ant:* break down

*Usage:* The commander *buttressed* the walls of the fort in hopes of keeping the villagers inside alive.

**CABAL** (n) *[kuh-BAL]*

*Syn:* small group of persons secretly united to promote their own interest

*Usage:* The police unearthed a heinous *cabal* to assassinate the president.

**CACHE** (n) *[kash]*

*Syn:* hiding place

*Ant:* open location

*Usage:* It was suspected that Jim Howard had stashed away the loot in a *cache* underneath his trailer.

**CACOPHONOUS** (adj) *[kuh-KOF-uh-nuh s]*

*Syn:* discordant; inharmonious

*Ant:* euphonious

*Usage:* I wonder how far she would get as a singer with that *cacophonous* voice.

**CADAVER** (n) *[kuh-DAV-er]*

*Syn:* corpse

*Ant:* living body

*Usage:* A partly mutilated *cadaver* lay on the table when I entered the autopsy room.

**CADENCE** (n) *[KEYD-ns]*

*Syn:* rhythmic rise and fall (of words or sounds); beat

*Usage:* The music had a very melodious *cadence*, making us all sway to it.

**CADGE** (v) *[kaj]*

*Syn:* beg; mooch; panhandle

*Ant:* lend

*Usage:* I believe he was able to *cadge* a lift on the bus.

**CAJOLE** (v) *[kuh-JOHL]*

*Syn:* coax; wheedle

*Ant:* scold; warn; blame; antagonize; displease; chide

*Usage:* We *cajoled* and persuaded her to accompany us to the picnic.

**CALIBER** (n) *[KAL-uh-ber]*

*Syn:* ability; quality

*Ant:* inability; incompetence

*Usage:* Peter underestimated his own *caliber*.

**CALLOW** (adj) *[KAL-oh]*

*Syn:* youthful; immature; inexperienced

*Ant:* mature; experienced

*Usage:* The young recruit was *callow* and immature.

**CALORIFIC** (adj) *[kal-uh-RIF-ik]*

*Syn:* heat-producing

*Ant:* cold-blooded

*Usage:* The doctor asked her to abstain from foods containing carbohydrates as they could be *calorific*.

**CAMEO** (n) *[KAM-ee-oh]*

*Syn:* shell or jewel carved in relief; star's special appearance in a minor role in a film

*Usage:* Valerie had been offered a *cameo* role in the film but she declined to accept it.

**CANARD** (n) *[kuh-NAHRD]*

*Syn:* false rumor

*Ant:* honesty; truth

*Usage:* His *canard* came back to haunt him when his friends discovered he was the source of the hurtful rumor.

**CANDOR** (n) *[KAN-der]*

*Syn:* frankness; open honesty

*Ant:* artifice; deception

*Usage:* I was pleased with her *candor* and frankness.

**CANTANKEROUS** (adj) *[kan-TANG-ker-uh s]*

*Syn:* ill-humored; irritable

*Ant:* amiable

*Usage:* With age, old man Jim has become *cantankerous* and troublesome.

**CANTATA** (n) *[kuh n-TAH-tuh]*

*Syn:* story set to music, to be sung by a chorus

*Usage:* We stood at the back of the auditorium to watch Priscilla's class perform the *cantata* telling the story of the town's origin.

**CANTO** (n) *[KAN-toh]*

*Syn:* division of a long poem

*Usage:* They recited the *canto* together melodiously.

**CAPACIOUS** (adj) *[kuh-PEY-shuh s]*

*Syn:* spacious; fickle; incalculable; ample

*Ant:* limited; shallow; restricted; narrow; petty; small

*Usage:* The man is built of *capacious* proportions.

**CAPITULATE** (v) *[kuh-PICH-uh-leyt]*

*Syn:* surrender

*Ant:* resist

*Usage:* Despite his unwillingness to take part in the games, eventually Paul *capitulated* to the pressure of his peers.

**CAPRICIOUS** (adj) *[kuh-PRISH-uh s]*

*Syn:* unpredictable; fickle; whimsical

*Ant:* steady; constant; dependable

*Usage:* Kenneth is too *capricious* to stay steady with the new job; he has been job-hopping continuously for the last two years.

**CARAFE** (n) [kuh-RAF]

Syn: glass water bottle

Usage: He poured warm water from the *carafe* into a glass and handed it to her saying it would soothe her sore throat.

**CARAPACE** (n) [KAR-uh-peys]

Syn: shell covering the back (of a turtle, crab, etc)

Ant: inside; interior

Usage: The turtle's body was trembling beneath its hard shell-like *carapace*.

**CARCINOGENIC** (adj) [kahr-suh-nuh-JEN-ik]

Syn: causing cancer

Ant: healing

Usage: The tumor was diagnosed to be *carcinogenic* and Martha had barely another six months to live.

**CAREEN** (v) [kuh-REEN]

Syn: lurch; sway from side to side

Ant: travel in a straight line

Usage: The car *careened* dangerously on its side, about to fall off the bridge any moment.

**CARICATURE** (n) [KAR-i-kuh-cher]

Syn: distortion; burlesque

Ant: reality; fact; truth

Usage: Little Mike was found drawing *caricatures* of his teachers in class.

**CARNAL** (adj) [KAHR-nl]

Syn: fleshly

Ant: spiritual; ethereal; exalted; refined; pure; temperate

Usage: A priest from that church was condemned and arrested for having indulged in *carnal* pleasures with a young devotee.

**CAROUSAL** (n) [kuh-ROU-zuh l]

Syn: drunken revelry

Ant: solemnity

Usage: The *carousal* and merry making to celebrate King George's victory lasted all night long.

**CARRION** (n) [KAR-ee-uh n]

Syn: rotting flesh of a dead body

Ant: living organism

Usage: Vultures are birds that love to feed on *carrion*.

**CARTOGRAPHER** (n) [kahr-TOG-ruh-feer]

Syn: map-maker

Usage: Mike loves maps with such passion that there is no doubt he'll grow up to be a *cartographer*.

**CASTE** (n) [kast]

Syn: one of the hereditary classes in Hindu society; social stratification; prestige

Usage: The application form contained a slot to fill in *caste* and religion.

**CASTIGATION** (n) [KAS-ti-gey shun]

Syn: punishment; severe criticism; chastisement; blame

Ant: exaltation; commendation; praise

Usage: Jenny knew she was in for a major *castigation* for having disobeyed the hostel warden's rules.

**CASUAL** (adj) [KAZH-oo-uh l]

Syn: accidental; not regular or permanent; careless; informal

Ant: intended; careful

Usage: The young men were dressed in *casual* attire comprising of jeans and T-shirts.

**CATACLYSM** (n) [KAT-uh-kliz-uh m]

Syn: upheaval; deluge

Ant: boon; happiness

*Usage:* We weren't prepared for the *cataclysm* that occurred suddenly throwing our lives totally out of gear.

**CATAPULT** (n) *[KAT-uh-puhlt]*

*Syn:* slingshot; a hurling machine

*Usage:* The boy's weapon of choice was a *catapult* with a leather sling.

**CATECHISM** (n) *[KAT-i-kiz-uh m]*

*Syn:* book for religious instruction; instruction by question and answer

*Usage:* Our new priest loves to preach about *catechism*.

**CATHARSIS** (n) *[kuh-THAHR-sis]*

*Syn:* purging or cleansing of any passage of the body

*Ant:* contamination

*Usage:* Shedding tears and giving vent to emotions, according to psychologists, is a form of *catharsis*; it heals us internally.

**CAUCUS** (n) *[KAW-kuh s]*

*Syn:* private meeting of members of a party to select officers or determine policy

*Usage:* The annual *caucus* was held in the basement of the council hall.

**CAULK** (v) *[kawk]*

*Syn:* make watertight by filling in cracks

*Ant:* loosen; unfasten

*Usage:* She instructed the kids to *caulk* the windows tightly for there was to be a thunderstorm.

**CAVALCADE** (n) *[kav-uh l-KEYD]*

*Syn:* procession; parade

*Usage:* The throngs gathered at the town square eagerly watched the colorful *cavalcade*.

**CAVIL** (v) *[KAV-uh l]*

*Syn:* make frivolous objections; criticize

*Ant:* support; approve; endorse

*Usage:* His pet pastime is to *cavil* upon everyone's speech, pointing out the faults in grammar and diction.

**CELIBATE** (adj) *[SEL-uh-bit]*

*Syn:* unmarried; abstaining from sexual intercourse

*Ant:* promiscuous

*Usage:* The man had taken an oath to stay *celibate* for a year and abstain from pleasures of the flesh.

**CENSORIOUS** (adj) *[sen-SAWR-ee-uh s]*

*Syn:* critical

*Ant:* complimentary; flattering

*Usage:* Her behavior is getting more *censorious* every day; she complains and is disparaging all the time.

**CENTAUR** (n) *[SEN-tawr]*

*Syn:* mythical figure; half man and half horse

*Usage:* Little Peter then drew a beautiful picture of a *centaur* and proceeded to fill it with colored crayons.

This page is intentionally left blank

# Chapter 4

## (Centrifuge – Concomitant)

*This chapter covers the following words along with their part of speech, pronunciation, synonyms and antonym, if applicable. Sample usage of the word is also illustrated.*

| | | |
|---|---|---|
| centrifuge | clamber | colossal |
| centripetal | clamor | comatose |
| centurion | clangor | comely |
| certitude | clarion | comestible |
| cessation | claustrophobia | comeuppance |
| chafe | clavicle | comity |
| chagrin | cleave | commemorate |
| chameleon | cleft | commensurate |
| chaotic | clemency | commodious |
| charisma | cliche | compact |
| charlatan | climactic | compelling |
| chary | clime | compendium |
| chase | clique | compilation |
| chassis | cloister | complacent |
| chastened | clout | complementary |
| chastise | coagulate | compliant |
| chauvinist | coalesce | component |
| cherubic | coda | composure |
| chicanery | coddle | compound |
| chide | codicil | compress |
| chimerical | coeval | comprise |
| choleric | cogitate | compromise |
| chortle | cognate | compunction |
| chronic | cognitive | concatenate |
| churlish | cognizance | concede |
| ciliated | cohabit | conceit |
| cipher | cohorts | concentric |
| circlet | coiffure | conception |
| circumlocution | colander | concession |
| circumscribe | collaborate | conclave |
| circumvent | collage | concoct |
| cistern | collate | concomitant |
| citadel | colloquial | |
| clairvoyant | colloquy | |

**CENTRIFUGE** (n) [SEN-truh-fyooj]
Syn: machine that separates substances by whirling them
Usage: The new machine acts like a *centrifuge* and spins very quickly, causing the solids and liquids inside it to separate by centrifugal action.

**CENTRIPETAL** (adj) [sen-TRIP-i-tl]
Syn: tending toward the center
Ant: centrifugal; tending toward the outside
Usage: The *centripetal* force was magnetizing and pulling her towards the door.

**CENTURION** (n) [sen-TOO R-ee-uh n]
Syn: Roman army officer
Usage: There was a carved stone statue of a *centurion* in full regalia.

**CERTITUDE** (n) [sur-ti-tood]
Syn: certainty
Ant: uncertainty
Usage: The comedy of forgiveness has no such luxurious *certitude*.

**CESSATION** (n) [se-SEY-shuh n]
Syn: stoppage
Ant: continuance; continuity.
Usage: After a full day, the storm still showed no signs of *cessation*.

**CHAFE** (v) [cheyf]
Syn: warm by rubbing; make sore (by rubbing)
Ant: soothe; smooth; calm; console
Usage: The fall down the cliff had badly *chafed* her hands and caused several bruises.

**CHAGRIN** (n) [shuh-GRIN]
Syn: vexation (caused by humiliation or injured pride); disappointment
Ant: delight; pleasure; happiness
Usage: To her great *chagrin*, the thief had stolen the bag containing her passport and tickets.

**CHAMELEON** (n) [kuh-MEE-lee-uh n]
Syn: lizard that changes color in different situations
Ant: permanence of color
Usage: Keith changes his opinions as fast as a *chameleon* changes color.

**CHAOTIC** (adj) [key-OT-ik]
Syn: in utter disorder
Ant: orderly
Usage: My schedule this week has been very *chaotic* and confusing.

**CHARISMA** (n) [kuh-RIZ-muh]
Syn: divine gift; great popular charm or appeal of a political leader
Ant: repulsion
Usage: Catherine's allure and *charisma* captivated Paul's attention so much that he never left her side all evening.

**CHARLATAN** (n) [SHAHR-luh-tn]
Syn: quack; pretender to knowledge
Ant: the real thing
Usage: The lady is a *charlatan*; no one trusts her to do legitimate business anymore.

**CHARY** (adj) [CHAIR-ee]
Syn: cautious; sparing or restrained about giving
Ant: culpable; liberal; lavish; profuse; eager
Usage: Jack is a bit *chary* of going to the local doctor after he read reports about someone dying there.

**CHASE** (v) [cheys]
Syn: ornament a metal surface by indenting
Usage: The jeweler *chased* our names inside our wedding

rings so they would be engraved there for eternity.

**CHASSIS** (n) *[CHAS-ee]*

*Syn:* framework and working parts of an automobile

*Ant:* automotive engine

*Usage:* They had to dismantle the *chassis* to get the body out from within it.

**CHASTENED** (adj) *[chey-suhn d]*

*Syn:* humbled; subdued; rebuked

*Ant:* encouraged; comforted

*Usage:* Martha was *chastened* for misbehaving with other girls in the class.

**CHASTISE** (v) *[chas-TAHYZ]*

*Syn:* punish

*Ant:* commend; flatter; indulge; pamper; spoil; demoralize; degrade

*Usage:* With sharp words, he *chastised* her for inviting strangers into the house in his absence.

**CHAUVINIST** (n) *[shoh-vuh-NIST]*

*Syn:* blindly devoted patriot; bigot

*Ant:* fair-minded person

*Usage:* To their immense dismay, the women discovered that the new mayor of the town was a *chauvinist*.

**CHERUBIC** (adj) *[chuh-ROO-bik]*

*Syn:* angelic; innocent-looking

*Ant:* devilish

*Usage:* The frescoes on the ceiling depicted three *cherubic* angels.

**CHICANERY** (n) *[shi-KEY-nuh-ree]*

*Syn:* trickery; deception

*Ant:* honesty

*Usage:* It's yet another of his tricks or *chicanery*; we refuse to believe him anymore.

**CHIDE** (v) *[chahyd]*

*Syn:* scold

*Ant:* hail

*Usage:* He *chided* her for inviting strangers into the house in his absence.

**CHIMERICAL** (adj) *[ki-MER-i-kuh l]*

*Syn:* fantastically improbable; highly unrealistic imaginative

*Ant:* real; ordinary

*Usage:* The whole episode was so unreal that it seemed *chimerical* to her.

**CHOLERIC** (adj) *[KOL-er-ik]*

*Syn:* hot-tempered

*Ant:* calm

*Usage:* His *choleric* attitude alienates people more than anything else.

**CHORTLE** (v) *[chawr-tl]*

*Syn:* chuckle with delight

*Usage:* She gave a mighty *chortle* and said, "I'm drunk as a skunk."

**CHRONIC** (adj) *[KRON-ik]*

*Syn:* long established as a disease; time after time; frequent; repeated

*Ant:* intermittent

*Usage:* Michael is a *chronic* gambler.

**CHURLISH** (adj) *[CHUR-lish]*

*Syn:* boorish; rude

*Ant:* captivating

*Usage:* We all wondered what had made Gary so *churlish*; normally he was so cheerful and pleasant-mannered.

**CILIATED** (adj) *[sil-ee-it]*

*Syn:* minute organism having minute hairs

*Usage:* An ameba, however, does not feed entirely on plants; it is also carnivorous, feeding on tiny *ciliated organisms.*

**CIPHER** (n) [SAHY-fer]

*Syn:* secret code

*Ant:* uncoded language.

*Usage:* The metal bracelet contained a secret *cipher* inside it.

**CIRCLET** (n) [SUR-klit]

*Syn:* small ring; band

*Usage:* The gold *circlet* on Anna's arm was badly damaged when she fell from the parapet, but she herself was barely injured.

**CIRCUMLOCUTION** (n) [sur-kuh m-loh-KYOO-shuh n]

*Syn:* indirect or roundabout expression

*Ant:* terseness; conciseness; directness; coherence; simplicity

*Usage:* The restless crowd was getting tired of the candidate's *circumlocution* and wanted shorter speeches.

**CIRCUMSCRIBE** (v) [SUR-kuh m-SKRAHYB]

*Syn:* limit; confine

*Ant:* allow; permit

*Usage:* The movements of the group have been severely *circumscribed* since the new laws came into effect.

**CIRCUMVENT** (v) [sur-kuh m-VENT]

*Syn:* outwit; baffle

*Ant:* aid; assist; comply with

*Usage:* Gordon was smart at *circumventing* the police despite the many barriers they erected.

**CISTERN** (n) [SIS-tern]

*Syn:* reservoir water tank

*Usage:* The woman collected rainwater in the *cistern* and then used it to wash her hair for a natural smoothness.

**CITADEL** (n) [SIT-uh-dl]

*Syn:* fortress

*Ant:* unprotected area

*Usage:* The women of the royal family huddled inside the *citadel* even as the kingdom was taken under siege by the enemy.

**CLAIRVOYANT** (adj) [klair-VOI-uh nt]

*Syn:* having foresight; fortunetelling

*Ant:* shortsighted

*Usage:* She must be *clairvoyant;* how else could she have predicted I was arriving in that city without even having met or called me?

**CLAMBER** (v) [KLAM-ber]

*Syn:* climb by crawling

*Usage:* As the fire began spreading, they *clambered* up the stairs leading to the terrace.

**CLAMOR** (n) [KLAM-er]

*Syn:* noise

*Ant:* silence; acquiescence; quiet; reticence

*Usage:* We raised our voices to the director in a *clamor* for more holidays.

**CLANGOR** (n) [KLANG-er]

*Syn:* loud; resounding noise

*Ant:* silence

*Usage:* The sudden heavy *clangor* of the bells at midnight awoke every villager.

**CLARION** (adj) [klar-ee-uhn]

*Syn:* shrill; trumpetlike sound

*Ant:* silence

*Usage:* The soldiers responded to the *clarion* call of the bugle and headed to the front to fight another day.

*(Centrifuge - Concomitant)*

**CLAUSTROPHOBIA** (n) [klaw-struh-FOH-bee-uh]

*Syn:* fear of enclosed spaces

*Ant:* agoraphobia; fear of open spaces

*Usage:* Wilma had a fear of *claustrophobia* so she refused to stay in the tiny room alone.

**CLAVICLE** (n) [KLAV-i-kuh l]

*Syn:* collarbone

*Usage:* The karate chop landed squarely on his *clavicle*, snapping it.

**CLEAVE** (v) [kleev]

*Syn:* split or sever; cling to; remain faithful to

*Ant:* remain whole

*Usage:* The butcher moved to *cleave* the carcass into smaller portions.

**CLEFT** (n) [kleft]

*Syn:* hollow; indentation

*Ant:* protuberance

*Usage:* The dark-haired man had a *cleft* in his chin.

**CLEMENCY** (n) [KLEM-uh n-see]

*Syn:* disposition to be lenient; mildness, as of the weather

*Ant:* severity

*Usage:* The prisoners petitioned the mayor for *clemency* and pardon.

**CLICHÉ** (n) [klee-SHEY]

*Syn:* phrase dulled in meaning by repetition

*Ant:* original expression

*Usage:* The statement was yet another *cliché*.

**CLIMACTIC** (adj) [klahy-MAK-tik]

*Syn:* relating to the highest point

*Ant:* anticlimactic

*Usage:* We waited with bated breath for the *climactic* ending.

**CLIME** (n) [klahym]

*Syn:* region; climate

*Usage:* We were unused to the tropical *climes* so we promptly fell ill.

**CLIQUE** (n) [kleek]

*Syn:* small exclusive group

*Ant:* open group

*Usage:* The cheerleaders formed a *clique* in the middle school.

**CLOISTER** (n) [KLOI-ster]

*Syn:* monastery or convent

*Usage:* Mary was then sheltered in the *cloister* with nuns watching over her.

**CLOUT** (n) [klout]

*Syn:* great influence (especially political or social)

*Ant:* inconsequentiality

*Usage:* John Matheson has a lot of *clout* and power in this city; he can get away with anything.

**COAGULATE** (v) [koh-AG-yuh-leyt]

*Syn:* thicken; congeal; clot

*Ant:* rarefy; expand; dissipate; thin; liquefy

*Usage:* The liquid gel was *coagulating* because of the cool temperature.

**COALESCE** (v) [koh-uh-LES]

*Syn:* combine; fuse

*Ant:* separate; divide

*Usage:* The two liquids were then *coalesced* into a congealed mass.

**CODA** (n) [KOH-duh]

*Syn:* concluding section of a musical or

literary composition

*Ant:* introduction

*Usage:* The *coda* is often more technically difficult to master than any other piece of music.

**CODDLE** (v) *[KOD-l]*

*Syn:* treat gently

*Ant:* treat roughly

*Usage:* The Berretts have *coddled* their children too much.

**CODICIL** (n) *[KOD-uh-suh l]*

*Syn:* supplement to the body of a will

*Ant:* main body of a document

*Usage:* A *codicil* was added to the will only yesterday.

**COEVAL** (adj) *[koh-EE-vuh l]*

*Syn:* living at the same time as; contemporary

*Ant:* non-contemporary

*Usage:* Although the two scientists were *coeval, they didn't know of each other's work* because of their vast geographic separation.

**COGITATE** (v) *[KOJ-i-teyt]*

*Syn:* think over

*Ant:* ignore

*Usage:* He needed a lot of privacy and silence to *cogitate* over this decision which could possibly alter his life.

**COGNATE** (adj) *[KOG-neyt]*

*Syn:* related linguistically; allied by blood; similar or akin in nature

*Ant:* dissimilar; unlike

*Usage:* They were just about as *cognate* with regards to each other as pea and pod.

**COGNITIVE** (adj) *[KOG-ni-tiv]*

*Syn:* having to do with knowing or perceiving; related to the mental processes

*Ant:* physical

*Usage:* Her *cognitive* abilities have won her the Best Intellectual of the Year award.

**COGNIZANCE** (n) *[KOG-nuh-zuh ns]*

*Syn:* knowledge

*Ant:* ignorance

*Usage:* Jack's sense of *cognizance* is exceptional; he is often sought after for advice.

**COHABIT** (v) *[koh-HAB-it]*

*Syn:* live together

*Ant:* live separately

*Usage:* The number of *cohabiting* couples is expected to double by 2021.

**COHORTS** (n) *[KOH-hawrts]*

*Syn:* companions; associates

*Ant:* enemies; opponents

*Usage:* The two men had been *cohorts* for many years and committed the crime together.

**COIFFURE** (n) *[kwah-FYOO R]*

*Syn:* hairstyle

*Usage:* She daintily touched her fingers to hair, appreciating the fresh *coiffure,* and preened in front of the mirror.

**COLANDER** (n) *[KUHL-uh n-der]*

*Syn:* container with perforated bottom used for straining

*Ant:* closed container

*Usage:* We had to use a *colander* to strain the pasta.

**COLLABORATE** (v) *[kuh-LAB-uh-reyt]*

*Syn:* work together

*Ant:* disagree

*Usage:* The two countries decided to *collaborate* on the new trade opportunities.

**COLLAGE** (n) *[kuh-LAHZH]*

*Syn:* work of art put together from fragments

*Usage:* We created a colorful *collage* using five of the photographs, some crayons, and a large colored sheet.

**COLLATE** (v) *[kuh-LEYT]*

*Syn:* examine in order to verify authenticity; arrange in order

*Ant:* disassemble

*Usage:* She was asked to *collate* the details of individual sales from each of the departments.

**COLLOQUIAL** (adj) *[kuh-LOH-kwee-uh l]*

*Syn:* pertaining to conversational or common speech

*Ant:* formal

*Usage:* The language they used was very *colloquial* and not in any way formal.

**COLLOQUY** (n) *[KOL-uh-kwee]*

*Syn:* informal discussion

*Ant:* silence

*Usage:* I enjoyed the local flavor of the *colloquy* among the tribes.

**COLOSSAL** (adj) *[kuh-LOS-uh l]*

*Syn:* huge

*Ant:* small

*Usage:* The movie he had in mind was a *colossal* epic.

**COMATOSE** (adj) *[KOM-uh-tohs]*

*Syn:* in a coma; extremely sleepy

*Ant:* conscious; awake

*Usage:* For years, he had been *comatose* and was being given food nutrients intravenously simply to keep his body alive.

**COMELY** (adj) *[KUHM-lee]*

*Syn:* attractive; agreeable

*Ant:* unseemly; ungraceful; unshapely

*Usage:* I couldn't believe that little Maria, who had been rather unattractive as a child, had grown up to become such a *comely* young woman.

**COMESTIBLE** (n) *[kuh-MES-tuh-buh l]*

*Syn:* something fit to be eaten

*Ant:* something unfit to eat

*Usage:* Faced with a variety of *comestible* delicacies we didn't know what to eat and what to leave out.

**COMEUPPANCE** (n) *[kuhm-UHP-uh ns]*

*Syn:* consequence; just desserts

*Usage:* For the amount of hard work he has put in, he hardly gets any favorable *comeuppance*.

**COMITY** (n) *[KOM-i-tee]*

*Syn:* courtesy; civility

*Ant:* discord

*Usage:* Michael's civility and *comity* had everyone smiling and beaming.

**COMMEMORATE** (v) *[kuh-MEM-uh-reyt]*

*Syn:* honor the memory of

*Ant:* forget

*Usage:* To *commemorate* the great man's life, a ceremony was held every year on the date of his death.

**COMMENSURATE** (adj) *[kuh-men-ser-it]*

*Syn:* equal in extent

*Ant:* unequal; lesser; greater

*Usage:* The letter said that the salary offered would be *commensurate* with the best in the industry.

**COMMODIOUS** (adj) *[kuh-MOH-dee-uh s]*

*Syn:* spacious and comfortable

*Ant:* cramped

*Usage:* His *commodious* apartment must have cost him a

fortune.

**COMPACT** (adj) *[kuhm-PAKT]*

*Syn:* tightly packed; firm; brief

*Ant:* loose; slack;

*Usage:* The mobile phone she carried was *compact* as well as trendy.

**COMPELLING** (adj) *[kuh m-PEL-ing]*

*Syn:* overpowering; irresistible in effect

*Ant:* weak; noninfluential

*Usage:* We demanded to know from the management a *compelling* reason for having dismissed the efficient accountant.

**COMPENDIUM** (n) *[kuh m-PEN-dee-uh m]*

*Syn:* brief; comprehensive summary; abstract; abridgement

*Ant:* expansion; addition

*Usage:* The students were asked to submit a brief *compendium* of their annual project to the departmental head.

**COMPILATION** (n) *[kom-puh-LEY-shuh n]*

*Syn:* collection

*Ant:* independent work

*Usage:* The book is nothing but a *compilation* of his previously published works.

**COMPLACENT** (adj) *[kuh m-PLEY-suh nt]*

*Syn:* self-satisfied; content

*Ant:* discontented

*Usage:* His laid-back, *complacent* attitude was the main reason why he hadn't progressed far in his career.

**COMPLEMENTARY** (adj) *[kom-pluh-MEN-tuh-ree]*

*Syn:* serving to complete something

*Ant:* independent; unrelated

*Usage:* Qualitative research approaches are considered as *complementary* to, and not in competition with, quantitative approaches.

**COMPLIANT** (adj) *[kuh m-PLAHY-uh nt]*

*Syn:* yielding

*Ant:* immutable

*Usage:* It is difficult to find a *compliant* maidservant these days; most of them seem to be haughty and overbearing.

**COMPONENT** (n) *[kuh m-POH-nuh nt]*

*Syn:* element; ingredient

*Ant:* whole

*Usage:* The program was merely one *component* of the entire software application.

**COMPOSURE** (n) *[kuh m-POH-zher]*

*Syn:* mental calmness

*Ant:* anxiety

*Usage:* Despite having received a great shock, it was remarkable how James retained his *composure* and calm.

**COMPOUND** (v) *[kom-POUND]*

*Syn:* combine; constitute; pay interest; increase

*Ant:* keep separate or simple

*Usage:* The fact that Jack abused his wife often *compounded* the crime, making him more guilty than ever.

**COMPRESS** (v) *[kuh m-PRES]*

*Syn:* close; squeeze; contract

*Ant:* expand; dilate; diffuse

*Usage:* The file size is too large and must be *compressed* before it can be copied to a disk.

**COMPRISE** (v) *[kuh m-PRAHYZ]*

*Syn:* include; consist of

*Ant:* exclude; except; omit; reject

*Usage:* The complete course is *comprised* of two short modules and one project.

**COMPROMISE** (v) *[KOM-pruh-mahyz]*

*Syn:* adjust or settle by making mutual concessions; endanger the interests or reputation of

*Ant:* aggravate; perpetuate; escalate

*Usage:* Gina refused to *compromise* on her principles simply to satisfy a handful of people.

**COMPUNCTION** (n) *[kuh m-PUHNGK-shuh n]*

*Syn:* remorse

*Ant:* defiance; immorality

*Usage:* He felt a terrible sense of *compunction* for his deed and begged forgiveness from the bereaved family.

**CONCATENATE** (v) *[kon-KAT-n-eyt]*

*Syn:* link as in a chain

*Ant:* let go; loose

*Usage:* She has decided to *concatenate* his name to her own without letting go of her maiden name.

**CONCEDE** (v) *[kuh n-SEED]*

*Syn:* admit; yield

*Ant:* infuriate

*Usage:* The government was determined not to *concede* to the terrorist's demands.

**CONCEIT** (n) *[kuh n-SEET]*

*Syn:* vanity or self-love; whimsical idea; extravagant metaphor

*Ant:* humility

*Usage:* Pride and *conceit* are things as alien to her nature as humanity to Mars.

**CONCENTRIC** (adj) *[kuh n-SEN-trik]*

*Syn:* having a common center

*Usage:* She wore a necklace shaped with a series of *concentric* circles.

**CONCEPTION** (n) *[kuh n-SEP-shuh n]*

*Syn:* beginning; forming of an idea

*Ant:* ending

*Usage:* From its *conception* to its implementation, the play was completely Jake's efforts.

**CONCESSION** (n) *[kuh n-SESH-uh n]*

*Syn:* an act of yielding

*Ant:* defiance

*Usage:* The government decided to make a *concession* to the plan after the public protests.

**CONCLAVE** (n) *[KON-kleyv]*

*Syn:* private meeting

*Ant:* open meeting

*Usage:* The writers' *conclave* at Detroit was a huge resounding success.

**CONCOCT** (v) *[kon-KOKT]*

*Syn:* prepare by combining; make up in concert

*Ant:* separate

*Usage:* Karen and Fred *concocted* a wicked plot.

**CONCOMITANT** (n) *[kon-KOM-i-tuh nt]*

*Syn:* that which accompanies

*Ant:* stranger; foe

*Usage:* Loss of memory is a natural *concomitant* of old age.

This page is intentionally left blank

# Chapter 5

## (Concord – Denigrate)

*This chapter covers the following words along with their part of speech, pronunciation, synonyms and antonym, if applicable. Sample usage of the word is also illustrated.*

| | | |
|---|---|---|
| concord | contentious | curmudgeon |
| concur | contiguous | cynosure |
| condescend | continence | dabble |
| condign | contraband | damp |
| condole | contrite | dank |
| condone | controvert | daunt |
| conducive | contumacious | dawdle |
| conduit | conundrum | debacle |
| confidant | converge | debauch |
| confiscate | convivial | debilitate |
| conflagration | convoluted | debunk |
| conflate | copious | debutante |
| confluence | coquette | decadence |
| conformity | cornucopia | decapitate |
| congeal | corporeal | declivity |
| congenial | corroborate | décolleté |
| congenital | coterie | decorum |
| congruent | covenant | decrepitude |
| conjugal | covetous | decry |
| connivance | cozen | deducible |
| connoisseur | crabbed | deference |
| connotation | crass | deflect |
| connubial | craven | defoliate |
| consanguinity | credo | defrock |
| conscientious | creed | defunct |
| consensus | crestfallen | deify |
| consequential | crone | deleterious |
| consonance | crotchety | delve |
| consort | crux | demagogue |
| consternation | crypt | demeanor |
| construe | cuisine | demoniac |
| consummate | culinary | denigrate |
| contagion | cull | |
| contention | culvert | |

**CONCORD** (n) *[KON-kawrd]*

*Syn:* harmony; agreement between people or things

*Ant:* discord; disagreement; variance; animosity

*Usage:* After years of discord, the two countries reached some *concord* amongst themselves.

**CONCUR** (v) *[kuh n-KUR]*

*Syn:* agree

*Ant:* differ; dissent; disagree; argue

*Usage:* We all *concurred* with the leader's decision.

**CONDESCEND** (v) *[kon-duh-SEND]*

*Syn:* bestow courtesies with a superior air

*Ant:* rise above

*Usage:* She *condescended* to attend the party even though she felt it was below her level to do so.

**CONDIGN** (adj) *[kuh n-DAHYN]*

*Syn:* adequate; fitting

*Ant:* improper; inappropriate

*Usage:* The occasion seemed *condign* for a speech so Mr. Tate rose to make one.

**CONDOLE** (v) *[kuh n-DOHL]*

*Syn:* express sympathetic sorrow

*Ant:* be indifferent; turn away; disdain

*Usage:* Though Peter pretended to *condole* with the Brown's grief, I knew that it was all a sham because he was as cold-hearted as a fish.

**CONDONE** (v) *[kuh n-DOHN]*

*Syn:* overlook; forgive; give tacit approval; excuse

*Ant:* disapprove

*Usage:* On seeing the mayor arriving at the town square, the prisoners broke down and begged him to *condone* their actions.

**CONDUCIVE** (adj) *[kuh n-DOO-siv]*

*Syn:* contributive; tending to

*Ant:* inhospitable

*Usage:* The atmosphere seemed *conducive* for a hearty debate.

**CONDUIT** (n) *[KON-dwit]*

*Syn:* aqueduct; passageway for fluids

*Ant:* barrier

*Usage:* She acted as a *conduit* between the cops and the smugglers, ferrying information from one to another.

**CONFIDANT** (n) *[KON-fi-dant]*

*Syn:* trusted friend

*Ant:* enemy; foe

*Usage:* Greg is Billy's closest *confidant*; Billy shares his life's events with him.

**CONFISCATE** (v) *[KON-fuh-skeyt]*

*Syn:* seize; commandeer

*Ant:* leave alone; return (goods)

*Usage:* The cops raided the shack and *confiscated* the gold bars hidden under the floorboards.

**CONFLAGRATION** (n) *[kon-fluh-GREY-shuh n]*

*Syn:* great fire

*Usage:* The *conflagration* started off shortly after they had left the club, scorching everything in its wake, leaving behind only ashes.

**CONFLATE** (v) *[kuhn-FLEYT]*

*Syn:* meld or fuse

*Ant:* separate

*Usage:* There is also a pronounced tendency to *conflate* a cultural idea with identities.

**CONFLUENCE** (n) *[KON-floo-uh ns]*

*Syn:* flowing together; crowd

*Ant:* separation

*Usage:* The *confluence* of the three rivers is a highly popular tourist spot.

**CONFORMITY** (n) *[kuh n-FAWR-mi-tee]*

*Syn:* harmony; agreement

*Ant:* difference

*Usage:* It's not possible for such a diverse group of people to have *conformity* among themselves.

**CONGEAL** (v) *[kuh n-JEEL]*

*Syn:* freeze; coagulate

*Ant:* melt; liquefy

*Usage:* The gel had *congealed* to become a thick brown mass.

**CONGENIAL** (adj) *[kuh n-JEEN-yuh l]*

*Syn:* pleasant; friendly

*Ant:* contentious

*Usage:* Joe is a friendly, *congenial* man.

**CONGENITAL** (adj) *[kuh n-JEN-i-tl]*

*Syn:* existing at birth

*Ant:* acquired

*Usage:* The baby was born with *congenital* defects.

**CONGRUENT** (adj) *[kong-GROO-uhnt]*

*Syn:* in agreement

*Ant:* incongruous

*Usage:* Use the conditions for *congruent* triangles in formal geometric proofs.

**CONJUGAL** (adj) *[KON-juh-guhl]*

*Syn:* pertaining to marriage

*Ant:* unmarried

*Usage:* They lived happily ever after in *conjugal* bliss.

**CONNIVANCE** (n) *[kuh-NAHY-vuh ns]*

*Syn:* assistance; pretense of ignorance of something wrong; permission to offend

*Ant:* ignorance

*Usage:* The appalling incident could only have happened with the *connivance* of the lady's in-laws.

**CONNOISSEUR** (n) *[kon-uh-SUR]*

*Syn:* person competent to act as a judge of art, etc.; a lover of an art

*Ant:* ignoramus

*Usage:* Ken Smith is a *connoisseur* of arts and culture.

**CONNOTATION** (n) *[kon-uh-TEY-shuh n]*

*Syn:* suggested or implied meaning of an expression

*Ant:* literal meaning

*Usage:* It was the hidden *connotations* in his speech that bothered me and made me uncomfortable.

**CONNUBIAL** (adj) *[kuh-NOO-bee-uhl]*

*Syn:* pertaining to marriage or the matrimonial state

*Ant:* nonmarried

*Usage:* The poor man has been married for a month but is yet to experience *connubial* pleasure with his wife.

**CONSANGUINITY** (n) *[kon-sang-GWIN-i-tee]*

*Syn:* kinship; harmony

*Ant:* antagonism; discord

*Usage:* The six brothers lived in great harmony and *consanguinity*.

**CONSCIENTIOUS** (adj) *[kon-shee-EN-shuh s]*

*Syn:* scrupulous; careful

*Ant:* indifferent

*Usage:* To such a morally rigid, *conscientious* man, even a small lie seemed a gross sin.

**CONSENSUS** (n) *[kuh n-SEN-suh s]*

*Syn:* general agreement

*Ant:* disagreement

*Usage:* The committee reached a *consensus* eventually, after hours of discussion on the issue, and passed the bill.

**CONSEQUENTIAL** (adj) *[kon-si-KWEN l]*

*Syn:* pompous; important; self important

*Ant:* inconsequential; unimportant

*Usage:* The *consequential* damage to the environment through the large-scale felling of trees is a very serious matter.

**CONSONANCE** (n) *[KON-suh-nuh ns]*

*Syn:* harmony; agreement

*Ant:* disagreement

*Usage:* I had never come across such peace and *consonance* in all my life.

**CONSORT** (v) *[kuh n-SAWRT]*

*Syn:* associate with

*Ant:* avoid

*Usage:* Eyewitness testified to having seen him *consort* with the lady in public on that issue.

**CONSTERNATION** (n) *[kon-ster-NEY-shuh n]*

*Syn:* anxiety, dismay

*Ant:* calm

*Usage:* To his extreme *consternation*, Peter found that he had lost his wallet somewhere on the train.

**CONSTRUE** (v) *[kuh n-STROO]*

*Syn:* explain; interpret

*Ant:* scramble

*Usage:* What she had actually said and what was being *construed* by the manager were two different things.

**CONSUMMATE** (adj) *[kuh n-SUHM-it]*

*Syn:* complete

*Ant:* imperfect; incomplete; unfinished

*Usage:* The man was a *consummate* professional, ensuring every detail was ready for the important meeting.

**CONTAGION** (n) *[kuh n-TEY-juh n]*

*Syn:* infection

*Usage:* The letter said that William had fatefully caught a *contagion* and was now on the verge of death.

**CONTENTION** (n) *[kuh n-TEN-shuh n]*

*Syn:* antagonism; strife; claim; thesis

*Ant:* accord; agreement; harmony

*Usage:* It was a close *contention* with each faction getting as many votes as the other.

**CONTENTIOUS** (adj) *[kuh n-TEN-shuh s]*

*Syn:* quarrelsome

*Ant:* congenial; obliging; considerate; easy; passive

*Usage:* From a peaceful discussion it soon rose to a *contentious*, hot argument with both parties swearing at each other.

**CONTIGUOUS** (adj) *[kuh n-TIG-yoo-uh s]*

*Syn:* adjacent to; touching upon

*Ant:* apart; separate

*Usage:* The troops were made to stand in a *contiguous* sequence along the fort walls.

**CONTINENCE** (n) *[KON-tn-uh ns]*

*Syn:* self-restraint; sexual chastity

*Ant:* indulgence

*Usage:* The degree to which he practices his self-restraint and *continence* is amazing and remarkable.

**CONTRABAND** (adj) *[KON-truh-band]*

*Syn:* illegally traded; smuggled

*Ant:* legitimate

*Usage:* Tim was arrested by the police for being in possession of *contraband* goods.

*(Concord - Denigrate)*

**CONTRITE** (adj) *[kuh n-TRAHYT]*

*Syn:* penitent

*Ant:* lacking remorse; unrepentant

*Usage:* Seeing her dismayed look on hearing my harsh words, I suddenly felt *contrite* and ashamed.

**CONTROVERT** (v) *[KON-truh-vurt]*

*Syn:* oppose with arguments; attempt to refute; contradict

*Ant:* agree; harmonize

*Usage:* They tried hard to make him confess but he *controverted* and opposed every statement they made and even brought in witnesses to support his logic.

**CONTUMACIOUS** (adj) *[kon-too-MEY-shuh s]*

*Syn:* disobedient; resisting authority; obstinate

*Ant:* obedient; subordinate

*Usage:* He was as stubborn and *contumacious* as an obstinate bull.

**CONUNDRUM** (n) *[kuh-NUHN-druh m]*

*Syn:* riddle; puzzle; secret

*Ant:* common understanding

*Usage:* Paul was facing a unique *conundrum*, something of the kind he had never faced before in life and would require all of his wits to solve.

**CONVERGE** (v) *[kuh n-VURJ]*

*Syn:* approach; tend to meet; come together

*Ant:* diverge

*Usage:* She asked him to wait near the spot where the two roads *converged*.

**CONVIVIAL** (adj) *[kuh n-VIV-ee-uh l]*

*Syn:* festive; gay; characterized by joviality

*Ant:* churlish; unsociable; ascetic; inhospitable; austere, reclusive

*Usage:* The *convivial* gathering of sundry cousins, aunts and uncles did quite a lot to lift Sara's spirits.

**CONVOLUTED** (adj) *[KON-vuh-loo-tid]*

*Syn:* coiled around; involved; intricate

*Ant:* direct; straight

*Usage:* The route was too *convoluted* and complex for us to understand, so we hired a guide to lead us to the hills.

**COPIOUS** (adj) *[KOH-pee-uh s]*

*Syn:* plentiful

*Ant:* destitute; sparse

*Usage:* She was weeping *copiously* and all Jack could do was to look at her in helplessness; he was at a loss for words.

**COQUETTE** (n) *[koh-KET]*

*Syn:* flirt

*Usage:* Betty was wrongly maligned by the townsfolk to be a *coquette* and a flirt when she truly was not.

**CORNUCOPIA** (n) *[kawr-nuh-KOH-pee-uh]*

*Syn:* horn overflowing with fruit and grain; symbol of abundance

*Ant:* scarcity

*Usage:* His cup of *cornucopia* flowed over; he was now king of the whole world.

**CORPOREAL** (adj) *[kawr-PAWR-ee-uh l]*

*Syn:* bodily; material

*Ant:* cerebral; mental

*Usage:* The man used cerebral skills in his new office job rather than the *corporeal* skills needed in his earlier landscaping position.

**CORROBORATE** (v) *[kuh-ROB-uh-reyt]*

*Syn:* confirm; support

*Ant:* contradict; refute; reject

*Usage:* The prosecution brought in eleven witnesses to *corroborate* the facts and support the conviction.

**COTERIE** (n) [KOH-tuh-ree]

Syn: group that meets socially; select circle

Usage: A *coterie* of poets gathered at the town square in the evening.

**COVENANT** (n) [KUHV-uh-nuh nt]

Syn: agreement

Ant: disagreement

Usage: They signed a *covenant* that would bind them to the contract for the next three years.

**COVETOUS** (adj) [KUHV-i-tuh s]

Syn: avaricious; eagerly desirous of

Ant: charitable; liberal; unselfish; profuse

Usage: The more I gazed at the necklace in the window the more it made me feel *covetous* of having that thing of beauty as my own.

**COZEN** (v) [KUHZ-uh n]

Syn: cheat; hoodwink; swindle; deceive

Ant: be honest

Usage: Polly is a very deceitful young woman; she has been known to *cozen* people out of their savings.

**CRABBED** (adj) [KRAB-id]

Syn: sour; peevish; difficult to understand

Ant: cheerful; clear

Usage: I couldn't make out the *crabbed* lettering on the wall; it was too illegible.

**CRASS** (adj) [kras]

Syn: very unrefined; grossly insensible

Ant: refined

Usage: His behavior was ungentlemanly and *crass*, shocking the women in the hall.

**CRAVEN** (adj) [KREY-vuh n]

Syn: cowardly

Ant: intrepid; bold

Usage: Gerald was such a cowardly, *craven* young man as compared to his gutsy brother Jeffrey.

**CREDO** (n) [kree-doh]

Syn: creed; belief

Usage: My *credo* for life is to seize each day and make the most of it because once a day is lost you cannot get it back.

**CREED** (n) [kreed]

Syn: system of religious or ethical belief

Usage: His unshakable values and *creed* are what set him apart in a crowd of peers.

**CRESTFALLEN** (adj) [KREST-faw-luh n]

Syn: dejected; dispirited

Ant: optimistic; cheerful

Usage: The children's faces turned *crestfallen* when their father refused permission for the summer camp.

**CRONE** (n) [krohn]

Syn: hag

Ant: beautiful young woman

Usage: The old *crone* had properly fooled all of us with her gait; she could actually walk well but had pretended to limp just to fool us.

**CROTCHETY** (adj) [KROCH-i-tee]

Syn: irritable

Ant: cheerful; happy pleasant

Usage: Every morning immediately after waking up, Bob is very *crotchety* and grumpy.

**CRUX** (n) [kruhks]

Syn: crucial point

Ant: nonconsequential element

Usage: Let's get to the *crux* of the matter.

*(Concord - Denigrate)*

**CRYPT** (n) *[kript]*

*Syn:* secret recess or vault; usually used for burial

*Usage:* They set out on an adventurous mission to unearth the *crypt* hidden in the hills.

**CUISINE** (n) *[kwi-ZEEN]*

*Syn:* style of cooking

*Usage:* I love experimenting with ethnic *cuisine*, especially Thai and Japanese dishes.

**CULINARY** (adj) *[KYOO-luh-ner-ee]*

*Syn:* relating to cooking

*Usage:* My *culinary* skills were not too good so I hired a cook for a month.

**CULL** (v) *[kuhl]*

*Syn:* pick out; reject

*Ant:* accept

*Usage:* They *culled* the rotting fruit from the fresh before making wine.

**CULVERT** (n) *[KUL-vert]*

*Syn:* artificial channel for water

*Usage:* HE said he would be waiting for her at the *culvert* near the road end.

**CURMUDGEON** (n) *[ker-MUHJ-uh n]*

*Syn:* churlish; miserly individual

*Ant:* contented person

*Usage:* They warned me against meeting Bart, saying that he was a *curmudgeon* and a rude fellow and to keep away from him.

**CYNOSURE** (n) *[SAHY-nuh-shoo r]*

*Syn:* the object of general attention

*Ant:* a nobody

*Usage:* Pretty and elegant Katrina was the *cynosure* of all eyes at the ball.

**DABBLE** (v) *[dab-uh]*

*Syn:* work at in a nonserious fashion

*Ant:* concentrate; focus; work systematically

*Usage:* I like to *dabble* with physics, but I'm no rocket scientist

**DAMP** (v) *[damp]*

*Syn:* lessen in intensity; diminish; mute

*Ant:* increase

*Usage:* Put these earplugs in to *damp* the sound of the rock band.

**DANK** (adj) *[dangk]*

*Syn:* damp

*Ant:* dry

*Usage:* The cabin was *dank* and musty, causing Heather to wheeze and cough.

**DAUNT** (v) *[dawnt]*

*Syn:* intimidate; frighten

*Ant:* embolden; encourage; inspire

*Usage:* It was bad of the woodcutter to *daunt* and scare the little kids with his big axe.

**DAWDLE** (v) *[DAWD-l]*

*Syn:* loiter; waste time

*Ant:* hurry

*Usage:* All Leroy does is *dawdle* and loiter whole day.

**DEBACLE** (n) *[dey-BAH-kuh l]*

*Syn:* collapse; sudden downfall; complete disaster

*Ant:* success

*Usage:* After his much publicized *debacle* all Ken wanted to do was to take a long break away from civilization.

**DEBAUCH** (v) *[di-BAWCH]*

*Syn:* corrupt; seduce from virtue

*Ant:* purify

*Usage:* The vile, perverted man attempted to *debauch* the young maiden.

**DEBILITATE** (v) *[di-BIL-i-teyt]*

*Syn:* weaken; enfeeble

*Ant:* strengthen

*Usage:* Krypton *debilitates* Superman, leaving him with less strength than normal men.

**DEBUNK** (v) *[di-BUHNGK]*

*Syn:* expose as false, exaggerated, worthless, etc; ridicule

*Ant:* prove; uphold

*Usage:* He *debunked* their arguments with just one sentence, which had them all gaping.

**DEBUTANTE** (n) *[DEB-yoo-tahnt]*

*Syn:* young woman making formal entrance into society

*Usage:* The lovely young *debutante* drew all the attention at the ball.

**DECADENCE** (n) *[DEK-uh-duh ns]*

*Syn:* decay

*Ant:* strength

*Usage:* The man who was once at the zenith of his career had now come down to such *decadence*.

**DECAPITATE** (v) *[di-KAP-i-teyt]*

*Syn:* behead

*Usage:* The crowds gasped in shock to see the head of the gladiator rolling down to the ground when the knight *decapitated* him with one stroke of his sharp sword.

**DECLIVITY** (n) *[di-KLIV-i-tee]*

*Syn:* downward slope

*Ant:* ascent; rise; mountain; verticality

*Usage:* The sales graph showed a sharp *declivity* for the last three months.

**DÉCOLLETÉ** (adj) *[dey-kol-TEY]*

*Syn:* having low necked dress

*Ant:* high-necked (clothing)

*Usage:* She loved to show off her well-boned shoulders by wearing *décolleté* gowns as often as possible.

**DECORUM** (n) *[di-KAWR-uh m]*

*Syn:* propriety; orderliness and good taste in manners

*Ant:* disorder; impropriety; disturbance

*Usage:* The pupils were sternly instructed to observe *decorum* in the auditorium.

**DECREPITUDE** (n) *[di-KREP-i-tood]*

*Syn:* state of collapse caused by illness or old age

*Ant:* youth; growth

*Usage:* I was saddened to see the *decrepitude* to which Anne's mother had been reduced.

**DECRY** (v) *[di-KRAHY]*

*Syn:* express strong disapproval of; disparage

*Ant:* laud; exalt; praise; commend; extol

*Usage:* The crowd outside the courtroom *decried* the verdict, criticizing the ineffective judicial process.

**DEDUCIBLE** (adj) *[dih-DOO-suh-buh l]*

*Syn:* derived by reasoning

*Ant:* ambiguous; uncertain

*Usage:* From the evidence gathered so far, it was *deducible* that the victim had committed suicide.

**DEFERENCE** (n) *[DEF-er-uh ns]*

*Syn:* courteous regard for another's wish

*Ant:* impoliteness; disobedience

*Usage:* In *deference* to the ladies present in the room, the men refrained from cracking lewd, bawdy jokes.

**DEFLECT** (v) *[di-FLEKT]*

*Syn:* turn aside; deviate

*Ant:* absorb; catch

*Usage:* The lens *deflected* the light from the sun.

**DEFOLIATE** (v) *[dee-FOH-lee-eyt]*

*Syn:* destroy leaves

*Usage:* The massive oak has been *defoliated* and rendered leafless.

**DEFROCK** (v) *[dee-FROK]*

*Syn:* strip a priest or minister of church authority

*Ant:* appoint

*Usage:* The former priest was then *defrocked* and barred from the church.

**DEFUNCT** (adj) *[di-FUHNGKT]*

*Syn:* dead; no longer in use or existence

*Ant:* active

*Usage:* The law for that particular crime is no longer valid and is *defunct*.

**DEIFY** (v) *[DEE-uh-fahy]*

*Syn:* turn into a god; idolize

*Usage:* The very same sports idols who were *deified* by the public into demi-gods last year are being criticized and lampooned this year.

**DELETERIOUS** (adj) *[del-i-TEER-ee-uh s]*

*Syn:* harmful

*Ant:* safe

*Usage:* The habit of smoking is *deleterious* not just to the people having the habit but to others around them as well.

**DELVE** (v) *[delv]*

*Syn:* dig; investigate

*Ant:* ignore; let lie

*Usage:* They needed more time to *delve* deeper into the facts and unearth the truth.

**DEMAGOGUE** (n) *[DEM-uh-gog]*

*Syn:* person who appeals to people's prejudice; false leader of people

*Ant:* follower

*Usage:* The arrested man was a *demagogue* and a fanatic who had killed seven people in the name of defending his religion.

**DEMEANOR** (n) *[di-MEE-ner]*

*Syn:* behavior; bearing; outward manner

*Usage:* She has a pleasing *demeanor* and very polite mannerisms.

**DEMONIAC** (adj) *[di-MOH-nee-ak]*

*Syn:* fiendish; cruel

*Ant:* charitable; kind

*Usage:* Jack's parents are alarmed to see him exhibiting signs of *demoniac* and evil behavior.

**DENIGRATE** (v) *[DEN-i-greyt]*

*Syn:* blacken; defame; slander

*Ant:* panegyrize; praise

*Usage:* Paul just loves to *denigrate* Kim's faults in public, to her extreme annoyance.

This page is intentionally left blank

# Chapter 6

# (Denouement – Epistemologist)

*This chapter covers the following words along with their part of speech, pronunciation, synonyms and antonym, if applicable. Sample usage of the word is also illustrated.*

| | | |
|---|---|---|
| denouement | disingenuous | egregious |
| depose | disjunction | elegy |
| depravity | disparage | elicit |
| deride | disparate | ellipsis |
| derision | disport | elliptical |
| derivative | disputatious | eloquence |
| desiccate | disseminate | elysian |
| desideratum | dissimulate | embargo |
| desperado | dissonance | embattled |
| despicable | distrait | embellish |
| despoil | diurnal | embroil |
| desultory | docket | emetic |
| detonation | doddering | emollient |
| detrimental | dogmatic | empirical |
| diadem | dolt | encipher |
| dialectic | dossier | encomium |
| diaphanous | dour | encroachment |
| diatribe | draconian | endemic |
| dichotomy | dross | enervate |
| didactic | drudgery | enfranchise |
| diffidence | dubious | enhance |
| diffusion | dulcet | enigma |
| digression | dyspeptic | ennui |
| dilettante | ebb | ensconce |
| diorama | ebullient | entomology |
| dirge | ecclesiastic | entrée |
| disapprobation | ecologist | environ |
| discernible | efface | eon |
| discombobulated | effeminate | epaulet |
| discordant | effete | ephemeral |
| discrepancy | efficacy | episodic |
| discrete | effluvium | epistemologist |
| discursive | effrontery | |
| disgruntle | egoism | |

**DENOUEMENT** (n) *[dey-noo-MAHN]*

*Syn:* outcome; final development of the plot of a play

*Ant:* beginning

*Usage:* When the final *denouement* was reached, the public heaved a sigh for the wait for a verdict had been too long.

**DEPOSE** (v) *[di-POHZ]*

*Syn:* dethrone; remove from office

*Ant:* enthrone; elect

*Usage:* The young prince *deposed* his own father to take over rule of the kingdom.

**DEPRAVITY** (n) *[di-PRAV-i-tee]*

*Syn:* extreme corruption; wickedness

*Ant:* nobility

*Usage:* I was saddened to see the *depravity* and degradation William had been reduced to after the death of his moralistic wife.

**DERIDE** (v) *[di-RAHYD]*

*Syn:* ridicule; make fun of; scoff

*Ant:* applaud

*Usage:* Little Paul was scared that his peers in school would *deride* him for his misshapen outfit.

**DERISION** (n) *[di-RIZH-uh n]*

*Syn:* ridicule

*Ant:* praise; compliments

*Usage:* He looked at her with scorn and *derision*.

**DERIVATIVE** (adj) *[di-RIV-uh-tiv]*

*Syn:* unoriginal; derived from another source

*Ant:* original

*Usage:* The *derivative* outcome of the bill is the massive surge in employment.

**DESICCATE** (v) *[DES-i-keyt]*

*Syn:* dry up

*Ant:* moisten

*Usage:* The recipe required the use of dry and *desiccated* coconut.

**DESIDERATUM** (n) *[di-sid-uh-REY-tuh m]*

*Syn:* a thing lacking, but desired or needed

*Ant:* neglect; avoidance; purposelessness

*Usage:* The *desideratum* or motive was the toughest to determine; everything else was easy.

**DESPERADO** (n) *[des-puh-RAH-doh]*

*Syn:* reckless outlaw

*Usage:* Gary Summers is wanted by the sheriff who claims that he is a *desperado* and a law-breaker.

**DESPICABLE** (adj) *[DES-pi-kuh-buh l]*

*Syn:* contemptible

*Ant:* commendable

*Usage:* The woman's behavior was utterly *despicable* and disgusting.

**DESPOIL** (v) *[di-SPOIL]*

*Syn:* plunder; pillage

*Ant:* build; construct; improve

*Usage:* The unruly, noisy crowd then went on a rampage and *despoiled* the palace.

**DESULTORY** (adj) *[DES-uh l-tawr-ee]*

*Syn:* aimless; haphazard; digressing at random

*Ant:* consecutive; serious; methodical; diligent; thorough; painstaking

*Usage:* They wandered *desultorily* and aimlessly for more than three hours in the woods before collapsing of fatigue near the stream.

**DETONATION** (v) *[det-n-EY-shuh n]*

*Syn:* explosion

*Usage:* The *detonation* of the mines coincided with the arrival of the oil ministry officials in the region.

**DETRIMENTAL** (adj) *[de-truh-MEN-tl]*

*Syn:* harmful; damaging

*Ant:* helpful

*Usage:* This decision she has taken is *detrimental* and harmful to her health.

**DIADEM** (n) *[DAHY-uh-dem]*

*Syn:* crown: control

*Ant:* weakness

*Usage:* She wore a glittering *diadem* and a lovely brocade gown.

**DIALECTIC** (n) *[dahy-uh-LEK-tik]*

*Syn:* art of debate

*Ant:* agreement

*Usage:* He was in an argumentative mood, so the critical statement pushed him into a hot *dialectic* with his colleague.

**DIAPHANOUS** (adj) *[dahy-AF-uh-nuhs]*

*Syn:* sheer; transparent

*Ant:* thick; opaque

*Usage:* He was embarrassed to see her clad in a *diaphanous* gown and politely refused to step inside the room.

**DIATRIBE** (n) *[DAHY-uh-trahyb]*

*Syn:* bitter scolding or harangue; invective; denunciation

*Ant:* praise; recommendation

*Usage:* Then there was an endless *diatribe* by his wife on why he should quit smoking.

**DICHOTOMY** (n) *[dahy-KOT-uh-mee]*

*Syn:* split; branching into two parts (especially contradictory ones)

*Ant:* unity

*Usage:* There is often a *dichotomy* between politicians' words and their deeds.

**DIDACTIC** (adj) *[dahy-DAK-tik]*

*Syn:* teaching; instructional

*Usage:* Nick has always been academically inclined so his *didactic* achievements were no surprise to his family.

**DIFFIDENCE** (n) *[DIF-i-duh ns]*

*Syn:* shyness; lack of confidence

*Ant:* audacity; arrogance; confidence

*Usage:* To alleviate the young boy's shyness and *diffidence*, George talked to him gently about books, music and other subjects which might draw the boy's attention.

**DIFFUSION** (n) *[di-FYOO-zhuh n]*

*Syn:* wordiness; spreading in all directions like a gas

*Ant:* concentration

*Usage:* The *diffusion* of the chemical slowly through the liquid in the beaker was interesting to watch.

**DIGRESSION** (n) *[di-GRESH-uh n]*

*Syn:* wandering away from the subject

*Ant:* directness; straightness

*Usage:* The *digression* of the speaker every now and then from the subject of the lecture was getting tiresome.

**DILETTANTE** (n) *[DIL-i-tahnt]*

*Syn:* aimless follower of the arts; amateur; dabbler

*Ant:* connoisseur

*Usage:* Nora is but a *dilettante*; she needs to learn so much more.

**DIORAMA** (n) *[dahy-uh-RAM-uh]*

*Syn:* life-size, three-dimensional scene from nature or history

*Usage:* At the exhibition hall, this weekend, there is a *diorama* of wildlife.

**DIRGE** (n) *[durj]*

*Syn:* sad song

*Usage:* The ladies of the dead tribesman's family wailed loudly in a *dirge*.

**DISAPPROBATION** (n) *[dis-ap-ruh-BEY-shuh n]*

*Syn:* disapproval; condemnation

*Ant:* approval

*Usage: Disapprobation* was strongly written on his face when he read the letter he'd seized from his daughter's fist.

**DISCERNIBLE** (adj) *[di-SUR-nuh-buh l]*

*Syn:* distinguishable; perceivable

*Ant:* indiscernible; invisible; impalpable; obscure; minute

*Usage:* He spoke so softly that his response was barely *discernible*.

**DISCOMBOBULATED** (adj) *[dis-kuh m BOB-yuh-leyt id]*

*Syn:* confused; discomposed

*Ant:* lucid; clear

*Usage:* The staff of the local county office was *discombobulated* and upset by the sudden unexpected arrival of the administration officials.

**DISCORDANT** (adj) *[dis-KAWR-dnt]*

*Syn:* not harmonious; conflicting

*Ant:* harmonious

*Usage:* In the midst of the lovely music suddenly some *discordant* tunes were heard, very jarring to the ears.

**DISCREPANCY** (n) *[di-SKREP-uh n-see]*

*Syn:* lack of consistency; difference

*Ant:* agreement consonance; similarity

*Usage:* There was a huge *discrepancy* between the original will and the recently prepared one.

**DISCRETE** (adj) *[di-SKREET]*

*Syn:* separate; discontinuous; unconnected

*Ant:* attached; combined; joined

*Usage: Discrete* particles hold a great fascination for Mark and he has chosen to conduct extensive research on them for his thesis.

**DISCURSIVE** (adj) *[di-SKUR-siv]*

*Syn:* digressing; rambling

*Ant:* focusing

*Usage:* His speech was long and *discursive*, often digressing from the main subject.

**DISGRUNTLE** (v) *[dis-GRUHN-tl]*

*Syn:* make discontented; disappoint; anger

*Ant:* appease

*Usage:* The new computer so *disgruntled* and dissatisfied the man that he decided to return it to the store.

**DISINGENUOUS** (adj) *[dis-in-JEN-yoo-uh s]*

*Syn:* not naive; sophisticated

*Ant:* naive; ingenuous

*Usage:* His *disingenuous* and insincere means of achieving the monthly targets soon came to the notice of the manager and he was dismissed from the job.

**DISJUNCTION** (n) *[dis-JUHNGK-shuhn]*

*Syn:* act or state of separation

*Ant:* joining; assembly

*Usage:* Several skills will be developed through experimentation but there will be a *disjunction* between aspiration and fulfillment.

**DISPARAGE** (v) *[di-SPAR-ij]*

*Syn:* belittle

*Ant:* tout

*Usage:* When Isabella further *disparaged* Michael's writing by poking fun and mocking several of the passages in the story, Margaret could take it no longer and begged her to stop.

**DISPARATE** (adj) *[DIS-per-it]*

*Syn:* unrelated; incomparable in quality; basically different

*Ant:* alike; equal; similar

*Usage:* They are as *disparate* as fire and ice.

**DISPORT** (v) *[di-SPAWRT]*

*Syn:* amuse

*Ant:* bore

*Usage:* The children loved to *disport* themselves with Lego kits and board games.

**DISPUTATIOUS** (adj) *[dis-pyoo-TEY-shuh s]*

*Syn:* argumentative; fond of arguing

*Ant:* agreeable

*Usage:* The scene between the two men was fast turning into a *disputatious* one, with both of them arguing vehemently and occasionally with violence.

**DISSEMINATE** (v) *[di-SEM-uh-neyt]*

*Syn:* distribute; spread; scatter (like seeds)

*Ant:* collect; gather

*Usage:* The news was then *disseminated* to all parts of the world through the various news channels.

**DISSIMULATE** (v) *[di-SIM-yuh-leyt]*

*Syn:* pretend; conceal by feigning; deceive

*Ant:* be honest

*Usage:* The thief deceived and *dissimulated* his way into a job as a bank teller so he could later empty the vaults.

**DISSONANCE** (n) *[DIS-uh-nuh ns]*

*Syn:* discord

*Ant:* agreement; concord; harmony

*Usage:* The *dissonance* and din were making it difficult for us to hear each other.

**DISTRAIT** (adj) *[di-STREY]*

*Syn:* absent-minded

*Ant:* focused

*Usage:* He is in a *distrait* mood today, preoccupied with something else.

**DIURNAL** (adj) *[dahy-UR-nl]*

*Syn:* daily

*Ant:* nocturnal; nightly

*Usage:* Bats are not *diurnal* creatures; rather they are nocturnal creatures.

**DOCKET** (n) *[DOK-it]*

*Syn:* program; as for trial; book where such entries are made

*Usage:* The regional *docket* for the training is not yet ready.

**DODDERING** (adj) *[DOD-er-ing]*

*Syn:* shaky; infirm from old age

*Ant:* firm; strong

*Usage:* The *doddering* old man could hardly be called as an opponent for mighty, powerful Richard.

**DOGMATIC** (adj) *[dawg-MAT-ik]*

*Syn:* opinionated; arbitrary; doctrinal

*Ant:* indecisive; flexible

*Usage:* Her *dogmatic* and rigid attitude often annoys the people around her.

**DOLT** (n) *[dohlt]*

*Syn:* stupid person

*Ant:* genius

*Usage:* Mike kicked the boy hard saying he was a *dolt* and an idiot for having made such a terrible error.

**DOSSIER** (n) *[DOS-ee-ey]*

*Syn:* file of documents on a subject

*Usage:* They had prepared an extensive *dossier* on the

criminal with complete information from his childhood background to his presently known activities.

**DOUR** (adj) *[doo r]*

*Syn:* sullen; stubborn

*Ant:* happy; pleasant; cheerul

*Usage:* Nora let out a sad sigh upon seeing Jack's *dour* temperament for she had been hoping fervently to find him in a pleasant, cheerful mood.

**DRACONIAN** (adj) *[drey-koh-nee-uhn]*

*Syn:* extremely severe

*Ant:* lax; lenient

*Usage:* The Drake opinion took steps toward making the recession remedy less *draconian*.

**DROSS** (n) *[draws]*

*Syn:* refuse; rubbish; waste matter; worthless impurities

*Ant:* items of value

*Usage:* All we could see at the site of the explosion was debris, rubble and *dross*.

**DRUDGERY** (n) *[DRUHJ-uh-ree]*

*Syn:* menial work

*Ant:* valuable, interesting work

*Usage:* For years she endured a life of *drudgery* to put her son through college.

**DUBIOUS** (adj) *[DOO-bee-uh s]*

*Syn:* questionable; filled with doubt

*Ant:* unquestionable; definite; positive; sure

*Usage:* He has risen to the top through *dubious* means.

**DULCET** (adj) *[DUHL-sit]*

*Syn:* sweet-sounding

*Ant:* cacophonous

*Usage:* Together, standing hand in hand on the dais, they sang a *dulcet* duet and charmed the crowd.

**DYSPEPTIC** (adj) *[dis-PEP-tik]*

*Syn:* suffering from indigestion; crabby; grouchy

*Ant:* irritable; pleasant; cheerful

*Usage:* The landlady was upset at having taken in a *dyspeptic*, bad-tempered tenant, for she feared the other tenants might be disturbed by his presence.

**EBB** (v) *[eb]*

*Syn:* recede; lessen

*Ant:* flow; increase

*Usage:* We decided to wait it out till the tide began to *ebb*.

**EBULLIENT** (adj) *[i-BUHL-yuh nt]*

*Syn:* showing excitement; overflowing with enthusiasm

*Ant:* lackluster

*Usage:* Her *ebullient* spirits and cheerful mood were contagious; soon the whole group was in a lively mood.

**ECCLESIASTIC** (adj) *[i-klee-zee-AS-tik]*

*Syn:* pertaining to the church

*Ant:* secular

*Usage:* The stranger introduced himself as an *ecclesiastic* scholar and said that he was looking for directions to the local church.

**ECOLOGIST** (n) *[ih-kol-uh-jee]*

*Syn:* a person concerned with the interrelationship between living organisms and their environment

*Usage:* Many an *ecologist* gathered at the annual ecological and environmental convention to discuss and share ideas about ways to preserve and conserve nature.

**EFFACE** (v) *[i-FEYS]*

*Syn:* rub out

*Ant:* restore; revive; portray; delineate; preserve; insert

*Usage:* The terrorists *effaced* every sign of civilization in the village, reducing it almost to a ghost town.

## Chapter 6

**EFFEMINATE** (adj) *[i-FEM-uh-nit]*

*Syn:* having womanly traits

*Ant:* masculine

*Usage:* Paul's *effeminate* mannerisms and girlish giggles annoyed Jim a great deal but he couldn't do anything about it.

**EFFETE** (adj) *[i-FEET]*

*Syn:* worn out; exhausted; barren

*Ant:* energetic; tireless

*Usage:* The efforts of the team have lately been *effete* with none of the targets accomplished.

**EFFICACY** (n) *[EF-i-kuh-see]*

*Syn:* power to produce desired effect

*Ant:* inefficiency; uselessness; futility

*Usage:* The young woman's *efficacy* and diligence impressed me; I decided to give her a year-end promotion.

**EFFLUVIUM** (n) *[i-FLOO-vee-uh m]*

*Syn:* noxious smell

*Ant:* bouquet; pleasant fragrance

*Usage:* The room was filled with strong fumes of *effluvium* and we were compelled to move out.

**EFFRONTERY** (n) *[i-FRUHN-tuh-ree]*

*Syn:* shameless boldness

*Ant:* diffidence

*Usage:* The manager was taken aback to see the newly appointed salesman's *effrontery*; he certainly hadn't expected this kind of brash behavior from a newcomer.

**EGOISM** (n) *[EE-goh-iz-uh m]*

*Syn:* excessive interest in one's self; belief that one should be interested in one's self rather than in others

*Ant:* selflessness

*Usage:* His pride and *egoism* will one day bring about his fall.

**EGREGIOUS** (adj) *[i-GREE-juh s]*

*Syn:* notorious; conspicuously bad or shocking

*Ant:* ordinary

*Usage:* He is an *egregious* boast and people take his words with a pinch of salt.

**ELEGY** (n) *[EL-i-jee]*

*Syn:* poem or song expressing lamentation; dirge; epitaph

*Ant:* celebration

*Usage:* The poet decided to compose an *elegy* for his friend's funeral.

**ELICIT** (v) *[ih-LIS-it]*

*Syn:* evoke; draw out by discussion

*Ant:* draw in

*Usage:* No matter what I said, I failed to *elicit* any kind of response from the child.

**ELLIPSIS** (n) *[i-LIP-sis]*

*Syn:* omission of words understood from a context as in 'if (it is) possible'

*Ant:* complete expression

*Usage:* The story was inundated with many an *ellipsis* causing a disjointed effect leaving sentences as though they were incomplete.

**ELLIPTICAL** (adj) *[i-LIP-ti-kuh l]*

*Syn:* oval; ambiguous, either purposely or because key words have been left out

*Ant:* square; complete

*Usage:* She wore an *elliptical*, conical hat with her golden brown locks tumbling out from the corners.

**ELOQUENCE** (n) *[EL-uh-kwuh ns]*

*Syn:* expressiveness; persuasive speech

*Ant:* speechlessness

*Usage:* We sat speechless, amazed and impressed by his *eloquence* and articulation.

**ELYSIAN** (adj) *[i-LIZH-uh n]*

*Syn:* relating to paradise; blissful

*Ant:* hellish

*Usage:* We were secretly ecstatic at the thought of experiencing *Elysian* pleasures.

**EMBARGO** (n) *[em-BAHR-goh]*

*Syn:* ban on commerce or other activity

*Ant:* allowance; permit

*Usage:* Unprepared for the *embargo* and prohibition, we were left without any supplies for a week, subsisting on whatever little we had at our disposal.

**EMBATTLED** (adj) *[em-BAT-ld]*

*Syn:* (of army, etc) ready for battle; in a state of defense

*Ant:* peaceful

*Usage:* An *embattled* management eventually had to give in to the demands of the workers.

**EMBELLISH** (v) *[em-BEL-ish]*

*Syn:* adorn; ornament

*Ant:* disfigure; deface; mar

*Usage:* Her gown was *embellished* with threaded designs of pure gold.

**EMBROIL** (v) *[em-BROLI]*

*Syn:* throw into confusion; involve in strife; entangle

*Ant:* extricate

*Usage:* Karen was *embroiled* in a nasty controversy when the press got hold of some indiscreet photographs from her youth.

**EMETIC** (n) *[uh-MET-ik]*

*Syn:* substance causing vomiting

*Usage:* Martha had no idea whatsoever that the liquid would act like an *emetic* and cause Noel to vomit profusely.

**EMOLLIENT** (n) *[i-MOL-yuh nt]*

*Syn:* soothing or softening remedy

*Ant:* abrasive substance

*Usage:* He applied a soothing *emollient* to the bruise on his arm.

**EMPIRICAL** (adj) *[em-PIR-i-kuh l]*

*Syn:* based on experience; practical

*Ant:* anecdotal; impractical; conjectural

*Usage:* The scientists based their conclusion on the *empirical* evidence from their many experiments.

**ENCIPHER** (v) *[en-SAHY-fer]*

*Syn:* encode

*Ant:* decode

*Usage:* The design is derived from the Enigma device, a machine used during World War II to *encipher* messages.

**ENCOMIUM** (n) *[en-KOH-mee-uh m]*

*Syn:* high praise; eulogy

*Ant:* condemnation; denunciation; vilification; censure

*Usage:* The senator was flattered to see the *encomium* and tributes being lavished upon him.

**ENCROACHMENT** (n) *[en-KROHCH-muh nt]*

*Syn:* gradual intrusion

*Ant:* maintenance of separation

*Usage:* The government needs to do something about the *encroachment* of the marshlands.

**ENDEMIC** (adj) *[en-DEM-ik]*

*Syn:* prevailing among a specific group of people or in a specific area or a country

*Ant:* widespread

*Usage:* The officials advised Karen to be quarantined in isolation because she had been diagnosed to have an *endemic* disease.

Chapter 6

**ENERVATE** (v) *[EN-er-veyt]*

*Syn:* weaken

*Ant:* strengthen; energize

*Usage:* A sleepless night had *enervated* Jim and made him listless in the morning.

**ENFRANCHISE** (v) *[en-FRAN-chahyz]*

*Syn:* admit to the rights of citizenship (especially the right to vote)

*Ant:* disenfranchise; withdraw citizenship or voting rights

*Usage:* The group of slaves beamed with gratitude for the white foreigner who had *enfranchised* them and given back their liberty and dignity.

**ENHANCE** (v) *[en-HANS]*

*Syn:* increase; improve

*Ant:* decrease; reduce; worsen

*Usage:* They have decided to *enhance* the features of the air-conditioning system to make it much more advanced and efficient.

**ENIGMA** (n) *[uh-NIG-muh]*

*Syn:* puzzle; mystery

*Ant:* known

*Usage:* Till her last, Sara remained an *enigma* to her neighbors who could never figure out much about her.

**ENNUI** (n) *[ahn-WEE]*

*Syn:* boredom

*Ant:* interest

*Usage:* Boredom and *ennui* engulfed Sam as he idled about on the little island with nothing at all to do.

**ENSCONCE** (v) *[en-SKONS]*

*Syn:* settle comfortably; hide away

*Ant:* unveil; uncover

*Usage:* To their extreme consternation, the man *ensconced* himself firmly on the boat, saying no one could stop him from journeying with the others.

**ENTOMOLOGY** (n) *[en-tuh-MOL-uh-jee]*

*Syn:* study of insects

*Usage:* Mr. Gordon was shocked to know that his son had chosen to specialize in *entomology* because as a child, Paul had always been terrified of insects.

**ENTRÉE** (n) *[AHN-trey]*

*Syn:* right to enter

*Ant:* rejection; blackballing

*Usage:* Only the swankiest and swishiest celebrities would gain *entrée* to the high profile dinner.

**ENVIRON** (v) *[en-VAHY-ruh n]*

*Syn:* enclose; surround

*Usage:* The course offered by the university did not *environ* the topics I'd anticipated but rather encompassed a wholly different range.

**EON** (n) *[EE-uh n]*

*Syn:* long period of time; an age

*Ant:* moment; short period of time

*Usage:* It was *eons* since I had stepped into a studio and everything seemed different to me.

**EPAULET** (n) *[EP-uh-let]*

*Syn:* ornament worn on the shoulder (of a uniform, etc.)

*Usage:* The sergeant commander's uniform bore three tasseled *epaulets*.

**EPHEMERAL** (adj) *[i-FEM-er-uh l]*

*Syn:* short-lived; fleeting

*Ant:* perpetual; endless; eternal; enduring; permanent

*Usage:* The pleasure was *ephemeral*, temporary and not long-lasting or enduring.

**EPISODIC** (adj) *[EP-uh-SOD-ik]*

*Syn:* loosely connected; divided into incidents

*Ant:* continuous

*Usage:* The producer suggested that they break the script to formulate an *episodic* serial with 100 episodes.

**EPISTEMOLOGIST** (n) *[ih-pis-tuh-MOL-uh-jist]*

*Syn:* philosopher who studies the nature of knowledge

*Usage:* Though qualified as a philosopher, Gia wants to further specialize as an *epistemologist* and study the nature of knowledge, its presuppositions, foundations, and validity.

# Chapter 7

## (Epitaph – Gawk)

*This chapter covers the following words along with their part of speech, pronunciation, synonyms and antonym, if applicable. Sample usage of the word is also illustrated.*

| | | |
|---|---|---|
| epitaph | exuberant | forswear |
| epithet | facetious | forte |
| epitome | facsimile | fortuitous |
| equanimity | factious | fractious |
| equestrian | factotum | fraudulent |
| equivocate | fallacious | frenetic |
| erratic | fallacy | fresco |
| erudite | fanaticism | frieze |
| eschew | fatuous | frivolous |
| esoteric | fawning | froward |
| etymology | fecundity | frugal |
| eugenic | fervid | frugality |
| eulogy | fiasco | frustrate |
| euphemism | fictitious | fulminate |
| euphoria | figurative | fulsome |
| euthanasia | filial | furor |
| evanescent | finicky | furtive |
| evocative | flaccid | fusillade |
| exacerbate | flagrant | futile |
| exchequer | flamboyant | gadfly |
| excoriate | fledgling | gaffe |
| exegesis | flippancy | gainsay |
| exigency | floe | gall |
| exiguous | flotsam | gambol |
| exonerate | flout | gamut |
| expatiate | flux | gargoyle |
| expatriate | foible | garner |
| expiate | foil | garnish |
| expository | foist | garrulity |
| expunge | foment | garrulous |
| extemporaneous | foppish | gauche |
| extraneous | forbearance | gawk |
| extrinsic | forestall | |
| extrude | forlorn | |

**EPITAPH** (n) *[EP-i-taf]*

*Syn:* inscription in memory of a dead person

*Ant:* biography; story of a living person

*Usage:* The *epitaph* on his tombstone was a glowing tribute to the fine gentleman that he had been.

**EPITHET** (n) *[EP-uh-thet]*

*Syn:* word or phrase characteristically used to describe a person or thing

*Usage:* They suffixed the *epithet* "The Conqueror" to the end of his name so he was known as Carl the Conqueror.

**EPITOME** (n) *[i-PIT-uh-mee]*

*Syn:* perfect example or embodiment

*Ant:* bad example

*Usage:* She was the *epitome* of perfection and efficiency.

**EQUANIMITY** (n) *[ee-kwuh-NIM-i-tee]*

*Syn:* calmness of temperament; composure; levelheadedness

*Ant:* agitation; anxiety

*Usage:* She did not lose her coolness and *equanimity* even in the face of such a terrible personal crisis.

**EQUESTRIAN** (n) *[i-KWES-tree-uh n]*

*Syn:* rider on horseback

*Usage:* Cody wants to grow up to be an *equestrian*; he is crazy about horses.

**EQUIVOCATE** (v) *[ih-KWIV-uh-keyt]*

*Syn:* avoid an issue; lie; mislead; attempt to conceal the truth

*Ant:* face; meet

*Usage:* I hadn't expected the Department of Justice to *equivocate* and evade the matter in this manner.

**ERRATIC** (adj) *[i-RAT-ik]*

*Syn:* odd; unpredictable

*Ant:* normal; predictable

*Usage:* The schedule is rather *erratic* and unpredictable.

**ERUDITE** (adj) *[ER-yoo-dahyt]*

*Syn:* learned; scholarly

*Ant:* ignorant

*Usage:* I had never come across such an *erudite*, intelligent person before.

**ESCHEW** (v) *[es-CHOO]*

*Syn:* avoid on purpose

*Ant:* seek out

*Usage:* He *eschewed* the temptation to join the political party despite their cajoling and pleading because he knew it would be detrimental to his long-term future.

**ESOTERIC** (adj) *[es-uh-TER-ik]*

*Syn:* hard to understand; known only to the chosen few

*Ant:* common; familiar; known

*Usage:* The trade agreement was framed in a rather *esoteric* manner according to Jake; it would be too difficult for a layman to understand it.

**ETYMOLOGY** (n) *[et-uh-MOL-uh-jee]*

*Syn:* study of word parts

*Usage:* He went through great efforts to trace the *etymology* of the word.

**EUGENIC** (adj) *[yoo-JEN-ik]*

*Syn:* pertaining to the designed improvement of race

*Ant:* naturally acquired improvement

*Usage:* The men in the lab were dedicated to the *eugenic* research that might possibly produce better calves and foal in future.

**EULOGY** (n) *[YOO-luh-jee]*

*Syn:* expression of praise; often on the occasion of someone's death

*Ant:* calumny; condemnation; criticism

*Usage:* On the spot, he decided to compose a *eulogy* in praise of the distinguished gentleman.

**EUPHEMISM** (n) [YOO-fuh-miz-uh m]

*Syn:* mild expression in place of an unpleasant one

*Ant:* bluntness

*Usage:* The prose was inundated with too many *euphemisms*, which was not to Neil's liking; he decided to edit the piece all over again with more direct language.

**EUPHORIA** (n) [yoo-FAWR-ee-uh]

*Syn:* feeling of great happiness and well-being (sometimes exaggerated)

*Ant:* sadness; depression

*Usage:* We were in a state of *euphoria* after our daughter's film was nominated for the Best Picture Oscar.

**EUTHANASIA** (n) [yoo-thuh-NEY-zhuh]

*Syn:* mercy killing

*Usage:* The pro-life activists had gathered near the governor's office to protest against the proposed bill allowing *euthanasia*.

**EVANESCENT** (adj) [ev-uh-NES-uh nt]

*Syn:* fleeting; vanishing

*Ant:* permanent

*Usage:* I wondered whether he had been a reality in my life or just an *evanescent*, fleeting episode like a whiff of a breeze.

**EVOCATIVE** (adj) [ih-VOK-uh-tiv]

*Syn:* tending to call up from memory; suggestive

*Ant:* different

*Usage:* Nature's harvest yields an abundance of *evocative* scents to woo our senses.

**EXACERBATE** (v) [ig-ZAS-er-beyt]

*Syn:* worsen; embitter

*Ant:* alleviate; soothe

*Usage:* Watching the movie *exacerbated* his passion against the terrorists and he decided to enlist in the armed services as soon as possible.

**EXCHEQUER** (n) [EKS-chek-er]

*Syn:* treasury; financial institution

*Usage:* The thieves had burgled the building at midnight and looted the contents of the *exchequer*.

**EXCORIATE** (v) [ik-SKAWR-ee-yet]

*Syn:* scold with biting harshness; strip the skin off

*Ant:* tout

*Usage:* The priest *excoriated* the man's crimes at the end of his sermon and exiled him from the congregation.

**EXEGESIS** (n) [ek-si-JEE-sis]

*Syn:* explanation; especially of biblical passages

*Usage:* Paul was facing difficulty with the *exegesis* of the biblical text so he enlisted Andrew's help for the same.

**EXIGENCY** (n) [EK-si-juh n-see]

*Syn:* urgency; difficulty

*Ant:* tranquility

*Usage:* I wished they would display more *exigency* in winding up the construction because we were short of time and the new residents were to arrive any day.

**EXIGUOUS** (adj) [ig-ZIG-yoo-uh s]

*Syn:* small; minute; scanty

*Ant:* plenty

*Usage:* Seeing their *exiguous* supplies but generous hearts, I was overwhelmed and humbled.

**EXONERATE** (v) [ig-ZON-uh-reyt]

*Syn:* acquit; exculpate

*Ant:* charge; accuse; condemn

*Usage:* At last after a long and tiring period of courtroom struggles, he was *exonerated* of all charges and declared a free man.

**EXPATIATE** (v) *[ik-SPEY-shee-eyt]*

*Syn:* talk at length

*Ant:* stay silent

*Usage:* During the course of lunch, he then *expatiated* wordily on the new policy.

**EXPATRIATE** (n) *[eks-PEY-tree-it]*

*Syn:* exile; someone who has withdrawn from his native land

*Ant:* homeland resident

*Usage:* We stood patiently with placards waiting to welcome the *expatriate*, who was returning back into his country after the long exile.

**EXPIATE** (v) *[EK-spee-eyt]*

*Syn:* make amends for (a sin)

*Ant:* sin; corrupt

*Usage:* The priest *expiated* the young man after he had begged forgiveness and repented for his sins.

**EXPOSITORY** (adj) *[ik-SPOZ-i-tawr-ee]*

*Syn:* explanatory; serving to explain

*Ant:* unclear

*Usage:* There was an *expository* seminar on exotic birds at the local hall.

**EXPUNGE** (v) *[ik-SPUHNJ]*

*Syn:* cancel; remove

*Ant:* keep active

*Usage:* They *expunged* his name from the list of nominees after he was publicly disgraced for his indiscretions.

**EXTEMPORANEOUS** (n) *[ik-stem-puh-REY-nee-uh s]*

*Syn:* impromptu; immediate

*Ant:* rehearsed; planned

*Usage:* The crowd heartily applauded the poet's *extemporaneous* efforts.

**EXTRANEOUS** (adj) *[ik-STREY-nee-uh s]*

*Syn:* not essential; superfluous

*Ant:* intrinsic; essential; vital; internal

*Usage:* We deleted the *extraneous* items from the list of supplies because we didn't want the backpacks to become too heavy.

**EXTRINSIC** (adj) *[ik-STRIN-sik]*

*Syn:* external; not essential; extraneous

*Ant:* intrinsic; necessary

*Usage:* The *extrinsic* factors were the primary obstacles in Adam's path towards achieving his goals.

**EXTRUDE** (v) *[ik-STROOD]*

*Syn:* force or push out

*Ant:* take in

*Usage:* Pieces of the plastic form were being *extruded* from the press.

**EXUBERANT** (adj) *[ig-ZOO-ber-uh nt]*

*Syn:* abundant; effusive; lavish

*Ant:* unexcited; bored

*Usage:* Being such an *exuberant* person, Kelly was full of cheer and in high spirits about the forthcoming journey.

**FACETIOUS** (adj) *[fuh-SEE-shuh s]*

*Syn:* joking (often inappropriately); humorous

*Ant:* grave; serious; dull; lugubrious

*Usage:* We all laughed at his *facetious* and hilarious attempt at poetry.

**FACSIMILE** (n) *[fak-SIM-uh-lee]*

*Syn:* exact copy

*Ant:* imperfect imitation

*Usage:* Benedict is a perfect *facsimile* of his brother

*(Epitaph - Gawk)*

Solomon so at times it becomes difficult to identify who is who.

**FACTIOUS** (adj) *[FAK-shuh s]*

*Syn:* inclined to form factions; causing dissension.

*Ant:* cooperative

*Usage:* Sam was charged with being *factious* and dissident by his superiors.

**FACTOTUM** (n) *[fak-TOH-tuh m]*

*Syn:* handyman; person who does all kinds of work

*Ant:* idler

*Usage:* Mr. Simons can rarely do without his personal assistant Gary, for the latter is a *factotum*, able to perform a wide variety of tasks easily.

**FALLACIOUS** (adj) *[fuh-LEY-shuh s]*

*Syn:* false; misleading

*Ant:* truthful

*Usage:* The firm was shocked to discover that the employee had supplied a *fallacious* background and gained a foothold into its fold.

**FALLACY** (n) *[FAL-uh-see]*

*Syn:* mistaken idea based on flawed reasoning

*Ant:* truth

*Usage:* Joe Cummins has exposed the *fallacy* of this claim.

**FANATICISM** (n) *[fuh-NAT-uh-sahyz-uh m]*

*Syn:* excessive zeal; extreme devotion to a belief or cause

*Ant:* disinterest

*Usage:* The degree of *fanaticism* in the young revolutionary astounded me and even terrified me to an extent.

**FATUOUS** (adj) *[FACH-oo-uh s]*

*Syn:* foolish; inane

*Ant:* intelligent; clever; sensible; knowledgeable

*Usage:* Freddie, being a *fatuous* and foolish boy, is always at the mercy of the other children who love to play silly pranks with him.

**FAWNING** (adj) *[fawn]*

*Syn:* courting favor by cringing and flattering; deferential; groveling

*Ant:* aloof; disinterested

*Usage:* I was irritated to see Mark flattering and *fawning* over Sara; she certainly didn't deserve the man's attentions.

**FECUNDITY** (n) *[fi-KUHN-di-tee]*

*Syn:* fertility; fruitfulness

*Ant:* infertility;

*Usage:* The *fecundity* of such an enormous sacrifice looked doubtful to me; I rather suspected there would be no fruitful event in its wake.

**FERVID** (adj) *[FUR-vid]*

*Syn:* ardent

*Ant:* cool; apathetic; indifferent; phlegmatic

*Usage:* His eager, *fervid* reply raised my suspicions and I grew a little sceptical.

**FIASCO** (n) *[fee-AS-koh]*

*Syn:* total failure

*Ant:* total success

*Usage:* After our *fiasco* and mishap at the amusement park, we abandoned plans to go further and returned back home.

**FICTITIOUS** (adj) *[fik-TISH-uh s]*

*Syn:* imaginary

*Ant:* factual; genuine; actual; authentic

*Usage:* The entire incident was *fictitious* and none of the facts she had stated were true.

**FIGURATIVE** (adj) [IG-yer-uh-tiv]

Syn: not literal, but metaphorical; using a figure of speech

Ant: literal; straightforward

Usage: I could grasp the literal meaning of the prose but not its *figurative* significance.

**FILIAL** (adj) [FIL-ee-uh l]

Syn: pertaining to a son or daughter

Ant: parental

Usage: He broke all his *filial* ties in one go and became a recluse on a remote island.

**FINICKY** (adj) [FIN-i-kee]

Syn: too particular; fussy

Ant: accepting; not picky

Usage: The landlady was rather *finicky* which made Ben dread her fussy attention.

**FLACCID** (adj) [FLAK-sid]

Syn: flabby

Ant: muscular

Usage: Her once-lustrous, bouncy hair now lay *flaccid* and dull upon her shoulders.

**FLAGRANT** (adj) [FLEY-gruh nt]

Syn: conspicuously wicked; blatant; outrageous

Ant: subservient

Usage: For his *flagrant* and outrageous behavior, Samuel was chastised by the mayor himself.

**FLAMBOYANT** (adj) [flam-BOI-uh nt]

Syn: ornate; colorful; flashy

Ant: moderate; tasteful

Usage: Gerald's *flamboyant* taste in clothes has earned him many funny nicknames and sobriquets.

**FLEDGLING** (adj) [FLEJ-ling]

Syn: inexperienced

Ant: expert; professional

Usage: They are a group of *fledgling*, budding writers.

**FLIPPANCY** (n) [FLIP-uh n see]

Syn: trifling gaiety

Ant: seriousness

Usage: The atmosphere was full of sauciness and *flippancy*, with the girls getting merrily sarcastic with the poor guys.

**FLOE** (n) [floh]

Syn: mass of floating ice

Ant: fixed; glacial mass

Usage: They were trapped on an ice *floe* in the middle of nowhere; mere survival seemed a distant possibility.

**FLOTSAM** (n) [FLOT-suh m]

Syn: drifting wreckage

Usage: The divers swam about near the *flotsam* in the hope of finding something valuable or unique.

**FLOUT** (v) [flout]

Syn: reject; mock

Ant: honor; respect

Usage: He is always *flouting* the rules that are laid down; someday he is bound to face trouble.

**FLUX** (n) [fluhks]

Syn: flowing; series of changes

Ant: constancy; stability

Usage: The constant *flux* in his personal life caused his work performance to suffer.

**FOIBLE** (n) [FOI-buh l]

Syn: weakness; slight fault

Ant: strength

Usage: We were all aware of old Ben's *foibles* and

peculiarities but he was such an adorable old man that no one minded him.

**FOIL** (n) [foil]

*Syn:* contrast

*Ant:* support; help

*Usage:* The young damsel proved a perfect *foil* for the prince's exploits.

**FOIST** (v) [foist]

*Syn:* insert improperly; palm off

*Ant:* leave alone

*Usage:* Jimmy's partner *foisted* unfair provisions into their partnership contract.

**FOMENT** (v) [foh-MENT]

*Syn:* stir up; instigate

*Ant:* dampen; dissuade

*Usage:* The movie *fomented* desires and passions that had been dormant within him.

**FOPPISH** (adj) [FOP-ish]

*Syn:* vain about dress and appearance

*Ant:* slovenly; disheveled

*Usage:* The young nobleman had a *foppish* manner.

**FORBEARANCE** (n) [fawr-BAIR-uhns]

*Syn:* patience

*Ant:* impatience

*Usage:* Her strength and *forbearance* are her biggest assets.

**FORESTALL** (v) [fohr-STAWL]

*Syn:* prevent by taking action in advance

*Ant:* enable; promote

*Usage:* Before they could move on further, he *forestalled* them, saying they could not enter the house now.

**FORLORN** (adj) [fawr-lawrn]

*Syn:* sad and lonely

*Ant:* happy

*Usage:* Now the trees stand *forlorn* in the gathering gloom.

**FORSWEAR** (v) [fawr-SWAIR]

*Syn:* renounce; abandon

*Syn:* support; advocate

*Usage:* His family felt that he made a big mistake by *forswearing* his hard-won wealth and riches and retiring into the mountains.

**FORTE** (n) [FAWR-tey]

*Syn:* strong point or special talent

*Ant:* weakness

*Usage:* Seeing the outline of the test, he relaxed and was confident about getting through because this field was his *forte* and he knew he would definitely do well.

**FORTUITOUS** (adj) [fawr-TOO-i-tuh s]

*Syn:* accidental; by chance

*Ant:* deliberate; intentional; calculated; purposeful

*Usage:* What a *fortuitous* event it was, to meet Jim there in the party when I hadn't even known that he was back from the States.

**FRACTIOUS** (v) [FRAK-shuh s]

*Syn:* unruly

*Ant:* blithesome; tractable; submissive; genial; pliant

*Usage:* The more she wrung her hands and whined incessantly, the more Paul was becoming *fractious*.

**FRAUDULENT** (adj) [FRAW-juh-luh nt]

*Syn:* cheating; deceitful

*Ant:* sincere; valid

*Usage:* He had secured entry into the most protected area of the factory through *fraudulent* means.

**FRENETIC** (adj) [fruh-NET-ik]

Syn: frenzied; frantic

Ant: calm; serene

Usage: Her *frenetic* activity was serving to irritate John because he wanted to relax in peace, at least for today.

**FRESCO** (n) [FRES-koh]

Syn: painting on plaster (usually fresh)

Usage: The fantastic *frescoes* on the ceiling of the chapel had us all gaping in awe.

**FRIEZE** (n) [freez]

Syn: ornamental band on a wall

Usage: The *friezes* on the outer walls of the ancient temple were intricate and well-carved.

**FRIVOLOUS** (adj) [FRIV-uh-luh s]

Syn: lacking in seriousness; self-indulgently carefree; relatively unimportant

Ant: serious,; earnest; grave; important

Usage: It is not appropriate of Heather to behave in such a *frivolous* manner in the presence of the elders.

**FROWARD** (adj) [FROH-werd]

Syn: stubbornly contrary

Ant: agreeable

Usage: The children reacted with *froward* rejection of the suggestion of one more boring visit to the museum.

**FRUGAL** (adj) [FROO-guh l]

Syn: thrifty; economic; cheap

Ant: altruistic

Usage: Through years of *frugal habits* the woman saved enough money to buy herself the piano she had always dreamed of having.

**FRUGALITY** (n) [froo-GAL-i-ty]

Syn: thrift; economy

Ant: generosity; wastefulness

Usage: His habit of *frugality* helped him during his economic crisis.

**FRUSTRATE** (v) [FRUHS-treyt]

Syn: thwart; defeat

Ant: support; enable

Usage: Staff can still become *frustrated* at the lack of cooperation between offices.

**FULMINATE** (v) [FUHL-muh-neyt]

Syn: thunder; explode

Ant: simmer

Usage: On seeing Tim there, he *fulminated* in a babble of angry words, venting out the rage he had been bottling within.

**FULSOME** (adj) [FOO L-suh m]

Syn: disgustingly excessive

Ant: thin

Usage: The meal was more than adequate; it was *fulsome*.

**FUROR** (n) [FYOO R-awr]

Syn: frenzy; great excitement

Ant: silence; indifference

Usage: Hearing the escape of the notorious criminal from the Mexican prison, there was a nationwide *furor*.

**FURTIVE** (adj) [FUR-tiv]

Syn: stealthy; sneaky

Ant: open; honest

Usage: He kept darting *furtive* looks at the door to see if anyone was approaching

**FUSILLADE** (adj) [FYOO-suh-leyd]

Syn: simultaneous firing or outburst (of missiles, questions, etc.)

Ant: single shot

*(Epitaph - Gawk)*

*Usage:* The sergeant barked his order and instantly there was a tumultuous *fusillade* from the troops, killing at least twenty men in the enemy ranks.

**FUTILE** (adj) *[FYOOT-l]*

*Syn:* useless; hopeless; ineffectual

*Ant:* effective; powerful; cogent; useful; solid; capable

*Usage:* No matter how hard she worked, her efforts seemed *futile* because nothing much was getting accomplished.

**GADFLY** (n) *[GAD-flahy]*

*Syn:* animal-biting fly; an irritating person; nuisance

*Usage:* She was such an annoying busybody that people called her a *gadfly* behind her back.

**GAFFE** (n) *[gaf]*

*Syn:* social blunder

*Ant:* correction

*Usage:* She was embarrassed at having made such a *gaffe* in front of the distinguished dignitaries.

**GAINSAY** (v) *[GEYN-sey]*

*Syn:* deny; contradict

*Ant:* affirm; verify; confirm; attest; witness

*Usage:* Her honesty meant no one could *gainsay* her conclusions.

**GALL** (v) *[gawl]*

*Syn:* annoy; chafe

*Ant:* please

*Usage:* I was *galled* by the total lack of the response to the diligently prepared questions.

**GAMBOL** (v) *[GAM-buh]*

*Syn:* frolic; jump and skip; leap playfully

*Ant:* flag; tire; work

*Usage:* The crowds *gambolled* about in the colorful carnival.

**GAMUT** (n) *[GAM-uh t]*

*Syn:* the entire range or extent; any complete musical scale

*Ant:* single item

*Usage:* The *gamut* of the policy encompassed the production, sales and finance departments.

**GARGOYLE** (n) *[GAHR-goil]*

*Syn:* waterspout carved in grotesque figures on a building

*Usage:* There was an ugly *gargoyle* carved and painted on the side of the door.

**GARNER** (v) *[GAHR-ner]*

*Syn:* gather; store up

*Ant:* disburse

*Usage:* He *garnered* many a laurel for his achievements.

**GARNISH** (v) *[GAHR-nish]*

*Syn:* decorate

*Ant:* strip; spoil; mark; pollute; deface; defile

*Usage:* They *garnished* the chocolate cake with pink icing on the top.

**GARRULITY** (n) *[guh-ROO-li-tee]*

*Syn:* talkativeness

*Ant:* silence; reticence

*Usage:* Keith is well-known for his *garrulity* so people take care not to give him much opportunity to talk.

**GARRULOUS** (adj) *[GAR-uh-luhs]*

*Syn:* loquacious; wordy; talkative

*Ant:* silent; speechless; taciturn; quiet

*Usage:* Nick is a *garrulous*, loquacious man who can barely resist an opening to start talking.

**GAUCHE** (adj) *[gohsh]*

*Syn:* unsophisticated; simple; erroneous

*Ant:* sophisticated

*Usage:* She was apprehensive of looking *gauche* and unsophisticated in front of the trendy, modern crowd.

# GAWK (v) [gawk]

*Syn:* stare foolishly; look in open-mouthed awe

*Ant:* ignore

*Usage:* The boys near the entrance of the building *gawked* and ogled at the attractive woman clad in a halter-top with white capris.

# Chapter 8

## (Genealogy – Impolitic)

*This chapter covers the following words along with their part of speech, pronunciation, synonyms and antonym, if applicable. Sample usage of the word is also illustrated.*

| | | |
|---|---|---|
| genealogy | hallucination | hyperbole |
| geniality | hap | hypochondriac |
| genteel | harangue | Hypocritical |
| genuflect | harbinger | ichthyology |
| germinal | harping | iconoclastic |
| gerontocracy | harrow | ideology |
| gerrymander | haughtiness | idiosyncratic |
| gesticulation | hazardous | idolatry |
| gibberish | headstrong | ignoble |
| giddy | heckler | illimitable |
| girth | hedonism | illusive |
| glacial | hegemony | imbecility |
| glean | heinous | imbroglio |
| glimmer | herpetologist | imminent |
| glossary | heterogeneous | immutable |
| glutinous | hew | impair |
| goad | hiatus | impalpable |
| granary | hieroglyphic | impassive |
| grandiloquent | hindrance | impeccable |
| grandiose | hirsute | impede |
| grate | hoard | impenetrable |
| gratuitous | hoary | imperiousness |
| gregarious | holocaust | Impermeable |
| grotesque | hone | imperturbable |
| gruel | hortatory | impetus |
| guffaw | hostility | impinge |
| guileless | hubbub | impious |
| gullible | hue | implacable |
| gustatory | humdrum | implicate |
| gusty | hummock | implicit |
| gyroscope | humus | implode |
| habituate | hurtle | impolitic |
| hackneyed | husbandry | |
| halcyon | hydrophobia | |

*www.vibrantpublishers.com*

**GENEALOGY** (n) *[jee-nee-OL-uh-jee]*

*Syn:* study of ancestry or family tree

*Usage:* His family tree or *genealogy* showed traces of royal blue blood in the early fifteen century.

**GENIALITY** (n) *[jee-nee-AL-i-tee]*

*Syn:* cheerfulness; kindliness; sympathy

*Ant:* unfriendliness; irritation; aloofness

*Usage:* After the death of his daughter, George lost his cheerfulness and *geniality* and became a withdrawn, silent man.

**GENTEEL** (adj) *[jen-TEEL]*

*Syn:* well-bred; elegant

*Ant:* boorish; clownish; rude; uncultivated

*Usage:* The old woman retained her *genteel*, well-bred behavior even though her sons had grown to be brash, rude young men.

**GENUFLECT** (v) *[JEN-yoo-flekt]*

*Syn:* bend the knee as in worship

*Ant:* stand erect

*Usage:* The young man *genuflected* in front of the emperor, his eyes downcast and manner respectful.

**GERMINAL** (adj) *[JUR-muh-nl]*

*Syn:* pertaining to a germ; creative

*Ant:* dying; shrinking

*Usage:* Jane Smith had been very active in the *germinal* stages of the space program.

**GERONTOCRACY** (n) *[jer-uh n-TOK-ruh-see]*

*Syn:* government ruled by old people

*Usage:* We had never before come across a nation with *gerontocracy*, where the government was formed wholly of elders.

**GERRYMANDER** (v) *[jer-i-man-der]*

*Syn:* change voting district lines in order to favor a political party

*Usage:* This redistricting looked like a clear attempt to *gerrymander* the boundaries to try to help the Conservatives.

**GESTICULATION** (n) *[je-stik-yuh-LEY-shuh]*

*Syn:* motion; gesture

*Usage:* She used a lot of *gesticulation* to convey her messages across the glass door.

**GIBBERISH** (n) *[GIB-er-ish]*

*Syn:* nonsense; babbling

*Ant:* sense; wisdom

*Usage:* The kids were speaking *gibberish* and the young mother laughed in delight at hearing their talk.

**GIDDY** (adj) *[GID-ee]*

*Syn:* light-hearted; dizzy

*Ant:* solemn; serious

*Usage:* The height of the tower was making her *giddy*.

**GIRTH** (n) *[gurth]*

*Syn:* distance around something; circumference

*Usage:* The man's *girth* had increased immensely since he had left the house and now his old trousers could no longer fit him.

**GLACIAL** (adj) *[GLEY-shuh,l]*

*Syn:* like a glacier; extremely cold

*Ant:* warm

*Usage:* His sea blue eyes had a *glacial*, icy look which made her shiver slightly.

**GLEAN** (v) *[gleen]*

*Syn:* gather leavings

*Ant:* abandon

*Usage:* They tried to *glean* any bit of information they could from him about the new proposed project.

# Chapter 8

**GLIMMER** (v) [GLIM-er]

*Syn:* shine erratically; twinkle

*Usage:* The lake *glimmered* as the sun's rays touched its surface.

**GLOSSARY** (n) [GLOS-uh-ree]

*Syn:* brief explanation of words used in the text

*Usage:* A self-explaining *glossary* was missing in the book, which made it difficult to comprehend the technical jargon.

**GLUTINOUS** (adj) [GLOOT-n-uh s]

*Syn:* sticky; viscous

*Ant:* slippery; dry

*Usage:* Walt stuck to Mary's side like a *glutinous* substance.

**GOAD** (v) [gohd]

*Syn:* urge on

*Ant:* discourage

*Usage:* They *goaded* and egged him on to win the race.

**GRANARY** (n) [GREY-nuh-ree]

*Syn:* storehouse for grain

*Usage:* Robbers ransacked the *granary* at midnight and made away with many sacks of grains.

**GRANDILOQUENT** (adj) [gran-DIL-uh-kwuh nt]

*Syn:* pompous; bombastic; using high-sounding language

*Ant:* humble; unpretentious; plain; unadorned

*Usage:* The wedding celebrations were in his inimitable, *grandiloquent* style.

**GRANDIOSE** (adj) [GRAN-dee-ohs]

*Syn:* pretentious; high-flown; ridiculously exaggerated; impressive

*Ant:* humble; unpretentious

*Usage:* His *grandiose* plans came to a standstill with his father's sudden death

**GRATE** (v) [greyt]

*Syn:* make a harsh noise; have an unpleasant effect; shred

*Usage:* The heavy noise on the street below the flat she had shifted to yesterday *grated* on her nerves.

**GRATUITOUS** (adj) [gruh-TOO-i-tuh s]

*Syn:* given freely; unwarranted; uncalled for

*Ant:* warranted

*Usage:* Many *gratuitous* favors were granted to her because she had been kind and helpful to the emperor in the past when he was exiled and in need of help.

**GREGARIOUS** (adj) [gri-GAIR-ee-uh s]

*Syn:* sociable; extroverted

*Ant:* introverted

*Usage:* Karen is such a *gregarious* person; she loves to be surrounded by people.

**GROTESQUE** (adj) [groh-TESK]

*Syn:* fantastic; comically hideous

*Ant:* beautiful

*Usage:* A huge, *grotesque* figure stood near the top of the hill in the darkness, frightening the young children.

**GRUEL** (v) [GROO-uh l]

*Syn:* liquid food made by boiling oatmeal; etc, in milk or water

*Usage:* She woke him and handed him some warm rice *gruel* saying she did not have good food supplies to cook a more healthy meal.

**GUFFAW** (n) [guh-FAW]

*Syn:* boisterous laughter

*Ant:* snicker; chuckle

*Usage:* The crowd *guffawed* loudly at the comedian's

jokes.

**GUILELESS** (adj) *[GAHYL-lis]*

*Syn:* without deceit; honest

*Ant:* artful; cunning; deceitful

*Usage:* I was taken aback by the sheer honesty and *guileless* attitude of the young man.

**GULLIBLE** (adj) *[GUHL-uh-buh l]*

*Syn:* easily deceived

*Ant:* discerning

*Usage:* Ben is too *gullible*; anyone can easily cheat him and get away with it too.

**GUSTATORY** (adj) *[GUHS-tuh-tawr-ee]*

*Syn:* affecting the sense of taste

*Ant:* bland

*Usage:* The lunch was sumptuous and *gustatory* so Harold had two helpings of the dishes.

**GUSTY** (adj) *[GUHS-tee]*

*Syn:* windy

*Ant:* windless; still

*Usage:* The air near the castle was *gusty* and blowing hard enough to make trees sway.

**GYROSCOPE** (n) *[JAHY-ruh-skohp]*

*Syn:* apparatus used to maintain balance, ascertain direction, etc.

*Usage:* For her fifteenth birthday, Jennifer's father bought her a *gyroscope*, which she could use to counteract the rolling movements of an object.

**HABITUATE** (v) *[huh-BICH-oo-yet]*

*Syn:* accustom or familiarize; addict

*Ant:* ignore

*Usage:* Discussion includes the move from the lecturer as expert to that of facilitator and questions concerning the need to *habituate* staff to new technology.

**HACKNEYED** (adj) *[HAK-need]*

*Syn:* commonplace; trite

*Ant:* fresh

*Usage:* The conversation was very *hackneyed*, with the three of them almost falling asleep due to fatigue and drowsiness.

**HALCYON** (adj) *[HAL-see-uh n]*

*Syn:* calm; peaceful

*Ant:* stormy

*Usage:* The Island was a serene, *halcyon* place.

**HALLUCINATION** (n) *[huh-loo-suh-NEY-shuh n]*

*Syn:* delusion

*Ant:* reality

*Usage:* The doctor was sure that the man had been seeing some *hallucination* because UFOs didn't exist in reality.

**HAP** (n) *[hap]*

*Syn:* chance; luck

*Ant:* plan

*Usage:* The report elaborates on the *hap* of being stranded of an island alone.

**HARANGUE** (n) *[huh-RANG]*

*Syn:* noisy speech; long lecture

*Ant:* conversation

*Usage:* Kenneth Parker then launched into a long and tiresome *harangue* on why the public should vote for the Democrats.

**HARBINGER** (n) *[HAHR-bin-jer]*

*Syn:* forerunner

*Ant:* follower

*Usage:* The uncle's visit was a *harbinger* of good news.

**HARPING** (n) *[HAHR-ping]*

*Syn:* tiresome dwelling on a subject

Ant: praise

Usage: Peter was annoyed at Nora's constant *harping* on the topic.

**HARROW** (v) *[HAR-oh]*

Syn: break up ground after plowing; torture

Ant: leave alone

Usage: It wasn't my intention to *harrow* him about the traumatic experience.

**HAUGHTINESS** (n) *[HAW-tee-nis]*

Syn: pride; arrogance

Ant: modesty; meekness; humility

Usage: I disliked her *haughtiness* and overbearing attitude.

**HAZARDOUS** (adj) *[HAZ-er-duh s]*

Syn: dangerous

Ant: safe

Usage: They had warned him that the trek was *hazardous* and full of perils and dangers, yet it was his lifetime ambition to fulfill it.

**HEADSTRONG** (adj) *[HED-strawng]*

Syn: stubborn; willful; unyielding

Ant: yielding; meek

Usage: He is hot-blooded, *headstrong.g* and stubborn.

**HECKLER** (n) *[HEK-ler]*

Syn: person who harasses others

Ant: fan; supporter

Usage: Jim Smith of Sunday Times is notorious for being a *heckler*; when he attends a press conference, the people groan in anticipation of his rude remarks.

**HEDONISM** (n) *[HEED-n-iz-uh m]*

Syn: belief that pleasure is the sole aim in life

Ant: spartanism

Usage: The way he indulges himself in all his favorite pleasures and pursuits is the height of *hedonism*.

**HEGEMONY** (n) *[hi-JEM-uh-nee]*

Syn: hedonism and asceticism are opposing philosophies of human behavior.

Usage: The man's *hegemony* to the topmost position in the corporate ladder is attributed to his sycophantic attitude.

**HEINOUS** (adj) *[HEY-nuh s]*

Syn: atrocious; hatefully bad

Ant: mild; good

Usage: They all agreed that it was a *heinous*, terrible crime.

**HERPETOLOGIST** (n) *[hur-pi-TOL-uh-jist]*

Syn: one who studies reptiles

Usage: The man channeled his affinity for snakes into a profession, that of a *herpetologist*.

**HETEROGENEOUS** (adj) *[het-er-uh-JEE-nee-uh s]*

Syn: dissimilar; mixed

Ant: homogeneous; same

Usage: The crowd was a *heterogeneous* mix of intellectuals, students and veteran professors.

**HEW** (v) *[hyoo]*

Syn: cut to pieces with ax or sword

Ant: make whole

Usage: The huge monolith was *hewn* out of a single rock.

**HIATUS** (n) *[hahy-EY-tuh s]*

Syn: interruption in duration or continuity; pause; a gap;

Ant: continuation

Usage: I decided to take brief *hiatus* from writing the novel and traveled to Japan for some idle sightseeing and relaxing.

**HIEROGLYPHIC** (n) *[hahy-er-uh-GLIF-ik]*

*Syn:* picture writing

*Usage:* The *hieroglyphic*s written on the inner walls of the tomb seemed to have a great significance so we decided to bring a team to decipher it.

**HINDRANCE** (n) *[HIN-druh ns]*

*Syn:* block; obstacle

*Ant:* support

*Usage:* Holly's presence was a *hindrance* to Jim's concentration but he couldn't summon the courage to ask her to leave.

**HIRSUTE** (adj) *[HUR-soot]*

*Syn:* hairy

*Ant:* bald; shorn

*Usage:* The man was huge, well built and *hirsute* to boot, with thick hair all over his burly arms.

**HOARD** (v) *[hawrd]*

*Syn:* stockpile; accumulate for future use

*Ant:* waste; squander; dissipate

*Usage:* The man is a miser and loves to *hoard* gold and silver rather than share it with those in need.

**HOARY** (adj) *[HAWR-ee]*

*Syn:* white with age

*Ant:* modern; young

*Usage:* A *hoary* old man opened the door in response to my knocks.

**HOLOCAUST** (n) *[HOL-uh-kawst]*

*Syn:* destruction by fire

*Usage:* The *holocaust* perpetrated by the Germans in Auschwitz was beyond anything the world had ever seen.

**HONE** (v) *[hohn]*

*Syn:* sharpen

*(Genealogy – Impolitic)*

*Ant:* dull

*Usage:* The writing workshop was intended to *hone* the skills of new writers.

**HORTATORY** (adj) *[HAWR-tuh-tawr-ee]*

*Syn:* encouraging; exhortive

*Ant:* discouraging; unsupportive

*Usage:* The *hortatory* speech by the electoral candidate had the crowd very enthused in his favor.

**HOSTILITY** (n) *[ho-stil-i-tee]*

*Syn:* unfriendliness; hatred

*Ant:* friendliness; calm; detente

*Usage:* Within the neighborhoods, living conditions are affected by competition and harsh *hostility* between different ethnic groups.

**HUBBUB** (n) *[HUHB-uhb]*

*Syn:* confused uproar

*Ant:* silence; calm

*Usage:* He missed the *hubbub* of the city while sitting in this quiet, idle countryside.

**HUE** (n) *[hyoo]*

*Syn:* color; aspect

*Ant:* colorlessness

*Usage:* The skies were colored with spectacular *hues* of orange and magenta.

**HUMDRUM** (adj) *[HUHM-druhm]*

*Syn:* dull; monotonous

*Ant:* exciting

*Usage:* The day-to-day *humdrum* routine was beginning to bore him now.

**HUMMOCK** (n) *[HUHM-uh k]*

*Syn:* small hill

*Ant:* depression (in the earth)

*Usage:* We trudged wearily up the *hummock* carrying our supplies and knapsacks.

**HUMUS** (n) *[HYOO-muh s]*

*Syn:* substance formed by decaying vegetable matter

*Usage:* The men unloaded three gunny bags of *humus*, which would be used as fertilizer for the crops.

**HURTLE** (n) *[HUR-tl]*

*Syn:* crash; rush

*Ant:* be still; stay at rest

*Usage:* With terrific speed, the car *hurtled* down the track.

**HUSBANDRY** (n) *[HUHZ-buh n-dree]*

*Syn:* frugality; thrift; agriculture

*Ant:* lavishness

*Usage:* John may look like a dunce but he is adept at home management and *husbandry*.

**HYDROPHOBIA** (n) *[hahy-druh-FOH-bee-uh]*

*Syn:* rabies; fear of water

*Usage:* He doesn't want his wife going near any dog for fear of contracting *hydrophobia*.

**HYPERBOLE** (n) *[hahy-PUR-buh-lee]*

*Syn:* exaggeration; overstatement

*Ant:* reality

*Usage:* Tom tends to use a lot of *hyperbole* in his statements, exaggerating ordinary events to make them sound extraordinary.

**HYPOCHONDRIAC** (n) *[hahy-puh-KON-dree-ak]*

*Syn:* person unduly worried about his health; worrier without cause about illness

*Ant:* truly sick individual

*Usage:* Gia is a *hypochondriac*; she often goes to the doctor for no reason at all, imagining she has some ailment.

**HYPOCRITICAL** (adj) *[hip-uh-KRIT-i-kuh l]*

*Syn:* pretending to be virtuous; deceiving

*Ant:* sincere

*Usage:* I could sense his *hypocritical* behavior even without getting close to him; he's too artificial and insincere.

**ICHTHYOLOGY** (n) *[ik-thee-OL-uh-jee]*

*Syn:* study of fish

*Usage:* She likes fish a lot so her uncle recommended that she take up *ichthyology* as her special subject under the major of zoology.

**ICONOCLASTIC** (adj) *[ahy-KON-uh-klast-ic]*

*Syn:* attacking cherished traditions; skeptical

*Ant:* traditionalist; orthodox

*Usage:* James Bean has always been *iconoclastic*, never conforming to the trend but always treading his own path.

**IDEOLOGY** (n) *[ahy-dee-OL-uh-jee]*

*Syn:* system of ideas of a group

*Usage:* He is very firm about his *ideologies* and beliefs.

**IDIOSYNCRATIC** (adj) *[id-ee-oh-sing-KRAT-it]*

*Syn:* private; peculiar to an individual

*Ant:* common; normal

*Usage:* We were amused at his peculiar and *idiosyncratic* behavior.

**IDOLATRY** (n) *[ahy-DOL-uh-tree]*

*Syn:* worship of idols; excessive admiration

*Ant:* disapproval

*Usage:* The college dean frowned at the girl's acts of *idolatry* in the presence of the visiting rock star.

**IGNOBLE** (adj) *[ig-NOH-buh l]*

*Syn:* of lowly origin; unworthy

*Ant:* noble; high-minded

*Usage:* He has been seen lately in *ignoble* company, which doesn't bode well for his future.

### ILLIMITABLE (adj) [i-LIM-i-tuh-buh l]

*Syn:* infinite

*Ant:* limited; finite

*Usage:* He pointed out that the possibilities are *illimitable* offering endless opportunities for the future.

### ILLUSIVE (adj) [ih-LOO-siv]

*Syn:* deceiving; fleeting

*Ant:* permanent

*Usage:* Happiness is an *illusive* goal; any temporary hold o it should be cherished before it slips away.

### IMBECILITY (n) [im-buh-SIL-i-tee]

*Syn:* weakness of mind

*Ant:* intelligence; soundness of mind

*Usage:* His latest mistake was the height of *imbecility* and stupidity.

### IMBROGLIO (n) [im-BROHL-yoh]

*Syn:* complicated situation; perplexity; entanglement

*Ant:* simplicity

*Usage:* The *imbroglio* and noisy fracas in the lobby was attracting a great deal of unwanted attention.

### IMMINENT (adj) [IM-uh-nuh nt]

*Syn:* near at hand; impending

*Ant:* unlikely

*Usage:* The *imminent* election was the cause for great excitement as well as apprehension for the senator.

### IMMUTABLE (adj) [ih-myoo-tuh-buhl]

*Syn:* unchangeable

*Ant:* changeable; flexible; variable

*Usage:* The point is that you can save yourself from many sorts of mistakes by making files *immutable*.

### IMPAIR (v) [im-PAIR]

*Syn:* worsen; diminish in value

*Ant:* enhance; improve; augment; repair; increase; build up; perfect

*Usage:* The chemicals had *impaired* his vision to some extent.

### IMPALPABLE (adj) [im-PAL-puh-buh l]

*Syn:* imperceptible; intangible

*Ant:* tangible

*Usage:* The *impalpable* and intangible implications of the event worried me a lot.

### IMPASSIVE (adj) [im-PAS-iv]

*Syn:* without feeling; imperturbable; stoical

*Ant:* passionate

*Usage:* Unperturbed, he shot an *impassive* look at her in response to her challenging statement.

### IMPECCABLE (adj) [im-PEK-uh-buh l]

*Syn:* faultless

*Ant:* flawed

*Usage:* His conduct is always flawless and *impeccable*.

### IMPEDE (v) [im-PEED]

*Syn:* hinder, block

*Ant:* assist

*Usage:* Nothing could now *impede* his progress since he was so determined to achieve his goal.

### IMPENETRABLE (adj) [im-PEN-i-truh-buh l]

*Syn:* not able to be pierced; entered beyond understanding

*Ant:* easily penetrated

*Usage:* The fort is *impenetrable* and impregnable.

**IMPERIOUSNESS** (n) *[im-PEER-ee-uh s]*

*Syn:* lordliness; domineering manner; arrogance

*Ant:* humility

*Usage:* I was fed up with his domineering manners and *imperiousness*.

**IMPERMEABLE** (adj) *[im-PUR-mee-uh-buh l]*

*Syn:* impervious; not permitting passage through as substance

*Ant:* permeable; passable

*Usage:* The covering was made of *impermeable* substance so that not a drop would leak through.

**IMPERTURBABLE** (adj) *[im-per-TUR-buh-buh l]*

*Syn:* calm; placid; composed

*Ant:* anxious

*Usage:* His face looked *imperturbable*, not giving away his response to the accusation.

**IMPETUS** (n) *[IM-pi-tuh s]*

*Syn:* incentive; stimulus; moving force

*Ant:* block; hindrance

*Usage:* A simple, modest lady was the main *impetus* behind the business tycoon's huge success.

**IMPINGE** (v) *[im-PINJ]*

*Syn:* infringe; touch; collide with

*Ant:* avoid; dodge

*Usage:* The trespassers *impinged* upon the government land too.

**IMPIOUS** (adj) *[IM-pee-uh s]*

*Syn:* irreverent

*Ant:* pious; sacred; godly; religious; reverent

*Usage:* The tribe did not tolerate any *impious* behavior; those who did not comply with the religious doctrine were immediately beheaded.

**IMPLACABLE** (adj) *[im-PLAK-uh-buhl]*

*Syn:* incapable of being pacified

*Ant:* easily pleased

*Usage:* The commander was *implacable*; no amount of cajoling would change his mind.

**IMPLICATE** (v) *[im-pli-keyt]*

*Syn:* incriminate; show to be involved

*Ant:* pardon; defend; support

*Usage:* The unions were deeply *implicated* in helping create a climate in which men's needs were seen to be paramount.

**IMPLICIT** (adj) *[im-PLIS-it]*

*Syn:* understood but not stated

*Ant:* explicit

*Usage:* Her assent was *implicit*. Although she did not explicitly agree, it was assumed that she'd said yes.

**IMPLODE** (v) *[im-PLOHD]*

*Syn:* burst inward

*Ant:* explode; burst outward

*Usage:* The bomb caused the mansion to *implode*.

**IMPOLITIC** (adj) *[im-POL-i-tik]*

*Syn:* not wise

*Ant:* tactful; politic

*Usage:* It was very unwise and rather *impolitic* of her to have broached the subject at the state dinner.

This page is intentionally left blank

# Chapter 9

## (Importune – Legerdemain)

*This chapter covers the following words along with their part of speech, pronunciation, synonyms and antonym, if applicable. Sample usage of the word is also illustrated.*

| | | |
|---|---|---|
| importune | ineluctable | invective |
| impregnable | inerrancy | inveigh |
| impromptu | inexorable | invidious |
| impropriety | infantile | irascible |
| improvise | infernal | iridescent |
| impudence | infinitesimal | irreconcilable |
| impugn | influx | irrepressible |
| inadvertently | infringe | irretrievable |
| incandescent | ingenuous | isthmus |
| incarcerate | ingratiate | itinerant |
| incendiary | inherent | jargon |
| incessant | inimical | jeopardy |
| inchoate | iniquitous | jingoism |
| incidental | innocuous | jocund |
| incipient | innuendo | juggernaut |
| inclement | insalubrious | junta |
| incognito | insensate | juxtapose |
| incommodious | insinuate | Knell |
| incongruity | insouciant | labile |
| inconsequential | insularity | lachrymose |
| incontinent | insurgent | laconic |
| incorporate | insurmountable | laggard |
| incorrigible | integral | lambaste |
| increment | integrate | languid |
| incrustation | intelligentsia | languor |
| incubus | interim | larceny |
| incursion | intermittent | lascivious |
| indemnify | interregnum | laudatory |
| indeterminate | intersperse | lax |
| indigence | intractable | laxative |
| indiscriminate | intransigence | lectern |
| indolent | intrinsically | legerdemain |
| indomitable | intuition | |
| inebriety | inundate | |

**IMPORTUNE** (v) *[im-pawr-TOON]*

*Syn:* beg persistently

*Ant:* give; answer

*Usage:* He continued to *importune* the judge to change his decision but to no avail.

**IMPREGNABLE** (adj) *[im-PREG-nuh-buh l]*

*Syn:* invulnerable

*Ant:* vulnerable

*Usage:* The fort is *impregnable*; no attack would break through its protective walls.

**IMPROMPTU** (adj) *[im-PROMP-too]*

*Syn:* extemporaneous; without previous preparation; off hand; on the spur of the moment

*Ant:* planned; rehearsed

*Usage:* We wrote an *impromptu* play and acted it out right there and then.

**IMPROPRIETY** (n) *[im-pruh-PRAHY-i-tee]*

*Syn:* improperness; unsuitableness

*Ant:* propriety; decorum

*Usage:* Mr. Thomas chastised his daughter for her *impropriety*; not at all suitable for the formal event.

**IMPROVISE** (v) *[IM-pruh-vahyz]*

*Syn:* compose on the spur of the moment

*Ant:* plan

*Usage:* The director asked the writer to *improvise* on the script a little more.

**IMPUDENCE** (n) *[IM-pyuh-duhns]*

*Syn:* impertinence; insolence; audacity

*Ant:* humility

*Usage:* Is not that the very man Frank had the *impudence* to bring here last Tuesday week against our wishes?

**IMPUGN** (v) *[im-PYOON]*

*Syn:* dispute or contradict (often in an insulting way); challenge; gainsay

*Ant:* confirm; prove; establish; evidence

*Usage:* He *impugned* the people to dare and prove his guilt.

**INADVERTENTLY** (adj) *[in-uh d-VUR-tnt-ly]*

*Syn:* unintentionally; by oversight; carelessly

*Ant:* intentionally

*Usage:* He *inadvertently* called her by her name even though she had forbidden him to do so.

**INCANDESCENT** (adj) *[in-kuh n-DES-uh nt]*

*Syn:* strikingly bright; shining with intense heat

*Usage:* There was an *incandescent* glow on her face in the candlelight that made her look very appealing.

**INCARCERATE** (v) *[in-KAHR-suh-reyt]*

*Syn:* imprison

*Ant:* set free

*Usage:* The notorious serial killer had been *incarcerated* in the city's most secluded prison.

**INCENDIARY** (n) *[in-SEN-dee-er-ee]*

*Syn:* arsonist

*Usage:* The man was arrested on charges of instigating an agitation primarily because he was an *incendiary* rebel.

**INCESSANT** (adj) *[in-SES-uh nt]*

*Syn:* uninterrupted; unceasing

*Ant:* stopped; intermittent

*Usage:* The *incessant* flow of repartees and rejoinders made the evening amusing and entertaining.

**INCHOATE** (adj) *[in-KOH-it]*

*Syn:* recently begun; rudimentary; elementary

*Ant:* long-lasting

*Usage:* The *inchoate* production of the play was enough to make us realize we would never wish to see the finished work.

**INCIDENTAL** (adj) [in-si-DEN-tl]

*Syn:* not essential; minor

*Ant:* essential; invariable; regular; irrelative; uniform; inherent; relevant

*Usage:* It was just *incidental* that he happened to be passing by on the same street that I was walking, for he had never come by that area in many years.

**INCIPIENT** (adj) [in-SIP-ee-uh nt]

*Syn:* beginning; in an early stage

*Ant:* ending; completed

*Usage:* The *incipient* visit of the cardinal was very successful but his later visits roused unwanted emotions and sentiments.

**INCLEMENT** (adj) [in-KLEM-uhnt]

*Syn:* stormy; unkind

*Ant:* mild; sunny; kind

*Usage:* The *inclement* weather has made Freda indisposed.

**INCOGNITO** (adj) [in-kog-NEE-toh]

*Syn:* with identity concealed; using an assumed name

*Ant:* known; openly

*Usage:* The criminal had got away by travelling *incognito* to the airport.

**INCOMMODIOUS** (adj) [in-kuh-MOH-dee-uh s]

*Syn:* not spacious; inconvenient

*Ant:* spacious

*Usage:* He couldn't bear to stay a day more in the *incommodious*, cramped apartment.

**INCONGRUITY** (n) [in-kuh n-GROO-i-tee]

*Syn:* lack of harmony; absurdity

*Ant:* sense; congruity

*Usage:* The *incongruity* and discrepancy in the two charts were very obvious.

**INCONSEQUENTIAL** (adj) [in-kon-si-KWEN-shuh l]

*Syn:* insignificant; unimportant

*Ant:* important; meaningful

*Usage:* One elderly woman's peaceful death in the city, at a time when it was being rocked by a hundred bombings every day, was but an *inconsequential* event.

**INCONTINENT** (adj) [in-KON-tn-uh nt]

*Syn:* lacking self-restraint; licentious

*Ant:* restrained

*Usage:* The old man found to his extreme embarrassment that he was becoming increasingly *incontinent* and losing control of his bladder.

**INCORPORATE** (v) [in-KAWR-puh-reyt]

*Syn:* introduce something into a larger whole; combine; unite

*Ant:* separate

*Usage:* We informed the director of the company that it would take a few weeks to *incorporate* his suggestions into the new system.

**INCORRIGIBLE** (adj) [in-KAWR-i-juh-buh l]

*Syn:* not correctable

*Ant:* correctable

*Usage:* Gary is an *incorrigible* liar, rarely telling the truth.

**INCREMENT** (n) [IN-kruh-muh nt]

*Syn:* increase

*Ant:* reduction; decrease

*Usage:* The software program expected numbers in *increments* of 10.

**INCRUSTATION** (n) [in-kruh-STEY-shuhn]

*Syn:* hard coating or crust

*Usage:* I have several times alluded to the surface of the

ground having an *incrust*ation of salt.

**INCUBUS** (n) *[IN-kyuh-buhs]*

*Syn:* evil spirit; burden; mental care; nightmare

*Ant:* angel; god

*Usage:* The woman screamed and claimed to have been attacked by an *incubus*.

**INCURSION** (n) *[in-KUR-zhuh n]*

*Syn:* temporary invasion

*Ant:* retreat; retirement; withdrawal; settlement

*Usage:* The sudden *incursion* by the Huns caused the villagers to panic.

**INDEMNIFY** (v) *[in-DEM-nuh-fahy]*

*Syn:* make secure against loss; compensate for loss

*Ant:* deprive; forfeit

*Usage:* He promised to *indemnify* the balance installments within the next two months.

**INDETERMINATE** (adj) *[in-di-TUR-muh-nit]*

*Syn:* uncertain; not clearly fixed; indefinite

*Ant:* definite; clear

*Usage:* The consequences of the event are *indeterminate* as of now.

**INDIGENCE** (n) *[IN-di-juh ns]*

*Syn:* poverty

*Ant:* affluence

*Usage:* Moved by the *indigence* and poverty he came upon during his visit, the President pledged to set aside a major chunk of funds for community development.

**INDISCRIMINATE** (adj) *[in-di-SKRIM-uh-nit]*

*Syn:* choosing at random; confused

*Ant:* careful; select; discerning; sorted; picked

*Usage:* The margin between the two senators in the gathered votes was minimal; it seemed that voters had been *indiscriminate* in making their choices.

**INDOLENT** (adj) *[IN-dl-uh nt]*

*Syn:* lazy; couch potato-ish

*Ant:* dynamic; energetic

*Usage:* He stretched out *indolently*, feeling too full of laziness to do anything productive on a Sunday.

**INDOMITABLE** (adj) *[in-DOM-i-tuh-buh l]*

*Syn:* unconquerable; unyielding

*Ant:* deferential

*Usage:* Her *indomitable* fighting spirit and courage have won

**INEBRIETY** (adj) *[in-i-BRAHY-i-tee]*

*Syn:* habitual intoxication; drunkenness

*Ant:* sobriety

*Usage:* He was eventually found guilty of having mowed down two people while driving rashly in a state of *inebriety*.

**INELUCTABLE** (adj) *[in-i-LUHK-tuh-buh l]*

*Syn:* irresistable; not to be escaped

*Ant:* escapable; resistable

*Usage:* The consequences were inevitable and *ineluctable*.

**INERRANCY** (n) *[in-ER-uh n-see]*

*Syn:* infallibility

*Ant:* misjudgment; frailty

*Usage:* His belief in the *inerrancy* of the Scriptures is unshakable.

**INEXORABLE** (adj) *[in-EK-ser-uh-buh l]*

*Syn:* relentless; unyielding; implacable

*Ant:* yielding; easily pleased

*Usage:* Under such *inexorable* circumstances, her feat is something of a marvel.

# Chapter 9

**INFANTILE** (adj) *[IN-fuh n-tahyl]*

*Syn:* childish

*Ant:* mature

*Usage:* Despite his huge build, his voice was *infantile* and his behavior childlike.

**INFERNAL** (adj) *[in-FUR-nl]*

*Syn:* pertaining to hell; devilish

*Ant:* celestial; godly; heavenly; saintly

*Usage:* The poor kids had to work in an *infernal*, suffocating environment.

**INFINITESIMAL** (adj) *[in-fin-i-TES-uh-muh l]*

*Syn:* very small

*Ant:* very large

*Usage:* The difference in the two rates was but *infinitesimal*, only pennies per hour.

**INFLUX** (n) *[IN-fluhks]*

*Syn:* inward flow

*Ant:* outflow

*Usage:* The *influx* of refugees into the nation from the war-ridden country was growing day by day.

**INFRINGE** (v) *[in-FRINJ]*

*Syn:* violate; encroach

*Ant:* leave alone

*Usage:* He had tried to *infringe* on Jim's privacy for which he was severely rebuked.

**INGENUOUS** (adj) *[in-JEN-yoo-uh s]*

*Syn:* naive and trusting; young; unsophisticated

*Ant:* disingenuous; sly; reserved; mean; insincere; crafty; cunning; urbane

*Usage:* The young lady is very naïve and *ingenuous*.

**INGRATIATE** (v) *[in-GREY-shee-eyt]*

*Syn:* become popular with

*Ant:* alienate

*Usage:* He put in a lot of efforts to *ingratiate* her to assent.

**INHERENT** (adj) *[in-HEER-uh nt]*

*Syn:* firmly established by nature or habit

*Ant:* acquired

*Usage:* His *inherent* honesty and diligence have stood him in good stead.

**INIMICAL** (adj) *[i-NIM-i-kuh l]*

*Syn:* unfriendly; hostile; harmful; detrimental

*Ant:* friendly; helpful

*Usage:* I did not anticipate such an *inimical* or adverse reaction from her.

**INIQUITOUS** (adj) *[i-NIK-wi-tuh s]*

*Syn:* wicked; immoral; unrighteous

*Ant:* moral; righteous

*Usage:* Her behavior was immoral and *iniquitous*.

**INNOCUOUS** (adj) *[i-NOK-yoo-uh s]*

*Syn:* harmless

*Ant:* hurtful; injurious; stimulating

*Usage:* Seemingly *innocuous* statements made by the president were contrived by the media to look sinister.

**INNUENDO** (n) *[in-yoo-EN-doh]*

*Syn:* hint; insinuation

*Ant:* direct statement

*Usage:* The movie was rife with *innuendo* and lewd dialogues.

**INSALUBRIOUS** (adj) *[in-suh-LOO-bree-uh s]*

*Syn:* unwholesome; not healthful

*Ant:* wholesome; healthful

*Usage:* The leaves of the shrub were found to be *insalubrious* and harmful to health.

**INSENSATE** (adj) *[in-SEN-seyt]*

*Syn:* without feeling

*Ant:* emotional

*Usage:* He is an unfeeling, *insensate* man.

**INSINUATE** (v) *[in-SIN-yoo-eyt]*

*Syn:* hint; imply; creep in

*Ant:* state; affirm; propound; announce; withdraw; retract; extract

*Usage:* He didn't dare openly accuse Benedict, but he did *insinuate* that many a wrongdoing had been attributed to him.

**INSOUCIANT** (adj) *[in-SOO-see-uh nt]*

*Syn:* heedless

*Ant:* discreet

*Usage:* Having fulfilled all his immediate responsibilities, he was, for the present *insouciant* and carefree.

**INSULARITY** (n) *[in-suh-LAR-i-tee]*

*Syn:* narrow-mindedness; isolation; xenophobia

*Ant:* open-mindedness

*Usage:* The *insularity* and narrow-mindedness of the community was growing each day.

**INSURGENT** (adj) *[in-SUR-juh nt]*

*Syn:* rebellious

*Ant:* cooperative; supportive

*Usage:* The unexpected *insurgent* attitude of the hitherto peaceful and quiet community caused the minister great concern.

**INSURMOUNTABLE** (adj) *[in-ser-moun-tuh-buhl]*

*Syn:* overwhelming; unbeatable

*Ant:* able to be overcome

*Usage:* What makes the problem almost *insurmountable* is the disparate base upon which the changes must be made.

**INTEGRAL** (adj) *[IN-ti-gruh l]*

*Syn:* complete; necessary for completeness

*Ant:* extrinsic; secondary

*Usage:* Diligence is an *integral* requirement for that kind of a job.

**INTEGRATE** (v) *[IN-ti-greyt]*

*Syn:* make whole; combine; make into one unit

*Ant:* break down; differentiate

*Usage:* More efforts are needed to *integrate* the area administration with the metro one.

**INTELLIGENTSIA** (n) *[in-tel-i-JENT-see-uh]*

*Syn:* the intelligent and educated classes (often used derogatorily)

*Ant:* ignoramuses

*Usage:* The gathering at the launch was an eclectic mix of *intelligentsia* and political bigwigs.

**INTERIM** (n) *[IN-ter-uh m]*

*Syn:* meantime

*Ant:* long term

*Usage:* In the *interim*, a lot had happened to the family.

**INTERMITTENT** (adj) *[in-ter-MIT-nt]*

*Syn:* periodic; on and off

*Ant:* chronic; continuous

*Usage:* The sighting of the meteor is an *intermittent* occurrence.

**INTERREGNUM** (n) *[in-ter-REG-nuh m]*

*Syn:* period between two reigns

*Ant:* period of rule

*Usage:* The *interregnum* has been long; we should have a government soon.

**INTERSPERSE** (v) *[in-ter-SPURS]*

*Syn:* scatter

*Ant:* collect; gather

*Usage:* Verbs and nouns were *interspersed* with adjectives in the English writing exercise.

**INTRACTABLE** (adj) *[in-TRAK-tuh-buh l]*

*Syn:* unruly; stubborn; unyielding

*Ant:* flexible; adaptable

*Usage:* At times, he can be *intractable* and obstinate to an annoying extent.

**INTRANSIGENCE** (n) *[in-TRAN-si-juh ns]*

*Syn:* refusal of any compromise; stubbornness

*Ant:* inclination

*Usage:* Her *intransigence* and wilfulness could someday bring her downfall.

**INTRINSICALLY** (adj) *[in-TRIN-si-kuh-lee]*

*Syn:* essentially; inherently; naturally

*Ant:* abnormally

*Usage:* The document is *intrinsically* such a strong piece of evidence that nothing more is required to prove Jim's guilt.

**INTUITION** (n) *[in-too-ISH-uh n]*

*Syn:* immediate insight; power of knowing without reasoning

*Ant:* reasoned knowledge

*Usage:* When asked how she had known about Sam's feelings for Martha, Peggy claimed it was her womanly *intuition* that had given her a clue.

**INUNDATE** (v) *[IN-uh n-deyt]*

*Syn:* overwhelm; flood; submerge

*Ant:* underwhelm

*Usage:* The town council's mailbox was *inundated* with complaints from the residents.

**INVECTIVE** (n) *[in-VEK-tiv]*

*Syn:* abuse

*Ant:* commendation; eulogy; panegyric; laudation; praise; encouragement

*Usage:* We hadn't expected or anticipated that Patrick would deliver such harsh *invective* in his restaurant critique.

**INVEIGH** (v) *[in-VEY]*

*Syn:* denounce; utter censure or invective

*Ant:* flatter; praise

*Usage:* It was mandatory for the newly elected king to *inveigh* some critical announcements about the deposed king's ineffective efforts.

**INVIDIOUS** (adj) *[in-VID-ee-uh s]*

*Syn:* designed to create ill will or envy

*Ant:* considerate; benevolent; charitable; generous

*Usage:* I was embarrassed by her *invidious* looks because I had nothing for her to envy.

**IRASCIBLE** (adj) *[i-RAS-uh-buh l]*

*Syn:* irritable; easily angered

*Ant:* courteous

*Usage:* Ken becomes *irascible* when someone talks about the war, hearing unspoken criticism because he didn't enlist.

**IRIDESCENT** (adj) *[ir-i-DES-uh nt]*

*Syn:* exhibiting rainbowlike colors

*Ant:* dull; lacking color

*Usage:* The night had an *iridescent*, shimmering glow because of the full moon.

**IRRECONCILABLE** (adj) *[i-REK-uh n-sahy-luh-buh l]*

*Syn:* incompatible; not able to be resolved

*Ant:* compatible; solvable

*Usage:* The couple divorced soon after, citing *irreconcilable* differences.

**IRREPRESSIBLE** (adj) [ir-i-PRES-uh-buh l]

Syn: unable to be restrained or held back

Ant: restrained; cowering

Usage: Her *irrepressible* enthusiasm soon had the whole gang amused and everyone's spirits was lifted within no time.

**IRRETRIEVABLE** (adj) [ir-i-TREE-vuh-buh l]

Syn: impossible to recover or regain; irreparable

Ant: recoverable

Usage: The flood had caused *irretrievable* damage to the land and property all over the state.

**ISTHMUS** (n) [IS-muh s]

Syn: narrow neck of land connecting two larger bodies of land

Usage: The Japanese created a negative *isthmus*, of sorts, on the Tsushima Islands, permanently dividing two islands joined by an isthmus by a 2 km wide channel.

**ITINERANT** (adj) [ahy-TIN-er-uh nt]

Syn: wandering; traveling

Ant: steady; staying in one place

Usage: Juanita's mother was not in favor of Paul as her son-in-law because of his *itinerant*, nomadic habits.

**JARGON** (n) [JAHR-guh n]

Syn: language used by a special group; technical terminology; gibberish

Ant: common language

Usage: The book was full of technical *jargon*, which I could not comprehend.

**JEOPARDY** (n) [JEP-er-dee]

Syn: exposure to death or danger

Ant: safety

Usage: The slight mistake she had committed now threatened to put her into great *jeopardy*.

**JINGOISM** (n) [JING-goh-iz-uh m]

Syn: extremely aggressive and militant patriotism

Ant: lack of bias

Usage: The *jingoism* and bigotry of the newly elected government is a huge disappointment to the public.

**JOCUND** (adj) [JOK-uh nd]

Syn: cheerful

Ant: melancholy; dull; grave; mournful; cheerless; sorrowful

Usage: The crowd was *jocund* and merry, having a lot of fun.

**JUGGERNAUT** (n) [JUHG-er-nawt]

Syn: massive, destructive force

Ant: saving force

Usage: The event was analogous to a *juggernaut* crushing everything else under its massive force.

**JUNTA** (n) [HOO N-tuh]

Syn: group of men joined in political intrigue; cabal

Usage: The *junta* was firmly opposed against the move.

**JUXTAPOSE** (v) [JUHK-stuh-pohz]

Syn: to place side by side

Ant: separate

Usage: They *juxtaposed* the background of the sea with the foreground shot of the actress.

**KNELL** (n) [nel]

Syn: tolling of a bell; especially to indicate a funeral; disaster, etc.; sound of the funeral bell

Usage: It was as though a death *knell* had sounded for him.

**LABILE** (adj) [LEY-buh l]

Syn: likely to change; unstable

Ant: permanent; steady

*Usage:* She is rather an emotionally *labile* woman.

**LACHRYMOSE** (adj) *[LAK-ruh-mohs]*

*Syn:* producing tears

*Ant:* happy

*Usage:* I couldn't bear to stay anymore in the *lachrymose* atmosphere with all the weeping and crying going on.

**LACONIC** (adj) *[luh-KON-ik]*

*Syn:* brief and to the point

*Ant:* authoritarian; verbose; garrulous; loquacious; prosy; lengthy

*Usage:* His replies were *laconic* and terse, so his audience refrained from asking too many questions.

**LAGGARD** (adj) *[LAG-erd]*

*Syn:* slow; sluggish

*Ant:* energetic

*Usage:* Kevin is known as being *laggard* and dawdling in his locality, always slow at things.

**LAMBASTE** (v) *[lam-BEYST]*

*Syn:* scold; censure

*Ant:* praise

*Usage:* He *lambasted* her for the gaffe she had made in front of the visiting President.

**LANGUID** (adj) *[LANG-gwid]*

*Syn:* weary; sluggish; listless

*Ant:* strong; healthy; robust; active

*Usage:* He was feeling rather *languid* and lethargic today so he called up the office to say he wouldn't report for work.

**LANGUOR** (n) *[LANG-ger]*

*Syn:* lassitude; depression

*Ant:* dynamism

*Usage:* Beset with *languor* and exhaustion, she could barely lift herself out of the chair to get herself some tea.

**LARCENY** (n) *[LAHR-suh-nee]*

*Syn:* theft

*Usage:* The duo was convicted on charges of robbery and *larceny*.

**LASCIVIOUS** (adj) *[luh-SIV-ee-uh s]*

*Syn:* showing uncontrolled sexual desire

*Ant:* chaste

*Usage:* The streets of Paris were teeming with pretty, sensual, and *lascivious* women.

**LAUDATORY** (adj) *[LAW-duh-tawr-ee]*

*Syn:* expressing praise

*Ant:* criticizing

*Usage:* His words were *laudatory* and full of praise.

**LAX** (adj) *[laks]*

*Syn:* careless

*Ant:* fastidious; coherent; compact; strict; rigid; severe; conscientious

*Usage:* John has everything going for him except his *lax* and negligent attitude, which will surely hinder his progress in any field.

**LAXATIVE** (adj) *[LAK-suh-tiv]*

*Syn:* facilitating evacuation of the bowels

*Usage:* The doctor prescribed him a *laxative* drug and asked him to take it at night after dinner.

**LECTERN** (n) *[LEK-tern]*

*Syn:* reading desk

*Usage:* He paused before the *lectern* on the dais, to take the wad of notes from his coat pocket and then, putting on his glasses, he began his speech.

**LEGERDEMAIN** (n) *[lej-er-duh-MEYN]*

*Syn:* sleight of hand

*Usage:* Gerry was skilled at *legerdemain* and could easily hoodwink the best of the players at a card game through his sleight of hand.

# Chapter 10

## (Lethargic – Nocturnal)

*This chapter covers the following words along with their part of speech, pronunciation, synonyms and antonym, if applicable. Sample usage of the word is also illustrated.*

| | | |
|---|---|---|
| lethargic | marital | monarchy |
| levee | maritime | monolithic |
| lewd | masochist | moratorium |
| lexicographer | matriarch | mordant |
| lexicon | matrix | moribund |
| libelous | maudlin | morose |
| libido | maverick | mortify |
| lien | mealymouthed | motley |
| lineaments | mediocre | mulct |
| litany | medley | mundane |
| lithe | megalomania | muse |
| loath | melee | mutter |
| longevity | mellifluous | myriad |
| loquacious | mendacious | narcissist |
| lucid | meretricious | nascent |
| lucre | mete | nautical |
| lugubrious | meteoric | navigable |
| lumen | metropolis | nebulous |
| lustrous | miasma | necromancy |
| macabre | militate | nemesis |
| macerate | millinery | neologism |
| machiavellian | minion | nepotism |
| madrigal | minutiae | nether |
| magnanimity | mirth | nettle |
| magniloquent | misapprehension | nexus |
| maim | miscegenation | nib |
| malapropism | misconstrue | nicety |
| malfeasance | misogamy | niggardly |
| malingerer | misogynist | niggle |
| malodorous | mitigate | nip |
| manacle | mitigation | nirvana |
| maniacal | modicum | nocturnal |
| manifesto | modulation | |
| manumit | mollycoddle | |

**LETHARGIC** (adj) *[luh-THAHR-jik]*

*Syn:* drowsy; dull; sluggish

*Ant:* energetic

*Usage:* It was a chilly wintry morning and she felt more *lethargic* than ever in her warm bed.

**LEVEE** (n) *[LEV-ee]*

*Syn:* earthen or stone embankment to prevent flooding

*Usage: Levees* are usually built by piling earth on a cleared, level surface near a waterway.

**LEWD** (adj) *[lood]*

*Syn:* lustful

*Ant:* clean; decent; moral

*Usage:* The tramp kept casting *lewd* glances at her making her more and more uncomfortable.

**LEXICOGRAPHER** (n) *[lek-si-KOG-ruh-fer]*

*Syn:* compiler of a dictionary

*Usage:* Peter Mark Roget was one of the most famous *lexicographers* and his dictionaries are even now in great demand all over the world.

**LEXICON** (n) *[LEK-si-kon]*

*Syn:* dictionary

*Usage:* He is working on a new English-Spanish *lexicon*, gathering new words that have crept into the language since the last dictionary was published.

**LIBELOUS** (adj) *[LAHY-buh-luh s]*

*Syn:* defamatory; injurious to the good name of a person

*Ant:* praising; honest; truthful

*Usage:* The industrialist was stunned to read the *libelous* account of his evening and declared angrily that he would sue the newspaper for libel.

**LIBIDO** (n) *[li-BEE-doh]*

*Syn:* emotional urges behind human activity

*Usage:* It is said that the *libido* of women decreases after childbirth perhaps because women do not want to risk another painful pregnancy.

**LIEN** (n) *[leen]*

*Syn:* legal claim or property

*Usage:* They staked a *lien* on the very first day, complete with a court decree and order.

**LINEAMENTS** (n) *[LIN-ee-uh-muh nts]*

*Syn:* features, especially of the face

*Ant:* rear

*Usage:* His *lineaments* and visage were perfectly captured on canvas by the skilled and talented artist.

**LITANY** (n) *[LIT-n-ee]*

*Syn:* supplicatory prayer

*Usage:* The air filled with a melodious *litany* emerging from the church.

**LITHE** (adj) *[lahyth]*

*Syn:* flexible; supple

*Ant:* inflexible

*Usage:* The *lithe* and supple young woman jumped over the wall in one quick movement.

**LOATH** (adj) *[lohth]*

*Syn:* reluctant; disinclined

*Ant:* eager; willing; alert; anxious

*Usage:* I am *loath* to say this, but I am not comfortable with Jim and his behavior.

**LONGEVITY** (n) *[lon-JEV-i-tee]*

*Syn:* long life

*Ant:* shortness of life

*Usage:* On his birthday, they blessed him and prayed for his *longevity*.

**LOQUACIOUS** (adj) [loh-KWEY-shuh s]

*Syn:* talkative

*Ant:* quiet; reticent

*Usage:* Nick is a *loquacious*, talkative person, always having something to talk about.

**LUCID** (adj) [LOO-sid]

*Syn:* easily understood; clear; intelligible

*Ant:* muddied; unclear; foggy

*Usage:* The report was very clear and *lucid*, providing adequate information to make the decision.

**LUCRE** (n) [LOO-ker]

*Syn:* money

*Usage:* He was tempted by the *lucre* and profits that the new venture promised to bring.

**LUGUBRIOUS** (adj) [loo-GOO-bree-uh s]

*Syn:* mournful

*Ant:* exhilarating; blithe

*Usage:* The *lugubrious* and depressing atmosphere in the hall dampened my good mood and enthusiasm.

**LUMEN** (n) [LOO-muh n]

*Syn:* unit of light energy (one candle's worth)

*Usage:* The *lumen* of the crystal almost blinded him.

**LUSTROUS** (adj) [LUHS-truh s]

*Syn:* shining

*Ant:* dull

*Usage:* Her long, *lustrous* locks were the envy of every woman at the party.

**MACABRE** (adj) [muh-KAH-bruh]

*Syn:* gruesome; grisly

*Ant:* common; normal

*Usage:* One of the major tourist sights in Moscow, however, is a somewhat *macabre* reminder of communist Russia's heyday.

**MACERATE** (v) [MAS-uh-reyt]

*Syn:* cause to become soft by being left in water; to waste away

*Ant:* harden

*Usage:* The piece of meat was then *macerated* and left overnight to marinate.

**MACHIAVELLIAN** (adj) [mak-ee-uh-VEL-ee-uh n]

*Syn:* crafty; double-dealing

*Ant:* gullible

*Usage:* His *Machiavellian* intentions were not unknown to me.

**MADRIGAL** (n) [MAD-ri-guh l]

*Syn:* pastoral song

*Usage:* The group then broke into a melodious *madrigal* bringing the night alive with their voices.

**MAGNANIMITY** (n) [mag-nuh-NIM-i-tee]

*Syn:* generosity; kindness

*Ant:* selfishness; malevolence

*Usage:* The nuns were overwhelmed by his *magnanimity*; none had ever before given their orphanage such an enormous sum of money along with the huge bounties of clothes and toys.

**MAGNILOQUENT** (adj) [mag-NIL-uh-kwuh nt]

*Syn:* boastful; pompous

*Ant:* humble

*Usage:* Lord James was the most *magniloquent* and pompous of them all.

**MAIM** (v) [meym]

*Syn:* mutilate; injure

*Ant:* mend; strengthen; restore

*Usage:* One of the primary rules of the game was that the

participants would not *maim* each other or cause any other form of physical damage.

**MALAPROPISM** (n) [MAL-uh-prop-iz-uh m]

*Syn:* comic misuse of a word

*Ant:* correct speech

*Usage:* Somehow the phrase sounded to me like a *malapropism*, as though it had been deliberately twisted to sound confusing.

**MALFEASANCE** (n) [mal-FEE-zuh ns]

*Syn:* wrongdoing

*Ant:* correct behavior

*Usage:* We knew he was up to some *malfeasance*, but what it was exactly, none of us had any clue.

**MALINGERER** (n) [muh-LING-ger-er]

*Syn:* one who feigns illness to escape duty; slacker; idler

*Ant:* go-getter; hard worker

*Usage:* Ken has acquired a reputation of sorts for being a *malingerer* and idler.

**MALODOROUS** (adj) [mal-OH-der-uh s]

*Syn:* foul-smelling

*Ant:* fragrant

*Usage:* The *malodorous* conditions of the room made it impossible for her to stay there though the rent was very cheap.

**MANACLE** (v) [MAN-uh-kuh l]

*Syn:* restrain; handcuff

*Ant:* set free

*Usage:* He was chained and *manacled* before being taken to court for the trial.

**MANIACAL** (adj) [muh-NAHY-uh-kuh l]

*Syn:* raving mad

*Ant:* sane

*Usage:* He has a *maniacal* side to his otherwise kind and sober personality.

**MANIFESTO** (n) [man-uh-FES-toh]

*Syn:* declaration; statement of policy

*Usage:* The *manifesto* was signed by the two Presidents.

**MANUMIT** (v) [man-yuh-MIT]

*Syn:* release from slavery; emancipate

*Ant:* enslave; imprison

*Usage:* The prisoners were *manumitted* on the fourth of July, not to be released for ten years.

**MARITAL** (adj) [MAR-i-tl]

*Syn:* pertaining to marriage

*Ant:* extramarital

*Usage:* They stressed that their *marital* conflicts were a private affair and that no one had any right to intervene.

**MARITIME** (adj) [MAR-i-tahym]

*Syn:* bordering on the sea; nautical

*Usage:* The *maritime* institute has inducted a new naval commander to train its students.

**MASOCHIST** (n) [MAS-uh-kist]

*Syn:* person who enjoys his own pain

*Ant:* sadist

*Usage:* His behavior as a harsh *masochist* has puzzled his family since he had always been such a gentle child.

**MATRIARCH** (n) [MEY-tree-ahrk]

*Syn:* woman who rules a family or larger social group

*Ant:* patriarch

*Usage:* The *matriarch* of the family was consulted and her opinions were weighed before the business empire was split into two halves.

**MATRIX** (n) *[MEY-triks]*

*Syn:* point of origin; array of numbers or algebraic symbols; mold or die

*Usage:* The orderly *matrix* was easy for the mathematician to understand, but it looked like a jumble of numbers to the rest of us.

**MAUDLIN** (adj) *[MAWD-lin]*

*Syn:* effusively sentimental

*Ant:* dispassionate

*Usage:* The play was overly *maudlin* and sentimental in my view.

**MAVERICK** (n) *[MAV-er-ik]*

*Syn:* rebel; nonconformist; radical

*Ant:* conformist

*Usage:* Jonah is a *maverick,* preferring to travel the world and learn new things and do odd jobs than stay stuck to a desk job.

**MEALYMOUTHED** (adj) *[MEE-lee-moutht]*

*Syn:* not outspoken; hypocritical; evasive

*Ant:* outspoken; bold

*Usage:* Beware of Mrs. Brown for she is *mealy-mouthed* and never sincere in her statements.

**MEDIOCRE** (adj) *[mee-dee-OH-ker]*

*Syn:* ordinary; commonplace

*Ant:* special; superlative

*Usage:* His performance had been average and *mediocre*, nothing special to talk about.

**MEDLEY** (n) *[MED-lee]*

*Syn:* mixture

*Ant:* classification; order; arrangement; grouping

*Usage:* The *medley* of tunes was used to make up a new musical composition.

**MEGALOMANIA** (n) *[meg-uh-loh-MEY-nee-uh]*

*Syn:* mania for doing grandiose things

*Ant:* altruism; humility

*Usage:* He suffers from *megalomania*, always having grand ideas.

**MELEE** (n) *[MEY-ley]*

*Syn:* fight

*Ant:* cooperation

*Usage:* The two brothers got so involved in the *melee* and fight that they failed to realize that people were gawking at them.

**MELLIFLUOUS** (adj) *[muh-LIF-loo-uh s]*

*Syn:* sweetly or smoothly flowing; melodious

*Ant:* cacophonous

*Usage:* Her voice was mellow and *mellifluous*.

**MENDACIOUS** (adj) *[men-DEY-shuh s]*

*Syn:* lying; habitually dishonest

*Ant:* trustworthy

*Usage:* Her *mendacious* statements shocked him for their total lack of foundation in truth and reality.

**MERETRICIOUS** (adj) *[mer-i-TRISH-uh s]*

*Syn:* flashy; tawdry; falsely attractive

*Ant:* genuine; real

*Usage:* Who could have predicted that the usually impeccable Gia would appear in such a *meretricious* and gaudy costume?

**METE** (v) *[meet]*

*Syn:* distribute; measure

*Ant:* withhold

*Usage:* He didn't deserve the treatment they had *meted* out to him.

**METEORIC** (adj) *[mee-tee-AWR-ik]*

*Syn:* swift; momentarily brilliant

*Ant:* slow

*Usage:* Mr. Pearson's rise from rags to riches had been sudden and *meteoric*.

**METROPOLIS** (n) *[mi-TROP-uh-lis]*

*Syn:* large city

*Ant:* suburb; countryside

*Usage:* In the urban *metropolis*, everything came with a price.

**MIASMA** (n) *[mahy-AZ-muh]*

*Syn:* swamp gas; heavy; vaporous atmosphere; often emanating from decaying matter; pervasive corrupting influence; effluvium

*Ant:* clearness; fragrance

*Usage:* Suffocated by the *miasma* and vapors he collapsed on the banks of the swamp.

**MILITATE** (v) *[MIL-i-teyt]*

*Syn:* work against; count

*Ant:* work against

*Usage:* The high attrition rate was soon *militated* by the high recruitment rate.

**MILLINERY** (n) *[MIL-uh-ner-ee]*

*Syn:* women's hats

*Usage:* Mrs. Marsh was a simple woman who disliked ornamentation and *millinery* of any kind.

**MINION** (n) *[MIN-yuh n]*

*Syn:* a servile dependent; sycophant

*Ant:* a leader

*Usage:* He was completely surrounded by his *minions*.

**MINUTIAE** (n) *[mi-NOO-shee-uh]*

*Syn:* petty details

*Ant:* core elements

*Usage:* The document contained a large amount of *minutiae* and trivia regarding the past employees.

**MIRTH** (n) *[murth]*

*Syn:* merriment; laughter

*Ant:* sadness; sorrow; trouble; gravity; sobriety; melancholy

*Usage:* He was overcome by a bout of *mirth* and laughter upon reading the passage.

**MISAPPREHENSION** (n) *[mis-ap-ri-HEN-shuhn]*

*Syn:* error; misunderstanding

*Ant:* correctness

*Usage:* On the other hand, there are grounds for saying that the judge suffered *misapprehen*sion of the material facts before him.

**MISCEGENATION** (n) *[mi-sej-uh-NEY-shuh n]*

*Syn:* intermarriage between persons of two different races

*Ant:* same race marriage

*Usage:* Racial bigots deplore *miscegenation*; their basic question is, "Why would a person of my race ever want to marry into another race?"

**MISCONSTRUE** (v) *[mis-kuh n-STROO]*

*Syn:* interpret incorrectly; misjudge

*Ant:* understand

*Usage:* He was irritated that his innocent statements were being *misconstrued* to mean something else.

**MISOGAMY** (n) *[mi-SOG-uh-mee]*

*Syn:* hatred of marriage

*Usage:* Paul James is a believer in *misogamy*; he is a die-hard bachelor and wishes to remain so forever.

**MISOGYNIST** (n) *[mi-SOJ-uh-nist]*

*Syn:* hater of women

*Ant:* philogynist

*Usage:* Nick Dean is often called a *misogynist* behind his back because of his phobia bordering on hatred for social activities involving women.

**MITIGATE** (v) *[MIT-i-geyt]*

*Syn:* lessen in intensity; moderate; appease

*Ant:* exacerbate; aggravate; increase; extend

*Usage:* The lawyer requested the judge to *mitigate* his client's punishment.

**MITIGATION** (n) *[MIT-i-geyt]*

*Syn:* abatement; lessening

*Ant:* aggravation

*Usage:* Risk *mitigation* plans were developed by the team for all identified risks.

**MODICUM** (n) *[MOD-i-kuh m]*

*Syn:* limited quantity

*Ant:* abundance

*Usage:* Not a *modicum* of modesty was in her as she proceeded to strip to prove she was still capable of drawing male attention.

**MODULATION** (n) *[moj-uh-LEY-shuh n]*

*Syn:* toning down; changing from one key to another

*Ant:* amplification

*Usage:* He conducts voice *modulation* therapy classes.

**MOLLYCODDLE** (v) *[MOL-ee-kod-l]*

*Syn:* pamper; indulge excessively

*Ant:* deprive

*Usage:* Since the very start of his career, I haven't *mollycoddled* him or given him easy fights to pad out his record.

**MONARCHY** (n) *[MAN-er-kee]*

*Syn:* government under a single hereditary ruler with varying degrees of power

*Ant:* democracy

*Usage:* The coup overthrew the *monarchy* and installed a revolutionary regime in its place.

**MONOLITHIC** (adj) *[mon-uh-LITH-ik]*

*Syn:* solidly uniform; unyielding

*Ant:* small; changing

*Usage:* The huge *monolithic* structure had been designed and executed by the city's most famous architect, John Fernandes.

**MORATORIUM** (n) *[mawr-uh-TAWR-ee-uh m-]*

*Syn:* legal delay of payment

*Ant:* continuation

*Usage:* Unable to take the *moratorium* that had been imposed on him, the investigating police officer resigned from the force seeking to operate independently as a private eye.

**MORDANT** (adj) *[MAWR-dnt]*

*Syn:* biting; sarcastic; stinging

*Ant:* praising

*Usage:* I could take the *mordant* remarks no longer and lashed back at her, matching caustic remark for remark.

**MORIBUND** (adj) *[MAWR-uh-buhnd]*

*Syn:* at the point of death

*Ant:* vibrant; alive

*Usage: Moribund* circumstances had led her to summon her estranged husband to look after her in her dying days.

**MOROSE** (adj) *[muh-ROHS]*

*Syn:* ill-humored; sullen; melancholy

*Ant:* genial; kindly; gentle; indulgent; joyous; merry; gay

*Usage:* I wanted to know why Karen looked so *morose* and sad.

**MORTIFY** (v) *[MAWR-tuh-fahy]*

*Syn:* humiliate; punish the flesh

*Ant:* please; gratify; delight; indulge; pamper; heal; recover

*Usage:* We had never intended to *mortify* Mrs. Howard; all we had wanted was to break the news to her before she heard a twisted version from someone else.

**MOTLEY** (adj) *[MOT-lee]*

*Syn:* multi-colored; mixed

*Ant:* uniform; homogeneous; alike

*Usage:* A *motley* crowd adorned the poolside where the party was in full swing.

**MULCT** (v) *[muhlkt]*

*Syn:* defraud a person of something

*Ant:* treat fairly

*Usage:* The officer *mulcted* the motorists for speeding when they were actually driving within the limits.

**MUNDANE** (adj) *[muhn-DEYN]*

*Syn:* worldly, as opposed to spiritual; boring; banal

*Ant:* exciting; extraordinary

*Usage:* Moira is planning to leave her current job because its *mundane* tasks bore her.

**MUSE** (v) *[myooz]*

*Syn:* ponder; think or say meditatively

*Ant:* stir; act; move; perform

*Usage:* John *muses* a lot about the future of his company.

**MUTTER** (v) *[MUHT-er]*

*Syn:* murmur or grumble

*Ant:* shout

*Usage:* Unable to stand her editor's nitpicking, Sara *muttered* something under her breath and left the meeting abruptly.

**MYRIAD** (n) *[MIR-ee-uh d]*

*Syn:* very large number

*Ant:* limited

*Usage:* The *myriad* hues and sounds of the mountains are truly rejuvenating.

**NARCISSIST** (n) *[NAHR-suh-sizt]*

*Syn:* conceited person; someone in love with his own image

*Ant:* selfless individual

*Usage:* He is a good actor, but is an insufferable *narcissist* at times. He thinks too much of himself.

**NASCENT** (adj) *[NAS-uh nt]*

*Syn:* incipient; coming into being

*Ant:* already established

*Usage:* The *nascent* peace process between the two countries is often threatened by bombings at public places.

**NAUTICAL** (adj) *[NAW-ti-kuh l]*

*Syn:* pertaining to ships or navigation

*Ant:* pertaining to land

*Usage:* Sailors at the academy were taught to read *nautical* charts of the regions they were set to sail.

**NAVIGABLE** (adj) *[NAV-i-guh-buhl]*

*Syn:* wide and deep enough to allow ships to pass through

*Ant:* blocked

*Usage:* To the west of Trent Bridge the river is still *navigable* for a short stretch.

**NEBULOUS** (adj) *[NEB-yuh-luh s]*

*Syn:* vague; hazy; cloudy; unclear

*Ant:* clear; easily understood

*Usage:* Modern art is often *nebulous*, subject to every individual's personal interpretation

**NECROMANCY** (n) *[NEK-ruh-man-see]*

*Syn:* black magic; dealings with the dead

*Usage:* Joan believed in *necromancy*. She would often sit alone at a table in front of a burning candle and try to communicate with her dead grandmother.

**NEMESIS** (n) *[NEM-uh-sis]*

*Syn:* someone seeking revenge; relentless pursuer of evildoers; jinx; bane

*Ant:* friend; supporter; compatriate

*Usage:* The imminent economic crisis may be the minister's *nemesis*, finally causing the church to run out of funds.

**NEOLOGISM** (n) *[nee-OL-uh-jiz-uh m]*

*Syn:* newly coined word or phrase

*Usage:* The magazine has started using a lot of *neologisms* making it difficult for many senior citizens to read words they have never seen before.

**NEPOTISM** (n) *[NEP-uh-tiz-uh m]*

*Syn:* favoritism (to a relative)

*Ant:* indifference

*Usage:* Many will regard the boss's son's appointment as *nepotism*, but the truth is that he is a really well-educated and talented person.

**NETHER** (adj) *[NETH-er]*

*Syn:* in the lower place

*Ant:* in the upper place

*Usage:* John escorted his girlfriend only till the *nether* part of her street.

**NETTLE** (v) *[NET-l]*

*Syn:* annoy; vex

*Ant:* conciliate

*Usage:* He was *nettled* by the way she totally ignored his presence and addressed her entire conversation to his friend.

**NEXUS** (n) *[nek-suhs]*

*Syn:* connection

*Ant:* separation

*Usage:* His essay focused on the *nexus* between the politicians and the State.

**NIB** (n) *[nib]*

*Syn:* beak; pen point

*Usage:* He was really annoyed when the *nib* of his pen broke midway through the examination.

**NICETY** (n) *[NAHY-si-tee]*

*Syn:* detail; nuance; precision; minute distinction

*Ant:* generality; whole

*Usage:* It took more than three months of hosting parties for her understand the *niceties* of serving food to the guests.

**NIGGARDLY** (adj) *[NIG-erd-lee]*

*Syn:* not willing to spend money; parsimonious

*Ant:* benevolent

*Usage:* Irene raised a hue and cry about the *niggardly* supply of hot water at the hotel.

**NIGGLE** (v) *[NIG-uh l]*

*Syn:* be over-elaborate on petty details; find fault in petty manner; nitpick

*Ant:* accept

*Usage:* The question that the teacher posed *niggled* away in Arnold's mind all night.

**NIP** (v) *[nip]*

*Syn:* stop something's growth or development

*Ant:* support; nurture

*Usage:* "We're going to *nip* this romance in the bud," said the overprotective father to his daughter's new boyfriend.

**NIRVANA** (n) *[nir-VAH-nuh]*

*Syn:* in Buddhist teachings; the ideal state in which the

individual loses himself in the attainment of an impersonal beatitude; enlightenment

*Ant:* hell

*Usage:* Harry spent more than a year at various Himalayan monasteries in search of *Nirvana*.

## NOCTURNAL (adj) *[nok-TUR-nl]*

*Syn:* done at night

*Ant:* diurnal; solar

*Usage:* At the beginning of her career in the Police Force, Irene found the dark *nocturnal* rounds quite scary.

*(Lethargic – Nocturnal)*

# Chapter 11

## (Noisome – Plauditory)

*This chapter covers the following words along with their part of speech, pronunciation, synonyms and antonym, if applicable. Sample usage of the word is also illustrated.*

noisome
nomadic
nomenclature
nominal
nonchalance
noncommittal
nondescript
nonentity
nonplus
nostalgia
nostrum
notoriety
noxious
numismatist
nutrient
obfuscate
objective
obliterate
obloquy
obscure
obsequious
obsession
obstreperous
obtrusive
occlude
odoriferous
oligarchy
onerous
onus
opiate
opprobrium
optometrist
oracular
oratorio

ordinance
ordination
orgy
ornate
orthography
osseous
ossify
ostentatious
oust
overhaul
overt
overwrought
ovoid
pachyderm
paean
pageant
palimpsest
palliate
panache
panegyric
paradigm
paranoia
paraphernalia
pariah
parochial
parquet
parsimonious
partisan
pastiche
patina
patois
paucity
peccadillo
pecuniary

pedagogue
pedant
pejorative
pellucid
penchant
penumbra
penurious
perception
peregrination
perfidious
perfunctory
peripheral
permeable
perspicuous
pertinacious
pest
pestilential
petrify
pharisaical
philanderer
philanthropist
philatelist
phoenix
physiognomy
piety
pillory
pinion
piquant
placate
placebo
platitude
plauditory

**NOISOME** (adj) *[NOI-suh m]*

*Syn:* foul-smelling; unwholesome

*Ant:* moral; upright

*Usage:* Sharon was surprised she loved him despite his *noisome* reputation.

**NOMADIC** (adj) *[noh-MAD-ik]*

*Syn:* wandering

*Ant:* entrenched; permanent

*Usage:* His father being an adventurer, John had a *nomadic* childhood.

**NOMENCLATURE** (n) *[NOH-muh n-kley-cher]*

*Syn:* terminology; system of names

*Usage:* Being unacquainted with the field of study, Irene found it quite difficult to understand all the chemical *nomenclature* in the book.

**NOMINAL** (adj) *[NOM-uh-nl]*

*Syn:* in name only; trifling; negligible

*Ant:* actual; real; true

*Usage:* The special edition was offered to subscribers at a *nominal* price.

**NONCHALANCE** (n) *[non-shuh-LAHNS]*

*Syn:* indifference; lack of concern; composure

*Ant:* caring; concern

*Usage:* His *nonchalant* attitude towards life irks his more serious mother.

**NONCOMMITTAL** (adj) *[non-kuh-MIT-l]*

*Syn:* neutral; unpledged; undecided

*Ant:* committed; biased

*Usage:* Her reply to his proposal was *noncommittal*, saying "I'll get back to you."

**NONDESCRIPT** (adj) *[non-di-SKRIPT]*

*Syn:* dull; undistinctive; ordinary

*Ant:* bright; striking

*Usage:* She lives in a modest, *nondescript* house at the other end of the street.

**NONENTITY** (n) *[non-EN-ti-tee]*

*Syn:* person of no importance or nonexistence

*Ant:* celebrity

*Usage:* He is a *nonentity* in the company, having no influence or even recognition of his presence.

**NONPLUS** (v) *[non-PLUHS]*

*Syn:* bring to halt by confusion; perplex; surprise

*Ant:* enlighten

*Usage:* His teetotalling fiancé *nonplussed* his steady composure when she asked him for a hard drink.

**NOSTALGIA** (n) *[no-STAL-juh]*

*Syn:* homesickness; longing for the past

*Usage:* Overcome by *nostalgia*, he decided to visit the farmhouse where he spent his childhood.

**NOSTRUM** (adj) *[NOS-truh m]*

*Syn:* quack remedy; pet scheme for political or social reform; cure-all; panacea

*Usage:* The company is bound to survive only if the Managing Director gives up his old school *nostrums* and adopts some real remedies.

**NOTORIETY** (n) *[noh-tuh-RAHY-i-tee]*

*Syn:* disrepute; ill fame

*Ant:* morality; righteousness

*Usage:* The evil Hitler's *notoriety* is bound to be discussed for many more years.

**NOXIOUS** (adj) *[NOK-shuh s]*

*Syn:* harmful

*Ant:* wholesome; healthy; useful; helpful; advantageous

*Usage:* She fainted on breathing in the *noxious* fumes that were emitted by the burning electrical appliance.

# Chapter 11

**NUMISMATIST** (n) *[noo-MIZ-muh-tist]*

*Syn:* Person who collects coins

*Usage:* The number of old coins that lay scattered on his table suggested that he may be a *numismatist*.

**NUTRIENT** (n) *[NOO-tree-uh nt]*

*Syn:* nourishing substance

*Ant:* poison

*Usage:* The manufacturer claims that his biscuits are loaded with essential *nutrients*.

**OBFUSCATE** (v) *[OB-fuh-skeyt]*

*Syn:* confuse; muddle; cause confusion; make needlessly complex

*Ant:* clarify

*Usage:* Despite his efforts to *obfuscate* the issue, the others were quite clear about what they wanted.

**OBJECTIVE** (n) *[uhb-jek-tiv]*

*Syn:* goal; aim

*Usage:* Her only *objective* in life was to become a famous and successful athlete.

**OBLITERATE** (v) *[uh-BLIT-uh-reyt]*

*Syn:* destroy completely

*Ant:* insert; mark

*Usage:* The invaders *obliterated* the entire tribal settlement.

**OBLOQUY** (n) *[OB-luh-kwee]*

*Syn:* strong words spoken against someone; tirade

*Ant:* praise; encomium; encouragement

*Usage:* The new secretary had to endure *obloquy* from her boss.

**OBSCURE** (v) *[uhb-SKYOOR]*

*Syn:* darken; make unclear

*Ant:* lighten; brighten; unveil; expose

*Usage:* The beautiful view was *obscured* by an ugly abandoned building.

**OBSEQUIOUS** (adj) *[uh b-SEE-kwee-uh s]*

*Syn:* slavishly attentive; servile; sycophantic

*Ant:* ignoring; indifferent

*Usage:* Harold was totally *obsequious* to John till he learned that he was also a laborer and not a supervisor.

**OBSESSION** (n) *[uh b-SESH-uh n]*

*Syn:* fixed idea; continued brooding

*Usage:* Philately has been his *obsession* ever since he was ten years old.

**OBSTREPEROUS** (adj) *[uh b-STREP-er-uh-s]*

*Syn:* boisterous; noisy

*Ant:* quiet

*Usage:* The customer became *obstreperous* when the waiter spilled soup on her table.

**OBTRUSIVE** (adj) *[uh b-TROO-siv]*

*Syn:* displeasingly noticeable

*Ant:* unobtrusive; unnoticeable

*Usage:* Today's appliances are less *obtrusive* and easy to store away when not needed.

**OCCLUDE** (v) *[uh-KLOOD]*

*Syn:* shut; close; block

*Ant:* open; allow; permit

*Usage:* He *occluded* the passage by lining the entrance with thorns.

**ODORIFEROUS** (adj) *[oh-duh-RIF-er-uh s]*

*Syn:* having a pleasant smell; odorous; fragrant

*Ant:* acrid; bland; unsavory

*Usage:* My grandmother had jars full of *odoriferous* spices that made my mouth water whenever they were opened.

**OLIGARCHY** (n) *[OL-i-gahr-kee]*

*Syn:* government by a privileged few

*Ant:* democracy

*Usage:* There was an uprising against the monarchy and *oligarchy* in the nation.

**ONEROUS** (adj) *[ON-er-uh s]*

*Syn:* burdensome

*Ant:* light; easy; trivial; slight

*Usage:* It really was an *onerous* task managing the naughty puppies.

**ONUS** (n) *[OH-nuh s]*

*Syn:* burden; responsibility

*Ant:* aid; benefit; blessing

*Usage:* The *onus* of creating a better living environment rests with the people.

**OPIATE** (n) *[OH-pee-it]*

*Syn:* medicine to induce sleep or deaden pain; something that relieves emotions or causes inaction

*Ant:* amphetamine

*Usage:* The doctor advised the patient never to use *opiates* when driving for she might fall asleep behind the wheel.

**OPPROBRIUM** (n) *[uh-PROH-bree-uh m]*

*Syn:* public shame; infamy; disgrace; scorn

*Ant:* honor; respect; glory; praise

*Usage:* The minister's misdeeds have attracted public *opprobrium*.

**OPTOMETRIST** (n) *[op-TOM-i-trist]*

*Syn:* one who fits glasses to remedy visual defects

*Usage:* The *optometrist* said Sara needs to wear corrective glasses only when reading.

**ORACULAR** (adj) *[aw-RAK-yuh-ler]*

*Syn:* prophetic; uttered as if with divine authority; mysterious or ambiguous

*Ant:* flippant; lighthearted

*Usage:* I can't understand any of the *oracular* sayings of the Victorian poets; give me something meaty.

**ORATORIO** (n) *[awr-uh-TAWR-ee-oh]*

*Syn:* dramatic poem set to music

*Usage:* He hopes to compose the first *oratorio* to be performed in zero gravity.

**ORDINANCE** (n) *[AWR-dn-uh ns]*

*Syn:* decree

*Ant:* custom;usage; prescription; convention

*Usage:* Many builders do not abide by the *ordinances* restricting building development.

**ORDINATION** (n) *[awr-dn-EY-shuh n]*

*Syn:* ceremony making someone a minister

*Ant:* defrocking

*Usage:* Father was very busy selecting candidates for *ordination*.

**ORGY** (n) *[AWR-jee]*

*Syn:* wild; drunken revelry

*Usage:* Mike's party turned to an *orgy*, where all guests were indulged in unrestrained merrymaking.

**ORNATE** (adj) *[awr-NEYT]*

*Syn:* excessively or elaborately decorated

*Ant:* simple

*Usage:* She really loved the *ornate* bead work in her fancy new dress.

**ORTHOGRAPHY** (n) *[awr-THOG-ruh-fee]*

*Syn:* art of writing words with the proper letters

*Usage:* After visiting the museum and seeing preserved scrolls, she has enrolled in a course to study the *orthography* of the ancient Egyptians.

**OSSEOUS** (adj) [OS-ee-uh s]

*Syn:* made of bone; bony

*Ant:* sinewy

*Usage:* She was cleaning the *osseous* piece of meat to cook it for dinner.

**OSSIFY** (v) [OS-uh-fahy]

*Syn:* change or harden into bone

*Ant:* soften

*Usage:* But for his wife's inspiration and encouragement, his career would have *ossified* long ago.

**OSTENTATIOUS** (adj) [os-ten-TEY-shuhs]

*Syn:* showy; pretentious; trying to attract attention

*Ant:* unpretentious

*Usage:* Her friend's wedding reception was *ostentatious*, complete with swans and a seven-tiered cake.

**OUST** (v) [oust]

*Syn:* expel; drive out

*Ant:* install; restore; reinstate

*Usage:* The tenants were *ousted* from the house because the owner's son was returning from abroad.

**OVERHAUL** (v) [oh-ver-HAWL]

*Syn:* thoroughly examine the condition of and repair if necessary; renovate

*Ant:* maintain as is

*Usage:* The electrician told us that the air conditioner needs to be *overhauled*.

**OVERT** (adj) [oh-VURT]

*Syn:* open to view; public; not secret

*Ant:* covert; secret; clandestine

*Usage:* His extreme opposition to the management's new policies was quite *overt*.

**OVERWROUGHT** (adj) [OH-ver-RAWT]

*Syn:* extremely agitated; hysterical

*Ant:* comfortable; at ease

*Usage:* It was difficult to console our *overwrought* neighbor after the burglary.

**OVOID** (adj) [OH-void]

*Syn:* egg-shaped

*Ant:* square

*Usage:* His face had such an *ovoid* appearance that they called him Humpty Dumpty.

**PACHYDERM** (n) [PAK-i-durm]

*Syn:* thick-skinned animal

*Usage:* I rode on the elephant just like the jungle hunter riding atop the back of the large pachyderm.

**PAEAN** (n) [PEE-uh n]

*Syn:* song of praise or joy

*Ant:* condemnation

*Usage:* The movie was a *paean* to deep, passionate love.

**PAGEANT** (n) [PAJ-uh nt]

*Syn:* a splendid public show and procession

*Usage:* Her grandmother did not approve of Sheila's participation in the beauty *pageant*.

**PALIMPSEST** (n) [PAL-imp-sest]

*Syn:* parchment used for second time after original writing has been erased

*Ant:* fresh sheet of paper; clean slate

*Usage:* She says researching a *palimpsest* is difficult because she has to read the many texts on it and also because the original is incomplete and difficult to read.

**PALLIATE** (v) [PAL-ee-eyt]

*Syn:* ease pain; make less severe or offensive

*Ant:* repulse; expose; denounce; exaggerate; aggravate

*Usage:* This pill will *palliate* your headache.

**PANACHE** (n) [puh-NASH]

Syn: flair; flamboyance

Ant: subtlety

Usage: She handled the interviews with ease and *panache*, enthralling all the normally cynical reporters.

**PANEGYRIC** (n) [pan-i-JIR-ik]

Syn: formal praise

Ant: satire; sarcasm; invective; tirade; condemnation

Usage: Many *panegyrics* on Roman rulers were written during their rule.

**PARADIGM** (n) [PAR-uh-dahym]

Syn: model; example; pattern

Ant: randomness

Usage: Ross found it difficult to remember the many *paradigms* of programming.

**PARANOIA** (n) [par-uh-NOI-uh]

Syn: psychosis marked by delusions of grandeur or persecution

Ant: security

Usage: All over the country, there is mounting *paranoia* of war.

**PARAPHERNALIA** (n) [par-uh-fer-NEYL-yuh]

Syn: equipment; odds and ends

Usage: The plumber arrived with all the *paraphernalia* for repairing the water pump.

**PARIAH** (n) [puh-RAHY-uh]

Syn: social outcast

Ant: life of the party

Usage: He treated his less fortunate brother like a *pariah*, avoiding him at all costs.

**PAROCHIAL** (adj) [puh-ROH-kee-uh l]

Syn: narrow in outlook; provincial; related to parishes

Ant: public; wide

Usage: The priest took a *parochial* view of the emergency, caring only how it would affect people in his church and ignoring the homeless.

**PARQUET** (n) [pahr-KEY]

Syn: floor made of wood strips inlaid in a mosic-like pattern.

Ant: continuous; unpatterned

Usage: In laying the floor, the carpenters combined redwood and oak in an elegant *parquet* pattern.

**PARSIMONIOUS** (adj) [pahr-suh-MOH-nee-uh s]

Syn: stingy; excessively frugal

Ant: generous; sharing

Usage: It took but one meeting for me to realize what a *parsimonious* person he was; he wouldn't even pay for lunch.

**PARTISAN** (adj) [PAHR-tuh-zuh n]

Syn: one-sided; prejudiced; committed to a party

Ant: independent

Usage: Having a *partisan* referee is the same as having none.

**PASTICHE** (n) [pa-STEECH]

Syn: imitation of another's style in musical composition or in writing

Ant: originality

Usage: His house is a *pastiche* of many brilliant architectural styles.

**PATINA** (n) [PAT-n-uh]

Syn: green crust on old bronze works; tone slowly taken by varnished painting

Ant: sheen

Usage: A *patina* of coffee covered the inside of the unwashed coffee cup.

**PATOIS** (n) *[PAT-wah]*

*Syn:* local or provincial dialect

*Ant:* official language

*Usage:* His years of study of the language at the university did not enable him to understand the *patois* of the natives.

**PAUCITY** (n) *[PAW-si-tee]*

*Syn:* scarcity; dearth

*Ant:* plenty

*Usage:* There was a *paucity* of imagination in the author's first dry and lifeless novel.

**PECCADILLO** (n) *[pek-uh-DIL-oh]*

*Syn:* slight offense

*Ant:* major offense

*Usage:* It's a sad thing that even the *peccadilloes* of public figures are publicized so much.

**PECUNIARY** (adj) *[pi-KYOO-nee-er-ee]*

*Syn:* pertaining to money

*Usage:* He says his new job offers more *pecuniary* benefits than his old one.

**PEDAGOGUE** (n) *[PED-uh-gog]*

*Syn:* teacher

*Ant:* student

*Usage:* He could never be a stuffy *pedagogue*; his classes were always lively and filled with humor.

**PEDANT** (n) *[PED-nt]*

*Syn:* scholar who overemphasizes book learning or technicalities

*Usage:* I am no *pedant* and avoid being dogmatic concerning old-school scientific theories and their complicated mathematical derivations.

**PEJORATIVE** (adj) *[pi-JAWR-uh-tiv]*

*Syn:* negative in connotation; having a belittling effect

*Ant:* praising

*Usage:* It's funny that some people look at "ambitious" as a *pejorative* term rather than seeing it as positive.

**PELLUCID** (adj) *[puh-LOO-sid]*

*Syn:* transparent; limpid; easy to understand

*Ant:* complex; confusing

*Usage:* He was head over heels in love with her from the first time he saw her *pellucid* eyes.

**PENCHANT** (n) *[PEN-chuh nt]*

*Syn:* strong inclination; liking

*Ant:* dislike; indifference; hatred

*Usage:* She has a *penchant* for collecting antique utensils.

**PENUMBRA** (n) *[pi-NUHM-bruh]*

*Syn:* partial shadow (in an eclipse)

*Ant:* brightness; sunlight

*Usage:* During an eclipse, we can see an area of total darkness and a lighter area, which is the *penumbra*.

**PENURIOUS** (adj) *[puh-NOO R-ee-uh s]*

*Syn:* very poor

*Ant:* prosperous

*Usage:* He lived in a most *penurious* manner, denying himself every indulgence.

**PERCEPTION** (n) *[per-SEP-shuh n]*

*Syn:* keen natural understanding

*Ant:* insensibility; ignorance; misapprehension

*Usage:* Her *perception* of the situation was very objective.

**PEREGRINATION** (n) *[per-i-gruh-NEY-shuh n]*

*Syn:* a long and winding journey; wandering

*Ant:* direct path

*Usage:* Thanks to his *peregrination*, he knows almost every nook and corner of the territory.

**PERFIDIOUS** (adj) [per-FID-ee-uh s]

*Syn:* treacherous; disloyal

*Ant:* staunch; faithful; honorable

*Usage:* She could never forgive her *perfidious* team members for their treachery.

**PERFUNCTORY** (adj) [per-FUHNGK-tuh-ree]

*Syn:* superficial; not thorough; lacking interest, care, or enthusiasm

*Ant:* heedful; careful; thoughtful; caring

*Usage:* I was disappointed to be greeted with no more than a *perfunctory* handshake.

**PERIPHERAL** (adj) [puh-RIF-er-uh l]

*Syn:* marginal; outer; of indirect importance; not central

*Ant:* central

*Usage:* I try to avoid *peripheral* and boring details in my lectures.

**PERMEABLE** (adj) [PUR-mee-uh-buh l]

*Syn:* penetrable; porous; allowing liquids or gas to pass through

*Ant:* impermeable; solid

*Usage:* Most clothing items are *permeable* to air and water, letting either through to the skin with just a short exposure.

**PERSPICUOUS** (adj) [per-SPIK-yoo-uhs]

*Syn:* having insight; penetrating; astute; clear; obvious

*Ant:* unclear; vague

*Usage:* The psychologist demonstrated a *perspicuous* understanding of the root cause of her depression.

**PERTINACIOUS** (adj) [pur-tn-EY-shuh s]

*Syn:* stubborn; persistent

*Ant:* inconstant; irresolute; volatile; unreliable

*Usage:* King Solomon was inspired by the *pertinacious* spider stubbornly rebuilding its web after daily removal.

**PEST** (n) [pest]

*Syn:* troublesome or annoying person

*Ant:* charmer

*Usage:* He was a real *pest* the other day, playing silly pranks on people and generally spoiling their moods.

**PESTILENTIAL** (adj) [pes-tl-EN-shuh l]

*Syn:* causing plague; baneful

*Ant:* healthful

*Usage:* They believed that the *pestilential* water of the stream was the reason for the epidemic.

**PETRIFY** (v) [PE-truh-fahy]

*Syn:* turn to stone

*Ant:* thaw

*Usage:* She remained in the haunted mansion in the amusement park *petrified*, unable to move, as if frozen in place.

**PHARISAICAL** (adj) [far-uh-SEY-ik-l]

*Syn:* pertaining to Pharisees, who paid scrupulous attention to tradition; self-righteous; hypocritical

*Ant:* reliable

*Usage:* Walter Lippmann has pointed out that moralists who do not attempt to explain the moral code they advocate are often regarded as *pharisaical*.

**PHILANDERER** (n) [fi-LAN-der er]

*Syn:* faithless lover; flirt

*Ant:* faithful lover

*Usage:* The married women steered clear of him, well knowing that he was a *philanderer*.

**PHILANTHROPIST** (n) [fi-LAN-thruh-pist]

*Syn:* lover of mankind; doer of good

*Ant:* hater of mankind; misanthropist

*Usage:* They were grateful to the *philanthropist* who gave them the money to rebuild their houses after the earthquake.

**PHILATELIST** (n) [fi-LAT-l-ist]

*Syn:* stamp collector

*Usage:* The children like spending time with him as he is a *philatelist* and shows them many interesting stamps from his collection.

**PHOENIX** (n) [FEE-niks]

*Syn:* symbol of immortality or rebirth

*Usage:* It's great to see the *phoenix* of his company rising yet again in the form of a website.

**PHYSIOGNOMY** (n) [fiz-ee-OG-nuh-mee]

*Syn:* face; visage; countenance

*Usage:* He was fascinated by her *physiognomy*. Her hard-set features seemed to complement her behavior.

**PIETY** (n) [PAHY-i-tee]

*Syn:* religious devotion; godliness

*Ant:* impiety; ungodliness; profanity; hypocrisy; irreverence

*Usage:* Her *piety* has gained her the respect of her church and the entire neighborhood.

**PILLORY** (v) [PIL-uh-ree]

*Syn:* attack someone with words so as to cause him disrespect among the public

*Ant:* praise; complimented

*Usage:* The actress committed suicide as a result of being *pilloried* by the press.

**PINION** (v) [PIN-yuh n]

*Syn:* restrain

*Ant:* set free

*Usage:* They *pinioned* his arms against his body but left his legs free so that he could move about.

**PIQUANT** (adj) [PEE-kuh nt]

*Syn:* pleasantly tart-tasting; stimulating

*Ant:* tame; dull; flat: insipid

*Usage:* At the dinner party, Betty served salad with an unusually *piquant* dressing.

**PLACATE** (v) [PLEY-keyt]

*Syn:* pacify; conciliate

*Ant:* snub

*Usage:* Betty smiled and spoke sweetly, trying to *placate* John after their fight

**PLACEBO** (n) [pluh-SEE-boh]

*Syn:* harmless substance prescribed as a dummy pill

*Ant:* poison; drug

*Usage:* Since the symptoms she described were not really serious, the doctor just pacified her and prescribed a few *placebos* to satisfy her request for treatment.

**PLATITUDE** (n) [PLAT-i-tood]

*Syn:* trite remark; commonplace statement

*Ant:* original idea

*Usage:* It is boring to listen to him spouting the same old *platitudes*.

**PLAUDITORY** (adj) [plaw-dih-TOH-ree]

*Syn:* approving; applauding

*Ant:* critical; disparaging; insulting

*Usage:* The theatrical company reprinted the *plauditory* comments of the critics in its advertisement.

This page is intentionally left blank

# Chapter 12

## (Plebeian – Repudiate)

*This chapter covers the following words along with their part of speech, pronunciation, synonyms and antonym, if applicable. Sample usage of the word is also illustrated.*

| | | |
|---|---|---|
| plebeian | proliferate | rapacious |
| plenitude | prologue | raspy |
| plethora | promulgate | raucous |
| podiatrist | propensity | ravenous |
| poignancy | prophylactic | realm |
| polemic | proponent | rebuttal |
| polyglot | propriety | recalcitrant |
| portend | prosaic | recidivism |
| poseur | proscribe | recondite |
| posture | protean | rectitude |
| poultice | protuberance | redoubtable |
| pragmatic | proviso | refectory |
| preamble | provoke | refraction |
| precarious | proxy | regatta |
| precedent | prune | regime |
| precept | prurient | regnant |
| precis | pseudonym | reiterate |
| precise | psychopathic | relegate |
| predetermine | puerile | remediable |
| predilection | pugilist | remorse |
| pre-eminent | purveyor | rendition |
| prefatory | putrid | reparable |
| premonition | pyre | repartee |
| prescience | pyromaniac | repercussion |
| prevaricate | quagmire | repertoire |
| primogeniture | quarantine | replica |
| primordial | queasy | reprieve |
| pristine | quiescent | reproach |
| proclivity | quietude | reprobate |
| procrastinate | quintessence | repudiate |
| prodigious | quisling | |
| profligate | quorum | |
| profound | raconteur | |
| progenitor | ramification | |
| proletarian | ramshackle | |

**PLEBEIAN** (adj) [pli-BEE-uh n]

Syn: common; pertaining to common people; not distinguished

Ant: autocratic; patrician; noble; aristocratic; high-horn

Usage: I was embarrassed by his alarmingly *plebeian* manners.

**PLENITUDE** (n) [PLEN-i-tood]

Syn: abundance; completeness

Ant: dearth; scarcity

Usage: The music brought Betty a feeling of *plenitude* and freedom.

**PLETHORA** (n) [PLETH-er-uh]

Syn: excess; overabundance

Ant: paucity

Usage: A *plethora* of imported appliances are available in the market.

**PODIATRIST** (n) [puh-DAHY-uh-trist]

Syn: doctor who treats ailments of the feet

Usage: In the teaching clinic, patients are treated by *podiatry* students under the supervision of staff.

**POIGNANCY** (n) [POIN-yuh n-see]

Syn: quality of being deeply moving; keenness of emotion

Ant: happiness; glee

Usage: He tried to disguise the *poignancy* of the situation by cracking ill-timed jokes.

**POLEMIC** (n) [puh-LEM-ik]

Syn: controversy; argument in support of point of view

Usage: The book is a passionate *polemic* for tolerance.

**POLYGLOT** (adj) [POL-ee-glot]

Syn: a person who knows several languages; linguist

Ant: monoglot

Usage: Being a multi-linguist, she enjoyed living among Chicago's *polyglot* population.

**PORTEND** (v) [pawr-TEND]

Syn: foretell; presage

Ant: avert; contradict; nullify; negate; preclude

Usage: The cloudy sky *portended* gloomy weather.

**POSEUR** (n) [poh-ZUR]

Syn: person who pretends to be sophisticated, elegant, etc. to impress others; pretender; hypocrite

Ant: genuine individual

Usage: As mayor Jean Valjean was a *poseur* as he was actually a poor plebeian who had spent years in prison.

**POSTURE** (v) [POS-cher]

Syn: assume an affected pose; act artificially

Ant: act genuinely

Usage: Betty's colleague was *posturing* to gain the manager's favor.

**POULTICE** (n) [POHL-tis]

Syn: soothing application applied to the inflamed portions of the body

Ant: irritant

Usage: Nancy applied a *poultice* to the soldier's wounds.

**PRAGMATIC** (adj) [prag-MAT-ik]

Syn: practical (as opposed to idealistic); concerned with the practical worth or impact of something

Ant: impractical; idealistic; unrealistic

Usage: Robin took a very *pragmatic* look at her situation, ready to start the necessary steps forward toward a workable solution.

**PREAMBLE** (n) [PREE-am-buh l]

Syn: introductory statement

Ant: peroration; finale; conclusion; essay; body

*Usage:* Rather than a brief introduction, the *preamble* turned out to last longer than the speech!

**PRECARIOUS** (adj) *[pri-KAIR-ee-uhs]*

*Syn:* uncertain; risky

*Ant:* safe; certain; assured; systematic; immutable; secure

*Usage:* Everybody's talking about the government's *precarious* position as rebels roam the streets.

**PRECEDENT** (n) *[pres-i-duh-nt]*

*Syn:* something preceding in time that may be used as an authority or guide for future action; antecedent

*Ant:* result

*Usage:* This court decision sets a *precedent* for future cases of a similar nature.

**PRECEPT** (n) *[PREE-sept]*

*Syn:* practical rule guiding conduct

*Ant:* suggestion; hint; prompting; impulse

*Usage:* His life is based on the *precepts* of Buddhism.

**PRECIS** (n) *[prey-see]*

*Syn:* concise summing up of main points

*Ant:* elaboration

*Usage:* The coach asked the students to prepare a *precis* of what they had learned during the two-day course.

**PRECISE** (adj) *[pri-SAHYS]*

*Syn:* exact

*Ant:* indefinite, vague; inexact; inaccurate; unceremonious

*Usage:* His replies are always very *precise* and succinct.

**PREDETERMINE** (v) *[pree-di-TUR-min]*

*Syn:* predestine

*Ant:* reflect (historically)

*Usage:* There's no way you can *predetermine* what shot to play.

**PREDILECTION** (n) *[pred-l-EK-shuhn]*

*Syn:* partiality; preference

*Ant:* impartiality

*Usage:* Until I fell in love, and begun to rhyme as a matter of consequence, I never had the least *predilection* for poetry.

**PREEMINENT** (adj) *[pree-EM-uh-nuh nt]*

*Syn:* outstanding; superior

*Ant:* inferior; low; unimportant

*Usage:* He was a *preeminent* political figure in the country.

**PREFATORY** (adj) *[PREF-uh-tawr-ee]*

*Syn:* introductory

*Ant:* concluding; summarizing

*Usage:* She requested her professor to write the *prefatory* section for her new book.

**PREMONITION** (n) *[pree-muh-NISH-uh n]*

*Syn:* forewarning

*Ant:* reflection; memory

*Usage:* Pay heed to her *premonitions*; they usually signal bad tidings for the family.

**PRESCIENCE** (n) *[PRESH-uh ns]*

*Syn:* ability to foretell the future

*Ant:* ignorance

*Usage:* He has demonstrated certain *prescience* in foreign affairs and has been able to head off hostilities.

**PREVARICATE** (v) *[pri-VAR-i-keyt]*

*Syn:* lie

*Ant:* affirm; maintain; prove; substantiate

*Usage:* The ministers continued to *prevaricate* despite the public queries about their truthfulness.

**PRIMOGENITURE** (n) *[prahy-muh-JEN-i-cher]*

*Syn:* seniority by birth

*Ant:* junior position by birth

*Usage:* By virtue of *primogeniture,* in some cultures the first-born child has many privileges denied his brothers and sisters.

**PRIMORDIAL** (adj) *[prahy-MAWR-dee-uh l]*

*Syn:* existing at the beginning (of time); rudimentary

*Ant:* fully developed

*Usage:* The lecture was about the original *primordial* explosion.

**PRISTINE** (adj) *[PRIS-teen]*

*Syn:* characteristic of earlier times; primitive; unspoiled

*Ant:* spoiled; polluted; dirty

*Usage:* He is always dressed in *pristine* white shirts, without a spot on them.

**PROCLIVITY** (n) *[proh-KLIV-i-tee]*

*Syn:* inclination; natural tendency

*Ant:* aversion; indisposition; disinclination

*Usage:* He has a *proclivity* to daydream.

**PROCRASTINATE** (v) *[proh-KRAS-tuh-neyt]*

*Syn:* postpone; delay or put off

*Ant:* hurry; complete; finish

*Usage:* He kept on *procrastinating* doing his homework and ultimately went to school without completing it.

**PRODIGIOUS** (adj) *[pruh-DIJ-uh s]*

*Syn:* marvelous; enormous

*Ant:* insignificant; meager

*Usage:* The money-laundering business generates cash in *prodigious* amounts.

**PROFLIGATE** (adj) *[PROF-li-git]*

*Syn:* dissipated; wasteful; wildly immoral

*Ant:* virtuous; honest; principled; conscientious; honorable

*Usage:* The factory consumes so much energy; the entire territory calls it *profligate.*

**PROFOUND** (adj) *[pruh-FOUND]*

*Syn:* deep; not superficial; complete

*Ant:* shallow; superficial; slight

*Usage:* She displays a *profound* understanding of the subject, able to answer any question from the audience.

**PROGENITOR** (n) *[proh-JEN-i-ter]*

*Syn:* ancestor

*Ant:* descendent

*Usage:* Ellen searched for her *progenitors,* hoping to find useful information about her genetic history.

**PROLETARIAN** (n) *[proh-li-TAIR-ee-uh n]*

*Syn:* member of the working class; blue collar person

*Ant:* aristocrat

*Usage:* The struggle between the management and the *proletarians* seems unending.

**PROLIFERATE** (v) *[pruh-LIF-uh-reyt]*

*Syn:* grow rapidly; spread; multiply

*Ant:* decline; decrease; limit

*Usage:* In his speech, the President condemned the *proliferation* of nuclear weapons, urging instead a mutual arms reduction.

**PROLOGUE** (n) *[PROH-lawg]*

*Syn:* introduction

*Ant:* summary; conclusion

*Usage:* Appetizing delicacies were the *prologue* to a long dinner.

**PROMULGATE** (v) *[PROM-uh l-geyt]*

*Syn:* proclaim a doctrine or law; make known by official publication

*Ant:* suppress; conceal; stifle; hush; discountenance

*Usage:* The Government *promulgated* the Information Technology Act as soon as it was passed in order to quickly provide guidelines in the market.

**PROPENSITY** (n) *[pruh-PEN-si-tee]*

*Syn:* natural inclination

*Ant:* aversion; disinclination; indisposition

*Usage:* It didn't take long to realize her *propensity* to lie; not a single word of truth crossed her lips!

**PROPHYLACTIC** (adj) *[proh-fuh-LAK-tik]*

*Syn:* used to prevent disease

*Ant:* communicating (disease)

*Usage:* Vaccination and other *prophylactic* measures must be carried out meticulously.

**PROPONENT** (n) *[pruh-POH-nuh nt]*

*Syn:* supporter; backer; opposite of opponent

*Ant:* critic; detractor

*Usage:* He is a leading *proponent* of the virtues of higher education.

**PROPRIETY** (n) *[pruh-PRAHY-i-tee]*

*Syn:* fitness; correct conduct

*Ant:* impropriety; misbehavior

*Usage:* He behaved with absolutely no sense of social *propriety*, to the great consternation of the other guests at the party.

**PROSAIC** (adj) *[proh-ZEY-ik]*

*Syn:* dull and unimaginative; matter-of-fact; factual

*Ant:* exciting

*Usage:* His letters are always dull and *prosaic*.

**PROSCRIBE** (v) *[proh-SKRAHYB]*

*Syn:* ostracize; banish; outlaw

*Ant:* prescribe; allow

*Usage:* In many countries members of the general public are *proscribed* from owning guns.

**PROTEAN** (adj) *[PROH-tee-uh n]*

*Syn:* versatile; able to take on many shapes

*Syn:* limited; inflexible

*Usage:* I am confident he can do any role—he is a *protean* actor.

**PROTUBERANCE** (n) *[proh-TOO-ber-uh ns]*

*Syn:* protrusion; bulge

*Ant:* depression (of a surface)

*Usage:* They need to operate a *protuberance* on her upper jawbone.

**PROVISO** (n) *[pruh-VAHY-zoh]*

*Syn:* a stipulation; a condition

*Ant:* freedom

*Usage:* With the *proviso* that Jane agreed, Robert also supported the plan.

**PROVOKE** (v) *[pruh-VOHK]*

*Syn:* stir to anger; cause retaliation

*Ant:* calm; quiet

*Usage:* He would not have become so violent if Robert had not *provoked* him with those rude remarks.

**PROXY** (n) *[PROK-see]*

*Syn:* authorized agent or vote

*Ant:* genuine person

*Usage:* The company allowed shareholders to vote by *proxy*.

**PRUNE** (v) *[proon]*

*Syn:* cut away; trim

*Ant:* add onto; graft

*Usage:* Harold ordered his gardener to *prune* the rose bushes.

**PRURIENT** (adj) *[PROOR-ee-uhnt]*

*Syn:* having or causing lustful thoughts and desires

*Ant:* lustless; chaste

*Usage:* Ron Davies, my friend, was now an item of *prurient* international news.

**PSEUDONYM** (n) *[SOOD-n-im]*

*Syn:* pen name

*Ant:* actual name

*Usage:* She writes all her mystery novels under the *pseudonym* Sharp rather than her true surname of Smith.

**PSYCHOPATHIC** (adj) *[sahy-kuh-PATH-ik]*

*Syn:* pertaining to mental derangement

*Usage:* There is a rumor that a *psychopathic* killer is on the rampage.

**PUERILE** (adj) *[PYOO-er-il]*

*Syn:* childish

*Ant:* manly; vigorous; powerful; cogent; strong; mature

*Usage:* The movie is *puerile*, but it's entertaining even for adults.

**PUGILIST** (n) *[PYOO-juh-list]*

*Syn:* boxer

*Ant:* pacifist; non-fighter

*Usage:* He is training to be a *pugilist*, in the sparring for hours every day.

**PURVEYOR** (n) *[per-VEY-er]*

*Syn:* furnisher of foodstuffs; caterer

*Ant:* receiver

*Usage:* Rob and Dallas are *purveyors* of gourmet foods.

**PUTRID** (adj) *[PYOO-trid]*

*Syn:* foul; rotten; decayed

*Ant:* fresh

*Usage:* A foul, *putrid* stench hung around the house for many days after the fire.

**PYRE** (n) *[pahy uhr]*

*Syn:* heap of combustible material; esp. for burning a corpse.

*Usage:* The tribal people built a funeral *pyre* and danced around it as the flames flickered to the sky.

**PYROMANIAC** (n) *[pahy-ruh-MEY-nee-uh]*

*Syn:* person with an insane desire to set things on fire

*Ant:* firefighter

*Usage:* The detectives searched the area for the *pyromaniac* who had set these costly fires.

**QUAGMIRE** (n) *[KWAG-mahy uhr]*

*Syn:* soft, wet, boggy land; complex or dangerous situation from which it is difficult to free oneself

*Ant:* blessing; solution; success

*Usage:* The industrialist complained of having been drawn into a political *quagmire*.

**QUARANTINE** (n) *[KWAWR-uh n-teen]*

*Syn:* isolation of person or ship to prevent spread of infection

*Ant:* commingling

*Usage:* The antivirus software *quarantined* the virus infected files.

**QUEASY** (adj) *[KWEE-zee]*

*Syn:* easily nauseated; squeamish; over-scrupulous; delicate

*Ant:* comfortable

*Usage:* He became *queasy* with seasickness within minutes of boarding the ship.

**QUIESCENT** (adj) *[kwee-ES-uh nt]*

*Syn:* at rest; dormant; temporarily inactive; motionless; still

*Ant:* active

*(Plebeian - Repudiate)*

*Usage:* She chose a *quiescent* beach resort instead of a popular and crowded one.

**QUIETUDE** (n) *[KWAHY-i-tood]*

*Syn:* tranquility

*Ant:* bustle; chaos; noise

*Usage:* After living in the bustling city, the *quietude* of the farm was unnerving.

**QUINTESSENCE** (n) *[kwin-TES-uh ns]*

*Syn:* purest and highest embodiment

*Ant:* extra

*Usage:* He was the *quintessence* of nastiness, a model for fictional tyrants.

**QUISLING** (n) *[KWIZ-ling]*

*Syn:* a traitor

*Ant:* loyalist

*Usage:* Thousands of people gathered to see the *quisling* being hanged after his treasonous a

**QUORUM** (n) *[KWAWR-uh m]*

*Syn:* number of members necessary to conduct a meeting

*Ant:* minority

*Usage:* The meeting was cancelled because enough people did not turn up to meet the *quorum*.

**RACONTEUR** (n) *[rak-uh n-TUR Fr]*

*Syn:* storyteller

*Usage:* My uncle is a *raconteur* and all my friends gather around him to listen to his many interesting tales.

**RAMIFICATION** (n) *[ram-uh-fi-KEY-shuh n]*

*Syn:* branching out; subdivision

*Ant:* limitation

*Usage:* The book analyzes the political and social *ramifications* of the war.

**RAMSHACKLE** (adj) *[RAM-shak-uh l]*

*Syn:* rickety; falling apart

*Ant:* sturdy

*Usage:* It's surprising that Bob decided to buy that *ramshackle* building since the rest of us worried it would soon fall apart.

**RAPACIOUS** (adj) *[ruh-PEY-shuh s]*

*Syn:* (typical of a person) who takes for himself everything he can, especially by force

*Ant:* frugal; contented; liberal; bountiful; generous

*Usage:* I hate his *rapacious* attitude towards hunting.

**RASPY** (adj) *[RAS-pee]*

*Syn:* grating; harsh

*Ant:* melodious

*Usage:* He sang in a deep, *raspy* tone.

**RAUCOUS** (adj) *[RAW-kuh s]*

*Syn:* harsh and shrill; disorderly and boisterous

*Ant:* subtle

*Usage:* They heard her screams and the *raucous* laughter of the murderer.

**RAVENOUS** (adj) *[REV-uh-nuh s]*

*Syn:* extremely hungry; rapacious

*Ant:* sated; satiated

*Usage:* You must have seen him eat *ravenously* at the party last night.

**REALM** (n) *[relm]*

*Syn:* kingdom; field or sphere of influence

*Ant:* outside of influence

*Usage:* Her research is mostly restricted to the *realm* of Physics.

**REBUTTAL** (n) *[ri-BUHT-l]*

*Syn:* refutation; response with contrary evidence

*Ant:* confirmation; support

*Usage:* He is making a point-by-point *rebuttal* of charges from former colleagues.

**RECALCITRANT** (adj) *[ri-KAL-si-truh nt]*

*Syn:* obstinately stubborn; determined to resist authority; unruly

*Ant:* hospitable

*Usage:* He can coax even the most *recalcitrant* employee to put in his best efforts.

**RECIDIVISM** (n) *[ri-SID-uh-viz-uh m]*

*Syn:* habitual return to crime

*Usage:* The basic criticism was that prisons do not reduce crime rate; they cause *recidivism*.

**RECONDITE** (adj) *[REK-uh n-dahyt]*

*Syn:* (of ideas, knowledge, etc) not commonly known; difficult to understand; profound; abstruse

*Ant:* obvious; simple; straightforward

*Usage:* I wonder how she manages to understand even *recondite* subject-matter with ease.

**RECTITUDE** (n) *[REK-ti-tood]*

*Syn:* uprightness; moral virtue; correctness of judgment

*Ant:* depravity

*Usage:* His respected acquaintances are all people of the utmost moral *rectitude*.

**REDOUBTABLE** (adj) *[ri-DOU-tuh-buh l]*

*Syn:* formidable; causing fear

*Ant:* pleasant; powerless

*Usage:* He is a *redoubtable* fighter, feared by all his opponents.

**REFECTORY** (adj) *[ri-FEK-tuh-ree]*

*Syn:* dining hall

*Usage:* The matron punished them for playing ping-pong ball on the *refectory* table since lunch was about to be served.

**REFRACTION** (n) *[ri-FRAK-shuh n]*

*Syn:* bending of a ray of light

*Ant:* straightness of a ray of light

*Usage:* The *refraction* of light on the dancing waves was interesting to watch.

**REGATTA** (n) *[ri-GAT-uh]*

*Syn:* boat race

*Usage:* They are for a celebratory sunset sail to celebrate because their team won the *regatta*.

**REGIME** (n) *[ruh-zheem]*

*Syn:* method or system of government

*Usage:* The people were happy during the benevolent former king's *regime*.

**REGNANT** (n) *[REG-nuh nt]*

*Syn:* reigning; predominant; prevalent; sovereign

*Ant:* humble

*Usage:* The first row at the theatre was reserved for the *regnant* queen.

**REITERATE** (v) *[ree-IT-uh-reyt]*

*Syn:* repeat

*Ant:* say only once

*Usage:* He *reiterates* the fact that beyond the time barrier, the children are quite safe.

**RELEGATE** (v) *[REL-i-geyt]*

*Syn:* banish to an inferior position; delegate; assign

*Ant:* promote; elevate

*Usage:* After a few days, the newspapers *relegated* the old news item to the middle pages.

**REMEDIABLE** (adj) [ri-MEE-dee-uh-buh l]

*Syn:* reparable

*Ant:* irreparable

*Usage:* Don't worry; the situation is *remediable*.

**REMORSE** (n) [ri-MAWRS]

*Syn:* guilt; self-reproach

*Ant:* indifference; complacency; self-approval

*Usage:* He has shown no *remorse* for his actions.

**RENDITION** (n) [ren-DISH-uh n]

*Syn:* translation; artistic interpretation of a song, etc.

*Ant:* obscurity; vagueness

*Usage:* I just listened to a beautiful *rendition* of some of Beethoven's symphonies.

**REPARABLE** (adj) [REP-er-uh-buh l]

*Syn:* capable of being repaired

*Ant:* irremediable

*Usage:* The mechanic assured me that the damage was *reparable*, although the fixes would be expensive!

**REPARTEE** (n) [rep-er-TEE]

*Syn:* a quick, amusing reply in a conversation

*Usage:* She was good at *repartee*, always having a quick retort for any comment.

**REPERCUSSION** (n) [ree-per-KUSHS-uh n]

*Syn:* rebound; reverberation; reaction

*Ant:* original action

*Usage:* She did not think about the *repercussions* of her act, only about the present moment.

**REPERTOIRE** (n) [REP-er-twahr]

*Syn:* list of works of music, drama, etc

*Usage:* She has thousands of songs in her *repertoire*.

**REPLICA** (n) [REP-li-kuh]

*Syn:* copy

*Ant:* original

*Usage:* I am sure it is only a *replica* of the original.

**REPRIEVE** (n) [ri-PREEV]

*Syn:* temporary stay or suspension of a punishment

*Ant:* conviction; condemnation

*Usage:* A man awaiting a death sentence was saved by a last minute *reprieve*.

**REPROACH** (v) [ri-PROHCH]

*Syn:* express disapproval or disappointment

*Ant:* approve; extol; laud

*Usage:* She *reproached* him for breaking his promise.

**REPROBATE** (n) [REP-ruh-beyt]

*Syn:* person hardened in sin; devoid of a sense of decency

*Ant:* paragon

*Usage:* He has turned out exactly like his father, a drunken *reprobate*.

**REPUDIATE** (v) [ri-PYOO-dee-eyt]

*Syn:* disown; disavow

*Ant:* acknowledge; avow; admit

*Usage:* The media urged people to turn out in large numbers to *repudiate* the violence.

This page is intentionally left blank

# Chapter 13

## (Requiem – Slew)

*This chapter covers the following words along with their part of speech, pronunciation, synonyms and antonym, if applicable. Sample usage of the word is also illustrated.*

| | | |
|---|---|---|
| requiem | rummage | seminary |
| requite | runic | sensitization |
| rescind | sacrilegious | sententious |
| resilient | sacrosanct | septic |
| resolution | sagacious | sepulcher |
| resolve | sage | sequester |
| resplendent | salacious | serendipity |
| restitution | salubrious | serrated |
| restraint | sanctimonious | servile |
| resume | sanguinary | severance |
| resurge | sanguine | severity |
| resuscitate | sardonic | sextant |
| reticent | satiate | shard |
| retraction | saturnine | sheaf |
| retrieve | satyr | sheathe |
| retroactive | savior | shirk |
| retrograde | scabbard | shrewd |
| revelry | scaffold | shun |
| reverent | scenario | shyster |
| reverie | schematic | sibling |
| rhapsodize | schism | sidereal |
| rhetoric | scourge | simian |
| ribald | scrupulous | simplistic |
| rife | scurrilous | sinewy |
| rigor | scurvy | skeptic |
| riveting | seamy | skinflint |
| rococo | secession | skulduggery |
| roseate | sedative | skulk |
| rostrum | sedulous | slake |
| rote | segregate | slapdash |
| rout | seine | sleazy |
| rubric | seismic | slew |
| rueful | semblance | |
| ruminate | seminal | |

**REQUIEM** (n) *[REK-wee-uh m]*

*Syn:* mass for the dead; dirge

*Usage:* People were very solemn when the *requiem* was being performed.

**REQUITE** (v) *[ri-kwahyt]*

*Syn:* repay; revenge

*Ant:* dissatisfy; refuse

*Usage:* I wonder if he can ever *requite* all the help that his father has done for him.

**RESCIND** (v) *[ri-SIND]*

*Syn:* cancel; repeal

*Ant:* continue; prolong

*Usage:* Because of the struggling economic recovery, people have been urging the government to *rescind* the price increase.

**RESILIENT** (adj) *[ri-ZIL-yuh nt]*

*Syn:* elastic; having the power of springing back

*Ant:* rigid

*Usage:* The chair is made of *resilient* plastic material.

**RESOLUTION** (n) *[rez-uh-LOO-shuh n]*

*Syn:* determination; resolve

*Ant:* indecision; composition; synthesis; inconsistency

*Usage:* She broke her New Year's *resolution* even before the end of January.

**RESOLVE** (n) *[ri-ZOLV]*

*Syn:* determination; firmness of purpose

*Ant:* indecision; uncertainty; lack of will

*Usage:* With that kind of firm *resolve*, she is sure to win.

**RESPLENDENT** (adj) *[ri-SPLEN-duh nt]*

*Syn:* dazzling; glorious; brilliant

*Ant:* dull; colorless; unimpressive

*Usage:* She arrived at the wedding, *resplendent* in her custom-made gown.

**RESTITUTION** (n) *[res-ti-TOO-shuh n]*

*Syn:* reparation; indemnification; compensation

*Ant:* dissatisfaction; fee; penalty

*Usage:* She filed a case for *restitution* of conjugal rights.

**RESTRAINT** (n) *[ri-STRYNT]*

*Syn:* moderation or self-control; controlling force; restriction

*Ant:* uncontrolled behavior

*Usage:* I advised him to exercise *restraint* when talking to his superiors.

**RÉSUMÉ** (n) *[REZ-oo-mey]*

*Syn:* a condensation; a précis

*Ant:* complete biography

*Usage:* His *résumé* is quite impressive.

**RESURGE** (v) *[ri-SURJ]*

*Syn:* rise again; flow to and fro

*Ant:* subside

*Usage:* They are sure their leader is going to *resurge* to power.

**RESUSCITATE** (v) *[ri-SUHS-i-teyt]*

*Syn:* revive; bring back to life

*Ant:* let die

*Usage:* The paramedic tried to *resuscitate* her

**RETICENT** (adj) *[RET-uh-suh nt]*

*Syn:* reserved; uncommunicative; inclined to silence

*Ant:* talkative

*Usage:* She is very *reticent* about her achievements.

**RETRACTION** (n) *[ri-TRAK-shuh n]*

*Syn:* withdrawal

*Ant:* confirmation

*Usage:* The actress said she expected an unqualified *retraction* of the journalist's comments within two days.

**RETRIEVE** (v) [ri-TREEV]

*Syn:* recover; find and bring in

*Ant:* lose; forfeit; impair; surrender

*Usage:* He jumped into the well to *retrieve* the cricket ball that had fallen inside.

**RETROACTIVE** (adj) [re-troh-AK-tiv]

*Syn:* of a law that dates back to a period before its enactment

*Ant:* current

*Usage:* The banks want a *retroactive* legislation to cover their past losses.

**RETROGRADE** (v) [RE-truh-greyd]

*Syn:* go backwards; degenerate

*Ant:* improve; increase; rise

*Usage:* I'm afraid her health is *retrograding*.

**REVELRY** (n) [REV-uh l-ree]

*Syn:* merrymaking

*Ant:* solemnity

*Usage:* The arrival of the warden at the scene put an end to all the holiday *revelry*.

**REVERENT** (adj) [REV-er-uh nt]

*Syn:* respectful; worshipful

*Ant:* irreverent

*Usage:* There was a *reverent* silence as the Principal entered the assembly hall.

**REVERIE** (n) [REV-uh-ree]

*Syn:* daydream; musing

*Ant:* focus; concentration

*Usage:* The noise broke her out of her *reverie*.

**RHAPSODIZE** (v) [RAP-suh-dahyz]

*Syn:* speak or write in an exaggeratedly enthusiastic manner

*Ant:* play down

*Usage:* She came into the hall *rhapsodizing* about Elvis Presley.

**RHETORIC** (n) [RET-er-ik]

*Syn:* art of effective communication; insincere language

*Ant:* sincerity of speech

*Usage:* Advertisements are often *rhetoric*.

**RIBALD** (adj) [RIB-uh ld]

*Syn:* profane; sexy

*Ant:* proper

*Usage:* He *ribald* comments about a guest's body language were embarrassing.

**RIFE** (adj) [rahyf]

*Syn:* abundant; current

*Ant:* scarce

*Usage:* Bribery and corruption were *rife* in the industry.

**RIGOR** (n) [RIG]

*Syn:* severity; lack of mercy

*Ant:* leniency; ease

*Usage:* The trainees took time to adjust to the *rigors* of army training.

**RIVETING** (adj) [riv-it ng]

*Syn:* absorbing; engrossing

*Ant:* distracting; uninteresting

*Usage:* The play was very *riveting*, holding our attention until the final curtain.

**ROCOCO** (adj) [ruh-KOH-koh]

*Syn:* highly ornamental; florid (of furniture, architecture, etc)

*Ant:* simple

*Usage:* The building was decorated with *rococo* furniture.

**ROSEATE** (adj) *[ROS-zee-it]*

*Syn:* rosy; optimistic

*Ant:* dour; pessimistic

*Usage:* She captured the *roseate* glow of dawn with her camera.

**ROSTRUM** (n) *[ROS-truh m]*

*Syn:* platform for speechmaking; pulpit

*Usage:* The *rostrum* for the graduation ceremony was very tastefully decorated.

**ROTE** (n) *[roht]*

*Syn:* repetition

*Ant:* single instance

*Usage:* Spending a little more time understanding what you learn is better than learning by *rote*.

**ROUT** (v) *[rout]*

*Syn:* stampede; drive out

*Ant:* gather in

*Usage:* The Chicago Bulls *routed* their opponents in the basketball match.

**RUBRIC** (n) *[ROO-brik]*

*Syn:* protocol; scoring guidelines

*Usage:* It took some time for the students to read the lengthy *rubric* on the first page of the quiz paper.

**RUEFUL** (adj) *[ROO-fuh l]*

*Syn:* regretful

*Ant:* proud; pleased

*Usage:* He grinned at her *ruefully*, sorry that he had upset her.

**RUMINATE** (v) *[ROO-muh-neyt]*

*Syn:* chew over and over (mentally, or, like cows, physically); mull over; ponder

*Ant:* accept unthinkingly

*Usage:* He *ruminated* on the teachings of the Bhagavad Gita

**RUMMAGE** (v) *[RUHM-ij]*

*Syn:* ransack; thoroughly search

*Usage:* He *rummaged* through his clothes looking for something to wear to the night's party.

**RUNIC** (v) *[ROO-nik]*

*Syn:* mysterious; set down in an ancient alphabet

*Ant:* clear; in plain language; readable; modern

*Usage:* There were a lot of plaques with *runic* inscriptions at the museum but I could not make sense of any of them.

**SACRILEGIOUS** (adj) *[sak-ruh-LIJ-uh s]*

*Syn:* desecrating; profane

*Ant:* respectful

*Usage:* The terrorists committed many *sacrilegious* acts, bringing great pain to the hearts of the spiritual churchgoers.

**SACROSANCT** (adj) *[SAK-roh-sangkt]*

*Syn:* most sacred; inviolable

*Ant:* touchable; able to be changed

*Usage:* The freedom of the press is *sacrosanct*.

**SAGACIOUS** (adj) *[suh-GEY-shuh s]*

*Syn:* perceptive; shrewd; having insight

*Ant:* dull; obtuse; stolid; unintelligent

*Usage:* He is a wise and *sagacious* leader.

**SAGE** (n) *[seyj]*

*Syn:* person celebrated for wisdom

*(Requiem - Slew)*

*Ant:* ignoramus; idiot

*Usage:* Ruth was inspired by the many stories she had read about ancient Chinese *sages* knowledgeable of complex subjects.

**SALACIOUS** (adj) *[suh-LEY-shuh s]*

*Syn:* lascivious; lustful

*Ant:* innocent

*Usage:* It was a wildly *salacious* novel.

**SALUBRIOUS** (adj) *[suh-LOO-bree-uh s]*

*Syn:* healthful

*Ant:* unhealthy; unwholesome

*Usage:* She enjoyed her stay at the *salubrious* hillside resort, welcoming the opportunity to heal her battered soul.

**SANCTIMONIOUS** (adj) *[sangk-tuh-MOH-nee-uh s]*

*Syn:* displaying ostentatious or hypocritical devoutness

*Ant:* pious

*Usage:* She found her neighbor to be a *sanctimonious* hypocrite.

**SANGUINARY** (adj) *[SANG-gwuh-ner-ee]*

*Syn:* fond of wounding and killing; bloodthirsty

*Ant:* peaceful

*Usage:* They were a *sanguinary* gang of ruffians.

**SANGUINE** (adj) *[SANG-gwin]*

*Syn:* cheerful; hopeful

*Ant:* pessimistic; desponding; distrustful; suspicious; misgiving

*Usage:* He has a very *sanguine* outlook to life.

**SARDONIC** (adj) *[sahr-DON-ik]*

*Syn:* disdainful; sarcastic; cynical

*Ant:* optimistic; sincere

*Usage:* He has a *sardonic* sense of humor.

**SATIATE** (v) *[SEY-shee-eyt]*

*Syn:* satisfy fully

*Ant:* stint; starve

*Usage:* There are enough apples on the tree to *satiate* all the children in the neighborhood.

**SATURNINE** (adj) *[SAT-er-nahyn]*

*Syn:* gloomy

*Ant:* optimistic

*Usage:* His manner was rather *saturnine*, after hearing the bad news.

**SATYR** (n) *[SEY-ter]*

*Syn:* half-human, half-bestial being in the court of Dionysus; portrayed as wanton and cunning

*Usage:* The children were amused by the picture of the *satyr* in the illustrated mythological story which they just read.

**SAVIOR** (n) *[SEYV-yer]*

*Syn:* a person who saves others from danger

*Ant:* victim

*Usage:* She regarded her fiancé as her *savior*.

**SCABBARD** (n) *[SKAB-erd]*

*Syn:* case for a sword blade; sheath

*Usage:* The pirate drew the sword from his *scabbard* and laughed wickedly.

**SCAFFOLD** (n) *[SKAF-uh ld]*

*Syn:* temporary platform for workers; bracing framework; platform for execution

*Usage:* The wind was blowing so fast that the whole *scaffold* swayed with it, causing the worker to lose his balance.

**SCENARIO** (n) *[si-NAIR-ee-oh]*

*Syn:* plot outline; screenplay; opera libretto

*Usage:* In the worst-case *scenario*, you might have to

remain in the hospital for a few more days.

**SCHEMATIC** (adj) [skee-MAT-ik]

*Syn:* relating to an outline or diagram; using a system of symbols

*Usage:* The concept is shown in the *schematic* diagram below.

**SCHISM** (n) [SIZ-uh m]

*Syn:* division; split

*Ant:* consolidation; joining

*Usage:* With all the infighting, the organization seems to be on the brink of *schism*.

**SCOURGE** (n) [skurj]

*Syn:* lash; whip; severe punishment

*Usage:* Drugs are a *scourge* that is devastating our society.

**SCRUPULOUS** (adj) [SKROO-pyuh-luh s]

*Syn:* conscientious; extremely thorough

*Ant:* reckless; slovenly; confident; self-complacent

*Usage:* I have been *scrupulous* about telling them the risks associated with the venture.

**SCURRILOUS** (adj) [SKUR-uh-luh s]

*Syn:* insolent; offensive; shameless

*Ant:* respectful; complimentary

*Usage:* She was upset by the *scurrilous* rumors.

**SCURVY** (adj) [SKUR-vee]

*Syn:* despicable; contemptible

*Ant:* laudable

*Usage:* What a *scurvy* attitude he has!

**SEAMY** (adj) [SEE-mee]

*Syn:* sordid; unwholesome

*Ant:* wholesome

*Usage:* She shielded her children from the *seamier* side of life.

**SECESSION** (n) [si-SESH-uh n]

*Syn:* withdrawal; official separation

*Ant:* unification; reunification

*Usage:* She was writing an essay on the impact of Ukraine's *secession* from the Soviet Union.

**SEDATIVE** (n) [SED-uh-tiv]

*Syn:* calming drug or influence

*Ant:* stimulant

*Usage:* She was so disturbed and uncooperative that the doctor had to administer a *sedative* to calm her.

**SEDULOUS** (adj) [SEJ-uh-luh s]

*Syn:* diligent; industrious

*Ant:* idle' wandering; distracted

*Usage:* He topped the class as a result of his *sedulous* efforts.

**SEGREGATE** (v) [SEG-ri-geyt]

*Syn:* separate

*Ant:* integrate; keep together

*Usage:* *Segregate* the damaged pieces from the good ones.

**SEINE** (n) [seyn]

*Syn:* net for catching fish

*Usage:* He cast the *seine* on the water hoping for a good catch.

**SEISMIC** (adj) [SAHYZ-mik]

*Syn:* pertaining to earthquakes

*Usage:* Earthquakes produce two types of *seismic* waves.

**SEMBLANCE** (n) [sem-bluhns]

*Syn:* outward appearance; guise

*Ant:* inner feelings

*Usage:* Harry hoped his claims would have a *semblance* of

authenticity.

**SEMINAL** (adj) [SEM-uh-nl]

Syn: germinal; influencing future developments; related to seed or semen

Ant: noninfluential

Usage: The reforms have been a *seminal* event in the political history of the nation.

**SEMINARY** (n) [SEM-uh-ner-ee]

Syn: school for training future ministers; academy for young women

Usage: He learns literature from a priest at the local *seminary*.

**SENSITIZATION** (n) [sen-si-tuh-ZEY-shuhn]

Syn: process of being made sensitive

Ant: desensitization

Usage: Once the team experienced *sensitization*, it was difficult for them to ignore the problem.

**SENTENTIOUS** (adj) [sen-TEN-shuh s]

Syn: terse; concise; aphoristic

Ant: lengthy

Usage: Most of her articles are *sententious*; only the most serious readers follow them to the end.

**SEPTIC** (adj) [SEP-tik]

Syn: infected

Ant: healthy

Usage: He is suffering from a *septic* toe.

**SEPULCHER** (n) [SEP-uh l-ker]

Syn: tomb

Usage: There were many ancient relics in the *sepulcher* that the archeologists unearthed.

**SEQUESTER** (v) [si-KWES-ter]

Syn: isolate; retire from public life; segregate; seclude

Ant: in the open

Usage: Everything he owned was *sequestered*.

**SERENDIPITY** (n) [ser-uh n-DIP-i-tee]

Syn: finding valuable or desirable things by accident; accidental good fortune or luck

Ant: bad luck; hardship

Usage: Archimedes' principle was an unexpected *serendipity*.

**SERRATED** (adj) [SER-ey-tid]

Syn: having a saw-toothed edge

Ant: smooth-edged

Usage: Bread knives should ideally have a *serrated* edge.

**SERVILE** (adj) [SUR-vil]

Syn: slavish; cringing

Ant: haughty; independent; refractory; stubborn; defiant; rebellious

Usage: He was subservient and *servile*.

**SEVERANCE** (n) [SEV-er-uh ns]

Syn: division; partition; separation

Ant: integration; joining

Usage: He was shocked by the sudden *severance* from his father's will.

**SEVERITY** (n) [suh-VER-i-tee]

Syn: harshness; intensity; sternness; austerity

Ant: mildness

Usage: They have not explained the *severity* of her health condition to Barbette.

**SEXTANT** (n) [SEK-stuh nt]

Syn: navigation tool used to determine a ship's latitude and longitude

Usage: The morning after the storm, the captain tried to

find the position of the ship using his *sextant*.

**SHARD** (n) *[shahrd]*

*Syn:* fragment, generally of pottery; small sample

*Ant:* whole

*Usage:* She wept over the *shards* of the heirloom vase that he had broken during the fight.

**SHEAF** (n) *[sheef]*

*Syn:* bundle of stalks of grain; any bundle of things tied together

*Ant:* separate elements

*Usage:* He brought in a *sheaf* of banknotes to pay the month's rent and other bills.

**SHEATHE** (v) *[sheeth]*

*Syn:* place into a case

*Ant:* leave in the open; unprotected

*Usage:* After cutting the fruits for desert, she carefully washed, wiped and *sheathed* the knife in its leather cover

**SHIRK** (v) *[shurk]*

*Syn:* avoid (responsibility, work, etc); malinger

*Ant:* accept (responsibility, work, etc.)

*Usage:* He *shirked* all his responsibilities and sailed overseas without even informing his family.

**SHREWD** (adj) *[shrood]*

*Syn:* clever; astute

*Ant:* dull-witted

*Usage:* The child is very *shrewd* for her age.

**SHUN** (v) *[shuhn]*

*Syn:* keep away from

*Ant:* accept; face; meet

*Usage:* He has always *shunned* publicity.

**SHYSTER** (n) *[SHAHY-ster]*

*Syn:* lawyer using questionable methods

*Ant:* trustworthy lawyer

*Usage:* Why did she choose that *shyster* to appear in court for her case?

**SIBLING** (n) *[SIB-ling]*

*Syn:* brother or sister

*Usage:* All his *siblings* live in the same city and they meet almost every weekend with their parents.

**SIDEREAL** (adj) *[sahy-DEER-ee-uh l]*

*Syn:* relating to the stars

*Usage:* He doesn't need a clock, he can tell *sidereal* time.

**SIMIAN** (adj) *[SIM-ee-uh n]*

*Syn:* monkeylike

*Usage:* She had a wrinkled, *simian* face.

**SIMPLISTIC** (adj) *[sim-PLIS-tik]*

*Syn:* oversimplified

*Ant:* complex

*Usage:* The logic is *simplistic* but quite acceptable.

**SINEWY** (adj) *[SIN-yoo-ee]*

*Syn:* tough; strong and firm

*Ant:* weak

*Usage:* He was a tall, *sinewy* young man.

**SKEPTIC** (n) *[SKEP-tik]*

*Syn:* doubter; person who suspends judgment until the evidence supporting a point of view has been examined

*Ant:* believer; proponent

*Usage:* It's going to be difficult convincing the *skeptics* about his plans.

**SKINFLINT** (n) *[SKIN-flint]*

*Syn:* stingy person; miser; niggard

*Ant:* magnanimous

*Usage:* I wonder how he managed to get a donation of even a dollar from that *skinflint*.

**SKULDUGGERY** (n) *[skuhl-DUHG-uh-ree]*

*Syn:* dishonest behavior

*Ant:* honest behavior

*Usage:* He had to face accusations of intimidation and political *skullduggery*.

**SKULK** (v) *[skuhlk]*

*Syn:* move furtively and secretly

*Ant:* show; parade; issue

*Usage:* Harry *skulked* off from the house to play soccer, unnoticed by his mother.

**SLAKE** (v) *[sleyk]*

*Syn:* quench; sate

*Ant:* deprive

*Usage:* I *slaked* my thirst with a large glass of lemonade.

**SLAPDASH** (adj) *[SLAP-dash]*

*Syn:* haphazard; careless; sloppy

*Ant:* careful; organized

*Usage:* His work methods seem amazingly *slapdash*.

**SLEAZY** (adj) *[SLEE-zee]*

*Syn:* flimsy; unsubstantial

*Ant:* substantial; upstanding

*Usage:* Greta's mother warned her not to associate with that *sleazy* fellow.

**SLEW** (n) *[sloo]*

*Syn:* large quantity or number

*Ant:* few

*Usage:* This year has seen a *slew* of articles about the former Beatle's life.

This page is intentionally left blank

# Chapter 14

## (Slough – Tensile)

*This chapter covers the following words along with their part of speech, pronunciation, synonyms and antonym, if applicable. Sample usage of the word is also illustrated.*

slough
sluggard
sluggish
smart
smattering
smirk
snivel
sobriety
sojourn
solecism
solicitous
soliloquy
solstice
somatic
somnambulist
sophist
sophistication
soporific
spangle
spasmodic
spatial
spatula
spawn
specious
spontaneity
sporadic
spurious
squabble
squander
staccato
staid
stanch
static
steadfast

stellar
stentorian
stereotyped
stigma
stipend
stipulate
stockade
stodgy
stolid
stolidity
stratagem
striated
stringent
strut
stultify
stygian
subaltern
suborn
subpoena
subservient
subsistence
substantiate
subsume
subtlety
succinct
suffragist
suffuse
sultry
sumptuous
superannuated
supercilious
superfluous
supernumerary
supplant

suppliant
supposition
suppress
surfeit
surmount
surreptitious
surveillance
suture
swelter
swindler
sybarite
sycophant
sylvan
symbiosis
synchronous
synthetic
tacit
taint
tangential
tantamount
tantrum
tarantula
tarry
taut
tautological
tedium
teetotalism
temerity
tempestuous
temporal
tenacity
tensile

**SLOUGH** (v) [slou]

*Syn:* cast off

*Ant:* take on

*Usage:* The geranium *sloughs* off the dry brown leaves at the base of its branches.

**SLUGGARD** (n) [SLUGH-erd]

*Syn:* lazy person

*Ant:* dynamo

*Usage:* Bob did not employ Don because he seemed like a *sluggard*.

**SLUGGISH** (adj) [SLUGH-ish]

*Syn:* slow; lazy; lethargic

*Ant:* energetic

*Usage:* The economy remains *sluggish*.

**SMART** (v) [smahrt]

*Syn:* be hurt in one's feeling

*Ant:* assuage; help; soothe

*Usage:* He is still *smarting* over the bad reviews that his book got.

**SMATTERING** (n) [SMAT-er-ing]

*Syn:* slight knowledge

*Ant:* abundance

*Usage:* I have good knowledge of English and a *smattering* of French grammar.

**SMIRK** (n) [smurk]

*Syn:* conceited smile

*Usage:* Her mouth was drawn back into a *smirk* of triumph.

**SNIVEL** (v) [SNIV-uh l]

*Syn:* run at the nose; snuffle; whine

*Usage:* I moved away as soon as Billy started to *snivel*.

**SOBRIETY** (n) [suh-BRAHY-i-tee]

*Syn:* moderation (especially regarding indulgence in alcohol); seriousness

*Ant:* levity

*Usage:* Society depends on certain values like *sobriety* and trust.

**SOJOURN** (n) [SOH-jurn]

*Syn:* temporary stay

*Ant:* residence

*Usage:* We resumed our journey after a short *sojourn* at a wayside inn.

**SOLECISM** (n) [SOL-uh-siz-uh m]

*Syn:* construction that is flagrantly incorrect grammatically

*Ant:* correct language usage

*Usage:* The English teacher made it clear that she would any more *solecisms* would earn students "F" grades.

**SOLICITOUS** (adj) [suh-LIS-i-tuh s]

*Syn:* worried; concerned

*Ant:* carefree; inconsiderate

*Usage:* He was so *solicitous* of his guests, anticipating their every need.

**SOLILOQUY** (n) [suh-LIL-uh-kwee]

*Syn:* talking to oneself

*Ant:* dialogue

*Usage:* His *soliloquy* brought tears to the audience's eyes.

**SOLSTICE** (n) [SOL-stis]

*Syn:* point at which the sun is farthest from the equator; height

*Ant:* depth

*Usage:* They have decided to hold their annual celebrations on the day of the summer *solstice* every year.

*(Slough - Tensile)*

**SOMATIC** (adj) *[soh-MAT-ik]*

*Syn:* corporeal; physical; of the body

*Ant:* intellectual

*Usage:* I think she is suffering from great *somatic* pain after running the marathon.

**SOMNAMBULIST** (n) *[som-NAM-byuh-liz-uh m]*

*Syn:* sleepwalker

*Usage:* Bob thinks Danny is a *somnambulist* for he finds him eating a sandwich in the kitchen nearly every morning at 2AM.

**SOPHIST** (n) *[SOF-ist]*

*Syn:* teacher of philosophy; quibbler; employer of fallacious reasoning

*Usage:* The author has collaborated with a reputed *sophist* for his next book.

**SOPHISTICATION** (n) *[suh-fis-ti-KEY-shuh n]*

*Syn:* artificiality; unnaturalness; act of employing sophistry in reasoning

*Ant:* innocence

*Usage:* Words can't describe the *sophistication* of the world's richest city.

**SOPORIFIC** (adj) *[sop-uh-RIF-ik]*

*Syn:* sleep-causing; marked by sleepiness

*Ant:* stimulating; invigorating

*Usage:* Bob did not know what he was blabbering while under the *soporific* effects of the alcohol.

**SPANGLE** (n) *[SPANG-guh l]*

*Syn:* small metallic piece sewn to clothing for ornamentation

*Usage:* She lay on the grass watching the dark night sky *spangled* with stars.

**SPASMODIC** (adj) *[spaz-MOD-ik]*

*Syn:* fitful; periodic; not continuous

*Ant:* continuous;

*Usage:* He managed to stifle the *spasmodic* sobs rising in his throat.

**SPATIAL** (adj) *[SPEY-shuh l]*

*Syn:* relating to space

*Usage:* He had to move his office to a different premise because of *spatial* constraints.

**SPATULA** (n) *[SPACH-uh-luh]*

*Syn:* broad-bladed instrument used for spreading or mixing

*Usage:* Betty smoothed the batter with a *spatula* before pushing the dish into the oven.

**SPAWN** (v) *[spawn]*

*Syn:* lay eggs in large quantities (like fish); create

*Ant:* destroy

*Usage:* His research has *spawned* a whole new branch of science.

**SPECIOUS** (adj) *[SPEE-shuh s]*

*Syn:* seemingly reasonable but incorrect; misleading (often intentionally)

*Ant:* genuine

*Usage:* Duke was not convinced by her *specious* arguments; he still doubted her intentions.

**SPONTANEITY** (n) *[on-tuh-NEE-i-tee]*

*Syn:* lack of premeditation; naturalness; freedom from constraint

*Ant:* premeditation; constraint

*Usage:* He had the *spontaneity* of a child.

**SPORADIC** (adj) *[spuh-RAD-ik]*

*Syn:* occurring irregularly

*Ant:* general; prevalent; continuous

*Usage:* The sound of *sporadic* shooting could still be heard at intervals through the night.

**SPURIOUS** (adj) [SPYOO r-ee-uh s]

Syn: false; counterfeit; forged; illogical

Ant: genuine; true; veritable; legitimate; authentic

Usage: He was arrested on spurious corruption charges.

**SQUABBLE** (n) [SKWOB-uh l]

Syn: minor quarrel; bickering

Ant: harmony

Usage: They are upset about a silly squabble.

**SQUANDER** (v) [SKWON-der]

Syn: waste

Ant: save; retain; hoard; hold; acquire; get

Usage: He has squandered away more than half of his inheritance within a year of his father's death.

**STACCATO** (adj) [stuh-KAH-toh]

Syn: played in an abrupt manner; marked by abrupt sharp sound

Ant: continuous and melodic

Usage: He spoke in short staccato bursts.

**STAID** (adj) [steyd]

Syn: dull and serious; sober; sedate

Ant: exuberant; flighty; indiscreet; eccentric; agitated

Usage: He had to spend the night at a staid wayside hotel in order to rest his horses and replenish his supplies.

**STANCH** (v) [stawnch]

Syn: check flow of blood

Usage: He stanched the flow of blood with a piece of cotton cloth.

**STATIC** (adj) [STAT-ik]

Syn: unchanging; lacking development

Ant: dynamic; changing

Usage: Both his paintings are of static subjects.

**STEADFAST** (adj) [STED-fast]

Syn: loyal; unswerving

Ant: obliging; wavering,;capricious; uncertain; dubious; irresolute

Usage: He remained steadfast in his love.

**STELLAR** (adj) [STEL-er]

Syn: pertaining to the stars; impressive

Ant: lowly

Usage: His was a real stellar rise to popularity.

**STENTORIAN** (adj) [sten-TAWR-ee-uh n]

Syn: very loud (voice)

Ant: quiet (voice)

Usage: He bellowed in a stentorian voice.

**STEREOTYPED** (adj) [STER-ee-uh-tahypt]

Syn: oversimplified; lacking individuality; seen as a type

Ant: unique

Usage: Scientists have always had the stereotyped image as complete nerds, despite their varied interests and talents.

**STIGMA** (n) [STIG-muh]

Syn: token of disgrace; brand

Ant: decoration; laurels; credit; renown

Usage: There is still a meaningless stigma attached to certain professions like acting, relegating them to lower levels of respect.

**STIPEND** (n) [STAHY-pend]

Syn: pay for services

Usage: He is able to live comfortably off the stipend the university paid him.

**STIPULATE** (v) [STIP-yuh-leyt]

Syn: make express conditions; specify

Ant: retract; decline; refuse; withdraw; disagree

*(Slough - Tensile)*

*Usage:* The match rules *stipulate* the number of extra golf clubs they can carry in their bags.

**STOCKADE** (n) [sto-keyd]

*Syn:* wooden enclosure or pen

*Ant:* open range

*Usage:* I had not gone a hundred yards when I reached the *stockade* where his prize stallion was secured

**STODGY** (adj) [STOJ-ee]

*Syn:* stuffy; boringly conservative

*Ant:* interesting

*Usage:* He was tired of having heard nothing but *stodgy* politicians the whole week.

**STOLID** (adj) [STOL-id]

*Syn:* dull; impassive

*Ant:* acute; quick; clever; bright; sensitive

*Usage:* He looked up at the *stolid* face of the doctor, unable to determine whether the diagnosis was good or bad.

**STOLIDITY** (n) [stuh-LID-i-tee]

*Syn:* dullness; impassiveness

*Ant:* excitement; passion

*Usage:* The *stolidity* of the parents after the loss of the child was a reflection of having been through so much trauma that they no longer felt anything.

**STRATAGEM** (n) [strat-uh-juhm]

*Syn:* clever trick

*Usage:* Various *stratagems* had been devised to conceal the withdrawals from the Ottoman Army.

**STRIATED** (adj) [STRAHY-ey-tid]

*Syn:* marked with parallel bands; grooved

*Ant:* smooth; solid

*Usage:* The geologist studied the *striated* rock to learn from its bands more about the history of the region.

**STRINGENT** (adj) [STRIN-juh nt]

*Syn:* binding; rigid

*Ant:* flexible

*Usage:* Ever since the bombing near the embassy, there have been *stringent* security measures.

**STRUT** (n) [struht]

*Syn:* supporting bar (secondary meaning)

*Usage:* The architect designed the main *strut* to support loads from wind, snow, people, and the building itself.

**STULTIFY** (v) [STUHL-tuh-fahy]

*Syn:* cause to seem foolish or useless

*Ant:* glorify

*Usage:* Too much of this drink can *stultify* your brain

**STYGIAN** (adj) [STIJ-ee-uh n]

*Syn:* literary dark

*Ant:* brightness

*Usage:* His antics seemed hellish and *stygian*, at times even macabre.

**SUBALTERN** (n) [suhb-AWL-tern]

*Syn:* navy officer; subordinate

*Usage:* The man told me he served the navy in the position of a *subaltern* and had come ashore just two days ago.

**SUBORN** (v) [suh-BAWRN]

*Syn:* persuade to act unlawfully (especially to commit perjury); incite

*Ant:* improve

*Usage:* Peter Jones was arrested on the charges of trying to *suborn* a government official.

**SUBPOENA** (n) [suh-PEE-nuh]

*Syn:* writ summoning a witness to appear; warrant; mandate

*Usage:* The entire staff of the company was served *subpoenas* to appear as witnesses for the prosecution.

**SUBSERVIENT** (adj) *[suh b-SUR-vee-uh nt]*

*Syn:* behaving like a slave; servile; obsequies

*Ant:* superior

*Usage:* The man's *subservient*, servile attitude was beginning to get on my nerves.

**SUBSISTENCE** (v) *[suh b-SIS-tuh ns]*

*Syn:* existence; means of support; livelihood

*Ant:* deadness

*Usage:* Even for the barest form of *subsistence*, he needed some money.

**SUBSTANTIATE** (v) *[suh b-STAN-shee-eyt]*

*Syn:* establish by evidence; verify; support

*Ant:* contradict; disprove

*Usage:* The evidence was too meager and trivial to *substantiate* the charges.

**SUBSUME** (v) *[suh b-SOOM]*

*Syn:* include; encompass

*Ant:* exclude

*Usage:* The project report will *subsume* a table of contents, a preface, thirty pages of research, and an appendix.

**SUBTLETY** (n) *[SUHT-l-tee]*

*Syn:* perceptiveness; ingenuity; delicacy

*Ant:* obviousness

*Usage:* The *subtlety* and delicacy with which she got Jack to agree to the plan was indeed remarkable.

**SUCCINCT** (adj) *[suh k-SINGKT]*

*Syn:* brief; terse; compact

*Ant:* prolix; diffuse; discursive; long

*Usage:* The speech was short, concise and *succinct*.

**SUFFRAGIST** (n) *[SUHF-ruh-jist]*

*Syn:* advocate of voting rights (for women)

*Usage:* In addition to being a reputed lawyer, Holly James was also a *suffragist* and often fought for women's rights.

**SUFFUSE** (v) *[suh-FYOOZ]*

*Syn:* permeate; to cover or spread over (esp. with a color or a liquid)

*Ant:* pull back to the core

*Usage:* Her voice was low and *suffused* with warmth.

**SULTRY** (adj) *[SUHL-tree]*

*Syn:* sweltering; hot and humid

*Ant:* cool and dry

*Usage:* The *sultry* equatorial conditions made the visitors feel tired for much of the day.

**SUMPTUOUS** (adj) *[SUHMP-choo-uh s]*

*Syn:* lavish; rich

*Ant:* poor; mean; inexpensive; sordid; beggarly; frugal

*Usage:* A large, *sumptuous* feast was laid out for them in the garden.

**SUPERANNUATED** (adj) *[soo-per-AN-yoo-ey-tid]*

*Syn:* retired on pension because of age

*Usage:* The infrastructure being used at the office was *superannuated* and obsolete.

**SUPERCILIOUS** (adj) *[soo-per-sil-ee-uhs]*

*Syn:* arrogant; condescending; patronizing

*Ant:* humble

*Usage:* His mother eyed my clothes with a *supercilious* air.

**SUPERFLUOUS** (adj) *[soo-PUR-floo-uh s]*

*Syn:* unnecessary; excessive; overabundant

*Ant:* essential; necessary; required; scant; deficient

*Usage:* The *superfluous* words of praise embarrassed the

humble servant.

**SUPERNUMERARY** (n) [soo-per-NOO-muh-rer-ee]

*Syn:* person or thing in excess of what is necessary

*Ant:* essential

*Usage:* As a *supernumerary* employee, he was the first to be fired when cost-cutting began.

**SUPPLANT** (v) [suh-PLANT]

*Syn:* replace; usurp; displace

*Ant:* include

*Usage:* The candidate from Texas *supplanted* the one from Montana.

**SUPPLIANT** (n) [SUHP-lee-uh nt]

*Syn:* beggar

*Usage:* The fact that he was a *suppliant* and often begged for favors from the higher ups didn't speak too highly about him.

**SUPPOSITION** (n) [suhp-uh-ZISH-uh n]

*Syn:* hypothesis; the act of supposing

*Ant:* proof

*Usage:* It was a mere *supposition* on his part; he had no proof to support his guesswork.

**SUPPRESS** (v) [suh-pres]

*Syn:* stifle

*Ant:* allow

*Usage:* Parents should not force children to *suppress* their curiosity.

**SURFEIT** (n) [SUR-fit]

*Syn:* excess

*Ant:* lack; deprivation

*Usage:* The grains at the warehouse were in huge surplus and *surfeit* this month.

**SURMOUNT** (v) [ser-MOUNT]

*Syn:* overcome

*Ant:* succumb; fail; miss; submit; lose

*Usage:* With a slow and deliberate effort, the army *surmounted* the enemy.

**SURREPTITIOUS** (adj) [sur-uh p-TISH-uh s]

*Syn:* secret; furtive; sneaky; hidden

*Ant:* open; frank; honest; ingenuous

*Usage:* He *surreptitiously* slid out the backdoor at midnight and walked to the highway where Jill said she'd be waiting with the car.

**SURVEILLANCE** (n) [ser-VEY-luh ns]

*Syn:* watching; guarding

*Ant:* privacy

*Usage:* The government ordered day and night *surveillance* on the former minister's residence even as charges were being prepared against him.

**SUTURE** (n) [SOO-cher]

*Syn:* stitches sewn to hold the cut edges of a wound or incision; material used in sewing

*Ant:* incision

*Usage:* The doctor then *sutured* her abdomen, thus signaling the end of the surgery.

**SWELTER** (v) [SWEL-ter]

*Syn:* be oppressed by heat

*Ant:* shiver

*Usage:* This summer, the heat is *sweltering* and stifling.

**SWINDLER** (n) [SWIN-dl]

*Syn:* cheat

*Ant:* honest person

*Usage:* He is a third-rate *swindler*, con-man and very disreputable.

**SYBARITE** (n) *[SIB-uh-rahyt]*

*Syn:* lover of luxury; hedonist

*Ant:* puritan

*Usage:* He is a *sybarite* and loves to enjoy the more sensual pleasures of life.

**SYCOPHANT** (n) *[SIK-uh-fuh nt]*

*Syn:* servile flatterer; follower

*Ant:* leader

*Usage:* His ingratiating and servile behavior makes him a *sycophant*, but if you tell him that he will never accept it.

**SYLVAN** (adj) *[SIL-vuh n]*

*Syn:* pertaining to the forest

*Ant:* urban

*Usage:* The quiet, *sylvan* and pleasing atmosphere was perfectly ideal for the writers to work on their stories.

**SYMBIOSIS** (n) *[sim-bee-OH-sis]*

*Syn:* cooperation of people or between animals or birds

*Ant:* conflict

*Usage:* The families of the two brothers lived in perfect harmony, mutual reliance and *symbiosis*.

**SYNCHRONOUS** (adj) *[SING-kruh-nuh s]*

*Syn:* similarly timed; simultaneous with

*Ant:* asynchronous

*Usage:* The two processes were running *synchronously*, and reached completion at the same time.

**SYNTHETIC** (adj) *[sin-THET-ik]*

*Syn:* combining parts into a whole; man-made

*Ant:* natural

*Usage:* Sonia's gown was tailored in genuine silk while Bella's outfit was made out of *synthetic* fabric.

**TACIT** (adj) *[TAS-it]*

*Syn:* understood; not put into words

*Ant:* open; avowed; declared; expressed

*Usage:* The husband and wife had a remarkable *tacit* understanding between themselves, sometimes making words unnecessary.

**TAINT** (v) *[teynt]*

*Syn:* contaminated; corrupt

*Ant:* purify; cleanse; disinfect; efface

*Usage:* She was *tainted* with a bad name for her misdeeds and driven out of the kingdom.

**TANGENTIAL** (adj) *[tan-JEN-shuh l]*

*Syn:* peripheral; only slightly connected; digressing

*Ant:* core; critical

*Usage:* The bullet had hit the door in a *tangential* shot, chipping off a scant millimeter of wood.

**TANTAMOUNT** (adj) *[TAN-tuh-mount]*

*Syn:* equivalent in force, effect, or value

*Ant:* different; opposite; reverse

*Usage:* His action, though small, was *tantamount* to sacrilege and the elders rebuked him for it.

**TANTRUM** (n) *[TAN-truh m]*

*Syn:* fit of petulance; caprice

*Usage:* The child was throwing too many *tantrums*, causing his mother to grow very frustrated.

**TARANTULA** (n) *[tuh-RAN-chuh-luh]*

*Syn:* venomous spider

*Usage:* To their horror they found a huge *tarantula* spider under the bed.

**TARRY** (v) *[TAR-ee]*

*Syn:* delay; dawdle

*Ant:* pres; push; speed; hasten

*Usage:* I did not comprehend their need to *tarry* the process; as far as I was concerned I wanted to hurry it up.

*(Slough - Tensile)*

# Chapter 14

**TAUT** (adj) *[tawt]*

*Syn:* tight; ready

*Ant:* loose

*Usage:* He tied one last *taut* knot, thus securing the bundle tightly around the bike and then set off on the road for the long journey.

**TAUTOLOGICAL** (adj) *[taw-TOL-uh-jee]*

*Syn:* needlessly repetitious

*Ant:* original

*Usage:* His speech was getting longwinded and *tautological*, causing a number of people in the audience to yawn.

**TEDIUM** (n) *[TEE-dee-uh m]*

*Syn:* boredom; weariness

*Ant:* interest

*Usage:* There seemed to be no end to the *tedium* and boredom at this backward place.

**TEETOTALISM** (n) *[TEE-toht-l-iz-uhm]*

*Syn:* practice of abstaining totally from alcoholic drinks

*Ant:* drunkenness

*Usage:* However, by the 1840s temperance societies began advocating *teetotalism*.

**TEMERITY** (n) *[tuh-MER-i-tee]*

*Syn:* boldness; rashness

*Ant:* timidity; caution; calculation

*Usage:* That such a puny little guest would have the *temerity* to talk back to the master of the household was shocking and unbelievable to him.

**TEMPESTUOUS** (adj) *[tem-pes-choo-uhs]*

*Syn:* stormy; impassioned

*Ant:* calm

*Usage:* I have become anxious watching the *tempestuous* relationship between these one-time friends.

**TEMPORAL** (adj) *[TEM-per-uh l]*

*Syn:* not lasting forever; limited by time

*Ant:* religious; eternal; sacerdotal

*Usage:* Some kind of *temporal* arrangements for shelter had been made for the flood victims.

**TENACITY** (n) *[tuh-NAS-i-tee]*

*Syn:* firmness; persistence

*Ant:* timidity

*Usage:* The man's *tenacity* and persistence are what took him to such great heights.

**TENSILE** (adj) *[TEN-suh l]*

*Syn:* capable of being stretched; pliable

*Ant:* brittle

*Usage:* The fabric's *tensile* strength was still to be measured.

This page is intentionally left blank

# Chapter 15

## (Tepid - Viscous)

*This chapter covers the following words along with their part of speech, pronunciation, synonyms and antonym, if applicable. Sample usage of the word is also illustrated.*

| | | |
|---|---|---|
| tepid | travesty | usurp |
| terse | treatise | uxorious |
| testator | tremulous | vagabond |
| tether | tribunal | vainglorious |
| thematic | trilogy | valor |
| thespian | trite | vanguard |
| threadbare | trivia | variegated |
| thrifty | truculence | vehement |
| throes | tumult | vendetta |
| throttle | turbulence | veneer |
| thwart | turgid | venerate |
| timid | tutelary | venison |
| timorous | ubiquitous | ventral |
| tipple | ulterior | ventriloquist |
| tirade | umbrage | veracious |
| titillate | unassailable | verbatim |
| titular | unconscionable | verbose |
| toga | unctuous | verge |
| tome | underscore | verisimilitude |
| tonsure | unequivocal | versatile |
| torpor | unfeigned | vertigo |
| torrent | unfettered | viable |
| torrid | unfrock | viand |
| tortuous | unguent | vicarious |
| touchstone | unimpeachable | vignette |
| tractable | unkempt | vindictive |
| traduce | unmitigated | viper |
| transcend | unpalatable | virile |
| transfigure | unprecedented | virtuoso |
| transgression | unrequited | visage |
| transitoriness | unsullied | visceral |
| transitory | untrammeled | viscous |
| transpire | upbraid | |
| traumatic | urbane | |

**TEPID** (adj) *[TEP-id]*

*Syn:* lukewarm

*Ant:* hot or cold

*Usage:* The tea was lukewarm and *tepid*.

**TERSE** (adj) *[turs]*

*Syn:* concise; abrupt; pithy

*Ant:* lengthy; long-winded; prolix

*Usage:* He replied in a *terse*, curt manner.

**TESTATOR** (n) *[TES-tey-ter]*

*Syn:* maker of a will

*Usage:* William James died after having made a valid will, thus making him a *testator* and saving his children lots of agony over a vague will.

**TETHER** (v) *[TATH-er]*

*Syn:* tie with a rope

*Ant:* ree; set loose

*Usage:* The man *tethered* the horse to the saloon rail.

**THEMATIC** (adj) *[thee-MAT-ik]*

*Syn:* relating to a unifying motif or idea

*Ant:* unrelated

*Usage:* The occasion seemed appropriate to bring up the *thematic* idea behind the novel.

**THESPIAN** (n) *[THES-pee-uh n]*

*Syn:* actor

*Usage:* Fans flocked eagerly to the famous *thespian* to get his autograph.

**THREADBARE** (adj) *[THRED-bair]*

*Syn:* worn through till the threads show

*Ant:* plush

*Usage:* The *threadbare* carpet was the only thing protecting them from the cold of the earthen floor.

**THRIFTY** (adj) *[THRIF-tee]*

*Syn:* careful about money; economical

*Ant:* prodigal; wasteful; extravagant; philanthropic

*Usage:* She is a *thrifty* woman and spends her money carefully.

**THROES** (n) *[throhs]*

*Syn:* violent anguish; pain

*Ant:* comfort

*Usage:* He was in the *throes* of a high fever.

**THROTTLE** (v) *[THROT-l]*

*Syn:* strangle

*Usage:* The thief tried to *throttle* the policeman attempting to arrest him.

**THWART** (v) *[thwawrt]*

*Syn:* baffle; frustrate

*Ant:* aid; support

*Usage:* He made a strong attempt to *thwart* the criminals but failed eventually.

**TIMID** (adj) *[TIM-id]*

*Syn:* easily frightened; apprehensive

*Ant:* brave

*Usage:* Peter is such a *timid* young man, it is difficult to imagine him performing even a remotely bold act, let alone committing a crime.

**TIMOROUS** (adj) *[TIM-er-uh s]*

*Syn:* fearful; demonstrating fear; nervous

*Ant:* valiant

*Usage:* She was trembling *timorously* with each rumble of the thunderstorm.

**TIPPLE** (v) *[TIP-uh l]*

*Syn:* imbibe; in the habit of drinking liquor

*Ant:* abstain (from alcohol)

*(Tepid - Viscous)*

*Usage:* He is a man known to spend his evenings at the local pub among his fellow miners, with a drink or two to *tipple* and some shared anecdotes to liven up the evening.

### TIRADE (n) [TAHY-reyd]

*Syn:* a long, angry, scolding speech; denunciation; harangue; outburst

*Ant:* calm; harmony; peace

*Usage:* The woman then launched into a lengthy *tirade* against him, listing out all his recent failures and mishaps.

### TITILLATE (v) [TIT-l-eyt]

*Syn:* tickle

*Ant:* bore

*Usage:* The films he makes generally cater to the masses only and are solely meant to *titillate* and entertain.

### TITULAR (adj) [TICH-uh-ler]

*Syn:* nominal holding of title without obligations

*Ant:* authentic

*Usage:* The gesture doesn't mean much to me for I know it's just *titular*, and not in deed.

### TOGA (n) [TOH-guh]

*Syn:* Roman outer robe

*Usage:* For the drama on Saturday, Julian has had a silk *toga* made to suit his part as the Roman Emperor.

### TOME (n) [tohm]

*Syn:* large volume

*Ant:* booklet

*Usage:* He looked frantically through the various racks in the bookshelf for the particular *tome* on herbal medicines.

### TONSURE (n) [TON-sher]

*Syn:* shaving of the head, especially by person entering religious orders

*Usage:* As a further insult to her, they chopped off her long, lovely tresses as *tonsure* before tying her to the stake in the public square.

### TORPOR (n) [TAWR-per]

*Syn:* lethargy; sluggishness; dormancy; apathy; inactivity

*Ant:* excitement; activity

*Usage:* She tried hard to wake him from his *torpor* and get him to do some chores, but he was feeling too lethargic and languid, so he resisted all her efforts.

### TORRENT (n) [TAWR-uh nt]

*Syn:* rushing stream; flood

*Ant:* drip

*Usage:* The rain lashed down in heavy *torrents*, pulling down even big trees.

### TORRID (adj) [TAWR-id]

*Syn:* passionate; hot or scorching; zealous

*Ant:* frigid; arctic; cold; cool; fresh; temperate; icy; freezing

*Usage:* The *torrid*, humid weather was causing havoc to her system since she was unused to anything but the mild-tempered climate of her native.

### TORTUOUS (adj) [TAWR-choo-uh s]

*Syn:* winding; full of curves

*Ant:* straight; direct

*Usage:* The route was a very twisted, *tortuous* one through the mountains.

### TOUCHSTONE (n) [TUHCH-stohn]

*Syn:* stone used to test the fineness of gold alloys; criterion; guide

*Usage:* They needed a better *touchstone* to use as a yardstick for the building construction.

## TRACTABLE (adj) [TRAK-tuh-buh l]

*Syn:* docile; easily managed

*Ant:* refractory; unmanageable; intractable; obstinate; stubborn

*Usage:* The new class seemed *tractable* so the teacher looked forward to the year, anticipating fewer discipline problems than in prior years.

## TRADUCE (v) [truh-DOOS]

*Syn:* slander; vilify

*Ant:* applaud; compliment

*Usage:* There was a covert attempt being made to *traduce* his name in the business circle because people were beginning to get jealous of his success.

## TRANSCEND (v) [tran-SEND]

*Syn:* exceed; surpass

*Ant:* fail

*Usage:* He wanted to *transcend* above the materialistic barriers and worldly barriers and move beyond into a greater realm.

## TRANSFIGURE (v) [trans-fig-yer]

*Syn:* transform outwardly, usually for the better

*Ant:* remain the same

*Usage:* The beautician gave her a makeover that dramatically *transfigured* her appearance.

## TRANSGRESSION (n) [trans-GRESH-uh n]

*Syn:* violation of a law; sin

*Ant:* upholding of a law; abidance

*Usage:* For his unwise *transgression*, Paul was convicted and sentenced to a year's imprisonment.

## TRANSITORINESS (n) [TRAN-si-tawr-ee-nis]

*Syn:* impermanence; brevity

*Ant:* permanence; longevity

*Usage:* The *transitoriness* of life sometimes depressed him to no end; he wished for immortality instead.

## TRANSITORY (adj) [TRAN-si-tawr-ee]

*Syn:* impermanent; fleeting

*Ant:* permanent; long-term

*Usage:* "Life is *transitory* so don't dwell too much on it," he said.

## TRANSPIRE (v) [tran-SAPHYUHR]

*Syn:* to become gradually known; occur; happen

*Usage:* They were very eager to know what had *transpired* behind the closed doors in the lawyer's office.

## TRAUMATIC (adj) [truh-MAT-ik]

*Syn:* pertaining to an injury caused by violence; scary; shocking

*Ant:* calming

*Usage:* The experience was *traumatic* enough to scar her for a lifetime.

## TRAVESTY (n) [TRAV-uh-stee]

*Syn:* comical parody; treatment aimed at making something appear ridiculous

*Ant:* seriousness

*Usage:* It was nothing but a sheer *travesty* of the immense honor that was supposed to have been given to him.

## TREATISE (n) [TREE-tis]

*Syn:* article treating a subject systematically and thoroughly

*Usage:* The graduate student submitted her *treatise* on global warming.

## TREMULOUS (adj) [TREM-yuh-luh s]

*Syn:* trembling; wavering

*Ant:* motionless; smooth; equable

*Usage:* She nodded shyly and *tremulously* in assent to his question.

## TRIBUNAL (n) [trahy-BYOON-l]

*Syn:* court of justice

*Usage:* The local *tribunal* decided to refer the matter to a higher court of justice.

**TRILOGY** (n) [TRIL-uh-jee]

*Syn:* group of three works

*Usage:* The Star Wars *trilogy* filmed by George Lucas was a huge worldwide success.

**TRITE** (adj) [trahyt]

*Syn:* hackneyed; commonplace

*Ant:* original; novel; startling; unusual

*Usage:* They were talking in a common, *trite* fashion which led Jane to believe that they knew each other well.

**TRIVIA** (n) [TRIV-ee-uh]

*Syn:* trifles; unimportant matters

*Ant:* serious matters

*Usage:* The fun quiz was full of *trivia* questions on movies.

**TRUCULENCE** (n) [TRUHK-yuh-luh ns]

*Syn:* aggressiveness; ferocity

*Ant:* passivity; cowardice

*Usage:* The fierce sense of *truculence* he exhibited at such a young age alarmed his parents, fearful of many schoolyard fistfights in the future.

**TUMULT** (n) [TOO-muh lt]

*Syn:* commotion; riot; noise

*Ant:* peace; quiet; order; tranquility

*Usage:* The chaos and *tumult* all around was preventing him from being able to focus clearly on work.

**TURBULENCE** (n) [TUR-byuh-luh ns]

*Syn:* state of violent agitation

*Ant:* smoothness; calm

*Usage:* The flight had some rough *turbulence* as they flew through the storm.

**TURGID** (adj) [TUR-jid]

*Syn:* swollen; distended

*Ant:* plain; simple

*Usage:* His feet had become swollen and *turgid*.

**TUTELARY** (adj) [TOOT-l-er-ee]

*Syn:* protective; pertaining to a guardianship

*Ant:* protected

*Usage:* His timely *tutelary* guidance was what led her to be such a successful dancer.

**UBIQUITOUS** (adj) [yoo-BIK-wi-tuh s]

*Syn:* being everywhere; omnipresent

*Ant:* rare

*Usage:* Unlike the *ubiquitous* glass-facaded towers now seen everywhere in the city, this place had houses with old-fashioned red tiled roofs.

**ULTERIOR** (adj) [uhl-TEER-ee-er]

*Syn:* situated beyond; unstated

*Ant:* immediate, obvious; stated

*Usage:* I suspected that he had some hidden *ulterior* motive in asking me about Jemma's whereabouts.

**UMBRAGE** (n) [UHM-brij]

*Syn:* offence; resentment; harsh feelings; shade

*Ant:* complacency; satisfaction; gratification

*Usage:* He took *umbrage* at the way they twisted his honorary title while announcing him to the crowd.

**UNASSAILABLE** (adj) [uhn-uh-SEY-luh-buh l]

*Syn:* not subject to question; not open to attack

*Ant:* above reproach; beyond attack

*Usage:* It was his ultimate dream to build an invincible, *unassailable* armed force.

**UNCONSCIONABLE** (adj) [uhn-KON-shuh-nuh-buh l]

*Syn:* unscrupulous; excessive; immoral

*Ant:* decent; good

*Usage:* He had secured the deal and contract through *unconscionable* means.

**UNCTUOUS** (adj) *[UHNGK-choo-uh s]*

*Syn:* oily; bland; insincerely suave

*Ant:* sincere

*Usage:* The man was sycophantic and *unctuous*, always running behind the big boss looking for opportunities to serve him.

**UNDERSCORE** (v) *[UHN-der-skawr]*

*Syn:* emphasize

*Ant:* ignore

*Usage:* He *underscored* the fact that had it not been for Tim, they might have never have made it back to the shore.

**UNEQUIVOCAL** (adj) *[uhn-i-KWIV-uh-kuh l]*

*Syn:* plain; obvious; unmistakable

*Ant:* unclear

*Usage:* There was *unequivocal* positive response to the poll.

**UNFEIGNED** (adj) *[uhn-FEYND]*

*Syn:* genuine; real

*Ant:* feigned; false

*Usage:* There was *unfeigned* surprise all over his face upon hearing the news.

**UNFETTERED** (adj) *[uhn-fet-er-d]*

*Syn:* unrestrained; unbound

*Ant:* constrained;

*Usage: Unfettered* free trade is an ideal, never achieved.

**UNFROCK** (v) *[uhn-FROK]*

*Syn:* strip a priest or minister of church authority

*Ant:* appoint

*Usage:* The priest looked different when *unfrocked*.

**UNGUENT** (n) *[UHNG-gwuh nt]*

*Syn:* ointment

*Usage:* He applied some soothing *unguent* to the wound.

**UNIMPEACHABLE** (adj) *[uhn-im-PEE-chuh-buh l]*

*Syn:* blameless and exemplary

*Ant:* at fault

*Usage:* The man was built of solid, *unimpeachable* character.

**UNKEMPT** (adj) *[uhn-KEMPT]*

*Syn:* disheveled; uncared for in appearance

*Ant:* clean and tidy

*Usage:* The man was not allowed into the hotel because he looked *unkempt* and his appearance was disheveled.

**UNMITIGATED** (adj) *[uhn-MIT-i-gey-tid]*

*Syn:* unrelieved or immoderate; absolute

*Ant:* limited

*Usage:* The *unmitigated* costs of residence deterred them from choosing to stay in the Pacific.

**UNPALATABLE** (adj) *[uhn-PAL-uh-tuh-buhl]*

*Syn:* distasteful; disagreeable

*Ant:* tasty

*Usage:* The food at the roadside joint was *unpalatable*.

**UNPRECEDENTED** (adj) *[uhn-PRES-i-den-tid]*

*Syn:* novel; unparalleled

*Ant:* unoriginal

*Usage:* The profits this year were totally *unprecedented* and surpassed all expectations.

**UNREQUITED** (adj) *[uhn-ri-KWAHY-tid]*

*Syn:* not reciprocated

*Ant:* reciprocated; returned

Chapter 15

*Usage:* *Unrequited* love, love that is not reciprocated, forms the theme of many a novel.

**UNSULLIED** (adj) *[uhn suhl-ee d]*

*Syn:* untarnished

*Ant:* tarnished; dirty

*Usage:* The firm has an *unsullied* reputation and boasts of the biggest clientele in the whole of the region.

**UNTRAMMELED** (adj) *[un-TRAM-uhld]*

*Syn:* without limits or restrictions

*Ant:* limited

*Usage:* The investors were in an *untrammeled* rush to purchase Apple stock after the latest product announcement.

**UPBRAID** (v) *[uhp-BREYD]*

*Syn:* severely scold; reprimand

*Ant:* praise

*Usage:* The old man *upbraided* the maid, taking her to task for having tried to steal from the pantry.

**URBANE** (adj) *[ur-BEYN]*

*Syn:* suave; refined; elegant

*Ant:* ingenuous

*Usage:* Michael Newman is a polite, *urbane* young man.

**USURP** (v) *[yoo-SURP]*

*Syn:* seize another's power or rank

*Ant:* receive; inherit; accept; yield; render; surrender

*Usage:* The insurgent rebels had attempted to *usurp* the power from the ruling monarchy.

**UXORIOUS** (adj) *[uhk-SAWR-ee-uh s]*

*Syn:* excessively devoted to one's wife

*Ant:* unfaithful; dominant

*Usage:* The man was *uxorious* and submissive to an extent that nauseated even his own wife.

**VAGABOND** (n) *[VAG-uh-bond]*

*Syn:* wanderer; tramp

*Ant:* homebody

*Usage:* The *vagabond* pursued his nomadic nature, never settling in one place.

**VAINGLORIOUS** (adj) *[veyn-GLAWR-ee-uh s]*

*Syn:* boastful; excessively conceited

*Ant:* humble

*Usage:* He began to strut in his new attire like a *vainglorious* peacock.

**VALOR** (n) *[VAL-er]*

*Syn:* bravery

*Ant:* cowardice; fear

*Usage:* For his timely courage and *valor* in saving three lives, the man was awarded a bravery medal.

**VANGUARD** (n) *[VAN-gahrd]*

*Syn:* forerunners; advance forces

*Ant:* followers

*Usage:* It was ironic that the *vanguards* of the state's most advanced security system were being convicted ten years later for a fraud.

**VARIEGATED** (adj) *[VAIR-ee-i-gey-tid]*

*Syn:* many-colored

*Ant:* same

*Usage:* She wore a black top and a cotton skirt with *variegated* colorful patterns on it.

**VEHEMENT** (adj) *[VEE-uh-muh nt]*

*Syn:* violent; forceful; intensely emotional; vigorous

*Ant:* mild; feeble; subdued; cold; passionless; weak

*Usage:* She carries a strong, *vehement* dislike for the Meltons.

**VENDETTA** (n) *[ven-DET-uh]*

*Syn:* blood feud

*Usage:* "Kill Bill" is the violent saga of personal *vendetta*.

**VENEER** (n) *[vuh-NEER]*

*Syn:* thin layer; cover

*Ant:* entirety; depth

*Usage:* His suave charm was merely a *veneer* for his malicious inner nature.

**VENERATE** (v) *[VEN-uh-reyt]*

*Syn:* revere

*Ant:* scorn; disparage

*Usage:* Several tribes in the Mayan civilization *venerated* elements of nature as their deities.

**VENISON** (n) *[VEN-uh-suh n]*

*Syn:* the meat of a deer

*Usage:* They feasted on *venison* freshly cooked over the campfire.

**VENTRAL** (v) *[VEN-truh l]*

*Syn:* abdominal

*Usage:* The *ventral* cavity had been cut open during the accident, causing him to bleed to death right there.

**VENTRILOQUIST** (n) *[ven-TRIL-uh-kwist]*

*Syn:* someone who can make his or her voice seem to come from another person or thing

*Usage:* Oliver works as a part-time *ventriloquist* because he is a marvel at throwing his voice.

**VERACIOUS** (adj) *[vuh-REY-shuh s]*

*Syn:* truthful

*Ant:* deceitful; imaginary; fictional; fraudulent; lying; untrue

*Usage:* What they liked best about him was his truthful, *veracious* nature.

**VERBATIM** (adj) *[ver-BEY-tim]*

*Syn:* word for word

*Ant:* paraphrased

*Usage:* He quoted the whole report *verbatim*.

**VERBOSE** (adj) *[ver-BOHS]*

*Syn:* wordy; loquacious

*Ant:* succinct; terse

*Usage:* He is not normally this *verbose*; perhaps the drinks have made him open up.

**VERGE** (n) *[vurj]*

*Syn:* border; edge

*Ant:* interior

*Usage:* He's on the *verge* of a nervous breakdown.

**VERISIMILITUDE** (n) *[ver-uh-si-MIL-i-tood]*

*Syn:* appearance of truth; likelihood

*Ant:* falseness

*Usage:* The *verisimilitude* of the ancient document was proven by carbon dating.

**VERSATILE** (adj) *[VUR-suh-tl]*

*Syn:* having many talents; capable of working in many fields

*Ant:* one-sided; uniform; narrow; limited; stolid; immobile

*Usage:* Little Mel is so *versatile*; he has a plethora of skills and is good at all of them.

**VERTIGO** (n) *[VUR-ti-goh]*

*Syn:* severe dizziness; giddiness

*Ant:* steadiness

*Usage:* She refused to climb further saying that she was prone to *vertigo* and dizziness at great heights.

**VIABLE** (adj) *[VAHY-uh-buh l]*

*Syn:* practical or workable; feasible; capable of

maintaining life

*Ant:* impractical; impossible

*Usage:* The venture seemed like a *viable* proposition so they decided to sign the contract.

## VIAND (n) [VAHY-uh nd]

*Syn:* food

*Usage:* After fortifying the famished soldiers with *viands* and foodstuffs they had brought with them, the commanders questioned them for hours on the activities in the past week.

## VICARIOUS (adj) [vahy-KAIR-ee-uh s]

*Syn:* acting as a substitute; done by a deputy

*Ant:* direct

*Usage:* The *vicarious* thrill people get at the matador exhibitions at the arena is at the cost of many a human life.

## VIGNETTE (n) [vin-YET]

*Syn:* picture; short literary sketch

*Usage:* She decided to submit a *vignette* based on events in her own life.

## VINDICTIVE (adj) [vin-DIK-tiv]

*Syn:* out for revenge; malicious

*Ant:* forgiving; generous; merciful; forbearing

*Usage:* Her *vindictive* and spiteful nature scares me.

## VIPER (n) [VAHY-per]

*Syn:* poisonous snake

*Usage:* News has come in that Jim was bitten by a *viper* in the jungle and succumbed to death immediately.

## VIRILE (adj) [VIR-uh l]

*Syn:* manly

*Ant:* weak; effeminate

*Usage:* The competition attracted many handsome, young, *virile* men to participate for the title.

## VIRTUOSO (n) [vur-choo-OH-soh]

*Syn:* highly skilled artist

*Ant:* tyro; novice

*Usage:* He bent forward to seek the *virtuoso's* blessings, the man who had inspired him for years.

## VISAGE (n) [VIZ-ij]

*Syn:* face; appearance

*Usage:* She had a kind weathered *visage*, with liquid brown eyes and a beautiful smile.

## VISCERAL (adj) [VIS-er-uh l]

*Syn:* felt in one's inner organs; instinctive

*Usage:* The *visceral* attacks left them chilled and cold.

## VISCOUS (adj) [VIS-kuh s]

*Syn:* sticky; gluey

*Usage:* The gel was sticky and *viscous*.

This page is intentionally left blank

# Chapter 16

## (Vitiate – Zephyr)

*This chapter covers the following words along with their part of speech, pronunciation, synonyms and antonym, if applicable. Sample usage of the word is also illustrated.*

vitiate
vitriolic
vivacious
vociferous
vogue
volatile
voluminous
voluptuous
vortex
votary
voyeur
waffle
waive
wanton
warble
warrant
wary
wastrel
wean
whelp
whimsical
whittle
winnow
winsome
withstand
wont
wrath
writhe
Xenophobia
yeoman
yokel
zeal
zealot
zephyr

**VITIATE** (v) [VISH-ee-eyt]

*Syn:* spoil the effect of; to weaken

*Ant:* strengthen

*Usage:* The harsh, tortuous life of Hell's Kitchen only served to *vitiate* his spirit and make him corrupt.

**VITRIOLIC** (adj) [vi-tree-OL-ik]

*Syn:* bitter; corrosive; sarcastic

*Ant:* sweet

*Usage:* Her temper is caustic and *vitriolic*.

**VIVACIOUS** (adj) [vi-VEY-shuh s]

*Syn:* gay; full of life; animated; lively

*Ant:* lifeless; dull; stolid; moody; heavy; sullen; torpid; sluggish

*Usage:* Kim has such a *vivacious* bubbly personality that it came as no surprise when she won the Miss Popular crown at college.

**VOCIFEROUS** (adj) [voh-SIF-er-uh s]

*Syn:* loudly vocal; clamorous; noisy

*Ant:* soft-spoken

*Usage:* They protested loudly and *vociferously* against the unfair treatment.

**VOGUE** (n) [vohg]

*Syn:* popular fashion

*Ant:* outmoded item

*Usage:* Long skirts are back in *vogue* this winter.

**VOLATILE** (adj) [VOL-uh-tl]

*Syn:* changeable; explosive; evaporating rapidly

*Ant:* stolid; impassive

*Usage:* His *volatile* temperament leaves them wondering what to expect each day.

**VOLUMINOUS** (adj) [vuh-LOO-muh-nuh s]

*Syn:* bulky; large

*Ant:* small

*Usage:* The jacket was *voluminous* even when folded neatly.

**VOLUPTUOUS** (adj) [vuh-LUHP-choo-uh s]

*Syn:* gratifying the senses

*Ant:* thin

*Usage:* He prefers *voluptuous* women to the slimmer ones.

**VORTEX** (n) [VAWR-teks]

*Syn:* whirlwind; whirlpool; center of turbulence; predicament into which one is inexorably plunged

*Usage:* He was caught treacherously in a *vortex* out of which he could not swim.

**VOTARY** (n) [VOH-tuh-ree]

*Syn:* eager admirer or supporter of some idea

*Ant:* skeptic

*Usage:* Jack Summers has always been a *votary* of Manchester United.

**VOYEUR** (n) [vwah-YUR]

*Syn:* Peeping Tom

*Usage:* Nick is a nasty *voyeur* and loves to peep into other's windows.

**WAFFLE** (v) [wof-uh l]

*Syn:* speak equivocally about an issue

*Ant:* decide

*Usage:* The politician *waffles* from one side of the issue to the other from one day to the next.

**WAIVE** (v) [weyv]

*Syn:* give up temporarily; yield

*Ant:* press; urge; claim; arrest; enforce

*Usage:* Hearing of her extreme financial difficulties, they *waived* the fees for the month.

**WANTON** (adj) *[WON-tn]*

*Syn:* unrestrained; willfully malicious; unchaste; excessive

*Ant:* staid; sober; demure; austere; formal; deliberate

*Usage:* The party revelers indulged in *wanton* drinking and dancing all night.

**WARBLE** (v) *[WAWR-buh l]*

*Syn:* sing; babble

*Usage:* Their jaws dropped in horror as he *warbled* out a loud country song.

**WARRANT** (v) *[WAWR-uh nt]*

*Syn:* justify; authorize

*Ant:* endanger; nullify; invalidate; repudiate

*Usage:* His misdeed had been mild and did not *warrant* such a heavy rigorous punishment.

**WARY** (adj) *[WAIR-ee]*

*Syn:* very cautious; careful

*Ant:* unwary; unsuspecting; heedless; unguarded; foolhardy; reckless; intrepid

*Usage:* The villagers are very *wary* of outsiders after the bombing occurred.

**WASTREL** (n) *[WEY-struh l]*

*Syn:* profligate

*Ant:* miser

*Usage:* The huge estate his father left him made him nothing but a good-for-nothing *wastrel*.

**WEAN** (v) *[ween]*

*Syn:* accustom a baby to not nurse; give up a cherished activity

*Ant:* continue a practice

*Usage:* It is important to start *weaning* a baby after six to eight months by feeding it solid food.

**WHELP** (n) *[hwelp]*

*Syn:* young wolf; dog; tiger, etc.

*Ant:* adult animal

*Usage:* The little *whelp* followed the old man all over the ranch even though he was a stranger to it.

**WHIMSICAL** (n) *[HWIM-zi-kuh l]*

*Syn:* capricious; fanciful

*Ant:* staid; serious; sober; sedate; orderly

*Usage:* His *whimsical*, weird nature often amuses people.

**WHITTLE** (v) *[HWIT-l]*

*Syn:* pare; cut off bits

*Ant:* build; rebuild

*Usage:* He *whittled* the long stick into a neat sharp wood knife.

**WINNOW** (v) *[WIN-oh]*

*Syn:* sift; separate good parts from bad

*Ant:* combine

*Usage:* It took them hours to *winnow* through the trash but they couldn't find the ring that had been accidentally discarded.

**WINSOME** (adj) *[WIN-suh m]*

*Syn:* agreeable; gracious; engaging

*Ant:* antagonistic

*Usage:* His suave, *winsome* charms have captured many a pretty girl's heart.

**WITHSTAND** (v) *[with-STAND]*

*Syn:* stand up against; successfully resist.

*Ant:* yield; submit; surrender; support; encourage; aid

*Usage:* To *withstand* such great pressure, the man must have been really strong and gutsy.

**WONT** (n) *[wawnt]*

*Syn:* difficulty; demand

*Ant:* ease

*Usage:* It was his *wont* to take on the hardest tasks for the group's efforts.

**WRATH** (n) *[rath]*

*Syn:* anger; fury

*Ant:* joy

*Usage:* He was loath to face the *wrath* of his angry grandfather.

**WRITHE** (v) *[rahyth]*

*Syn:* twist in coils; contort in pain

*Ant:* quiet; soothe; calm; rest

*Usage:* The snake *writhed* in agony for a few seconds before becoming still in death.

**XENOPHOBIA** (n) *[zen-uh-FOH-bee-uh]*

*Syn:* fear or hatred of foreigners

*Ant:* tolerance; respect

*Usage:* The degree to which she practices *xenophobia* makes others see her as a strong racist.

**YEOMAN** (n) *[YOH-muh n]*

*Syn:* worker; middle-class farmer; petty officer in the navy

*Usage:* The *yeoman* was recognized as the hardest worker in the crew.

**YOKEL** (n) *[YOH-kuh l]*

*Syn:* rusty country bumpkin

*Ant:* sophisticate

*Usage:* They made fun and mocked at the *yokel* who was unaccustomed to the city.

**ZEAL** (n) *[zeel]*

*Syn:* eager enthusiasm; keenness

*Ant:* apathy; indifference; coldness; detachment; torpor

*Usage:* He has a great undying *zeal* for life and lives each day to the fullest

**ZEALOT** (n) *[ZEL-uh t]*

*Syn:* fanatic; person who shows excessive zeal

*Ant:* renegade; traitor; deserter

*Usage:* The *zealots* were gathering at the town square displaying their religious fanaticism openly.

**ZEPHYR** (n) *[ZEF-er]*

*Syn:* gentle breeze; west wind

*Usage:* She is like a *zephyr*, a hint of a summer breeze in my life.

Made in the USA
San Bernardino, CA
30 December 2018